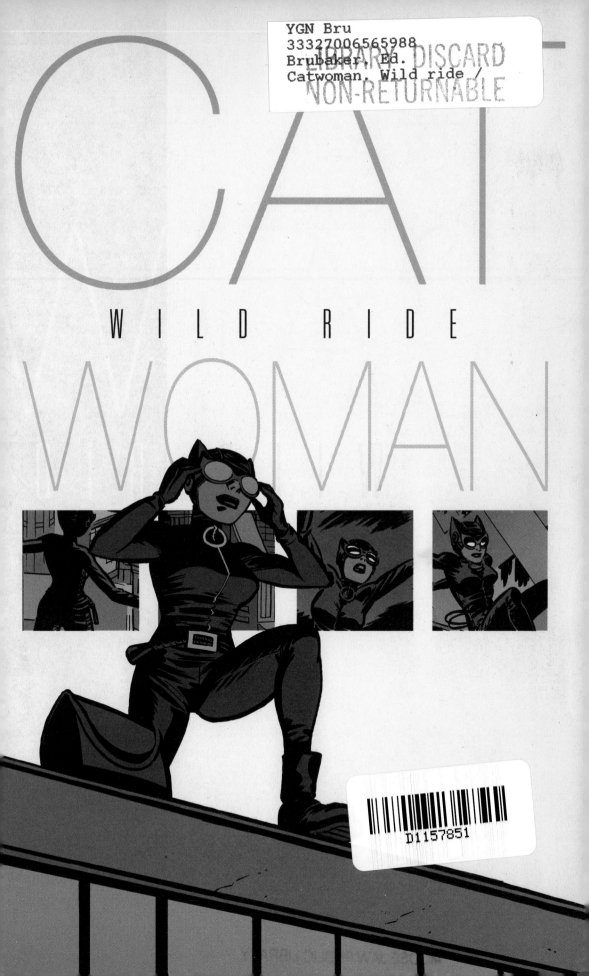

CAT
WILD RIDE
WOMAN

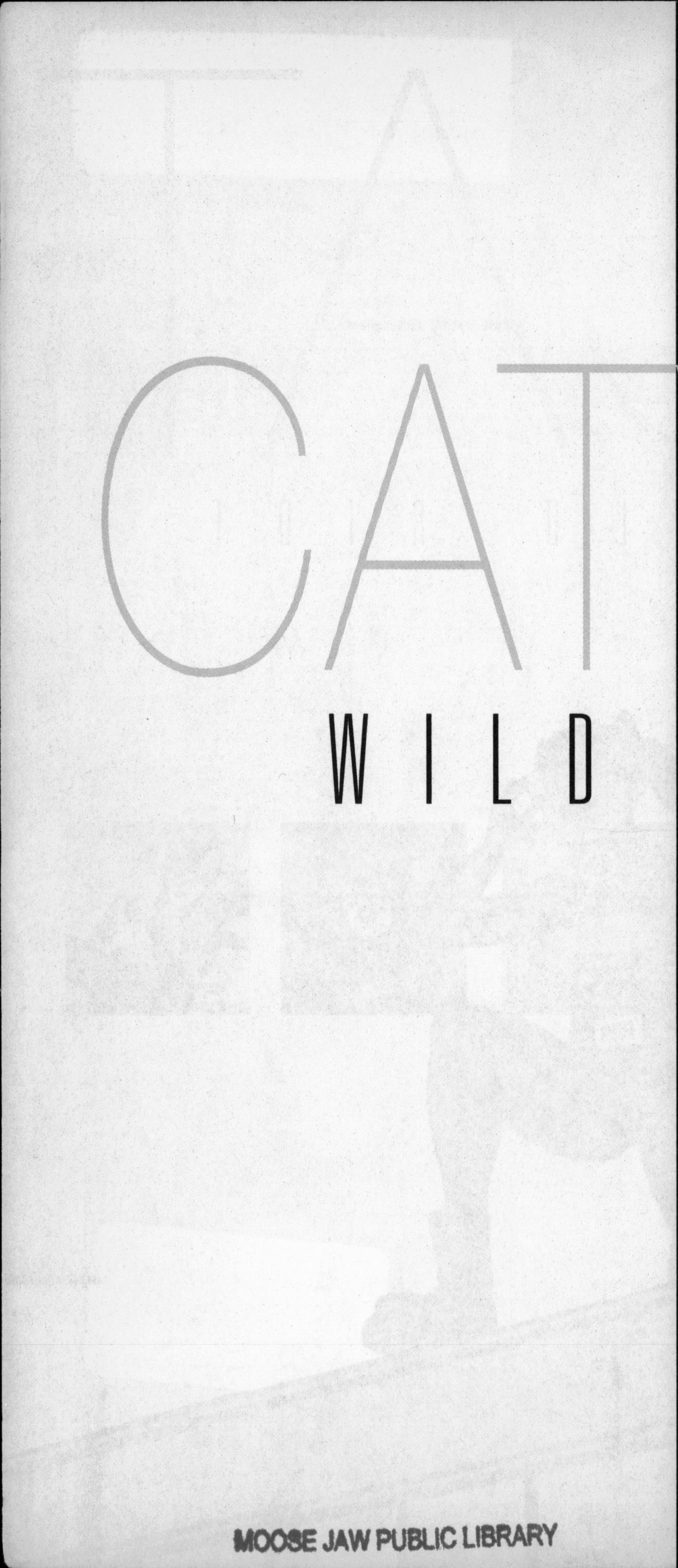

CATW

WILD RID

OMAN

ED **BRUBAKER** WRITER   CAMERON **STEWART** ARTIST   GUY **DAVIS** NICK **DERINGTON**

Additional Layouts   MATT **HOLLINGSWORTH** LEE **LOUGHRIDGE** COLORISTS

SEAN **KONOT** LETTERER CAMERON **STEWART** ORIGINAL COVERS

CATWOMAN: WILD RIDE

Published by DC Comics. Cover and compilation copyright © 2005
DC Comics. All Rights Reserved.

Originally published in single magazine form in CATWOMAN SECRET
FILES #1, CATWOMAN #20-24. Copyright © 2002, 2003 DC Comics.
All Rights Reserved. All characters, their distinctive likenesses and
related elements featured in this publication are trademarks of
DC Comics. The stories, characters and incidents featured in this
publication are entirely fictional. DC Comics does not read or
accept unsolicited submissions of ideas, stories or artwork.

DC Comics, 1700 Broadway, New York, NY 10019
A Warner Bros. Entertainment Company
Printed in Canada. First Printing.
ISBN: 1-4012-0436-8
Cover art by Cameron Stewart

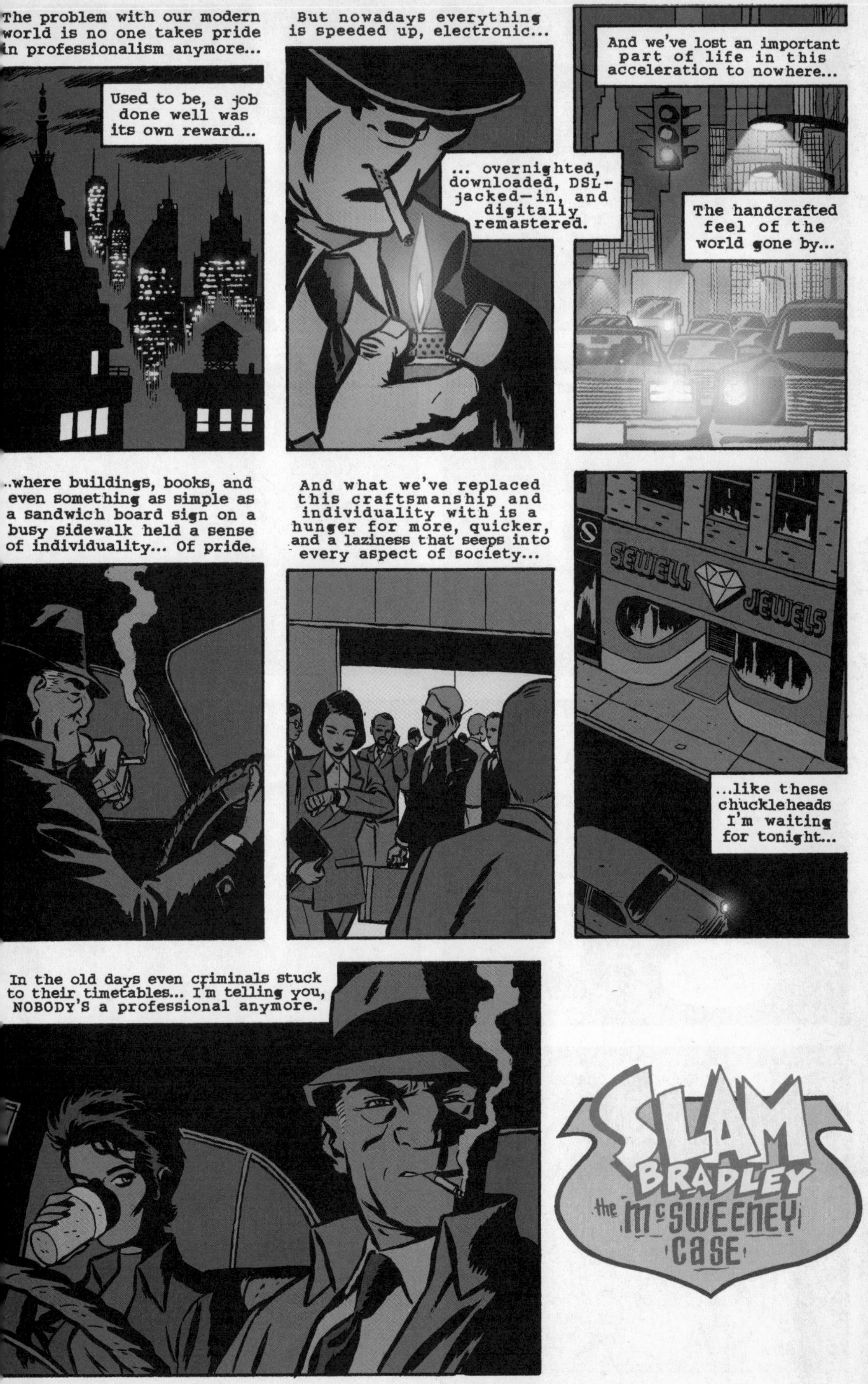

The problem with our modern world is no one takes pride in professionalism anymore...
Used to be, a job done well was its own reward...
But nowadays everything is speeded up, electronic...
... overnighted, downloaded, DSL-jacked—in, and digitally remastered.
And we've lost an important part of life in this acceleration to nowhere...
The handcrafted feel of the world gone by...
..where buildings, books, and even something as simple as a sandwich board sign on a busy sidewalk held a sense of individuality... Of pride.
And what we've replaced this craftsmanship and individuality with is a hunger for more, quicker, and a laziness that seeps into every aspect of society...
SEWELL JEWELS
...like these chuckleheads I'm waiting for tonight...
In the old days even criminals stuck to their timetables... I'm telling you, NOBODY'S a professional anymore.
SLAM BRADLEY
the McSWEENEY CASE

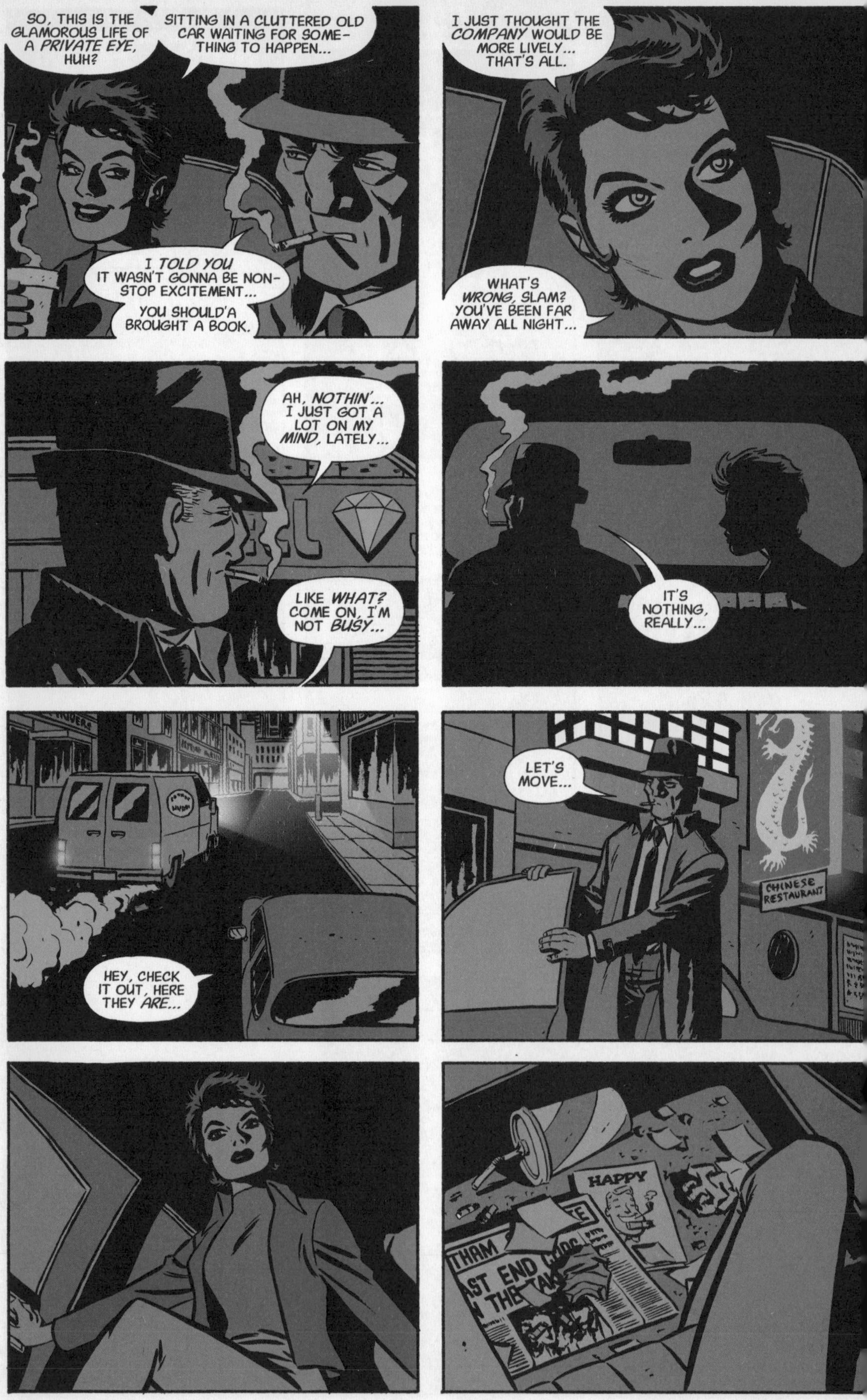
SO, THIS IS THE GLAMOROUS LIFE OF A PRIVATE EYE, HUH?
SITTING IN A CLUTTERED OLD CAR WAITING FOR SOME-THING TO HAPPEN...
I TOLD YOU IT WASN'T GONNA BE NON-STOP EXCITEMENT...
YOU SHOULD'A BROUGHT A BOOK.
I JUST THOUGHT THE COMPANY WOULD BE MORE LIVELY... THAT'S ALL.
WHAT'S WRONG, SLAM? YOU'VE BEEN FAR AWAY ALL NIGHT...
AH, NOTHIN'... I JUST GOT A LOT ON MY MIND, LATELY...
LIKE WHAT? COME ON, I'M NOT BUSY...
IT'S NOTHING, REALLY...
HEY, CHECK IT OUT, HERE THEY ARE...
LET'S MOVE...
CHINESE RESTAURANT
HAPPY

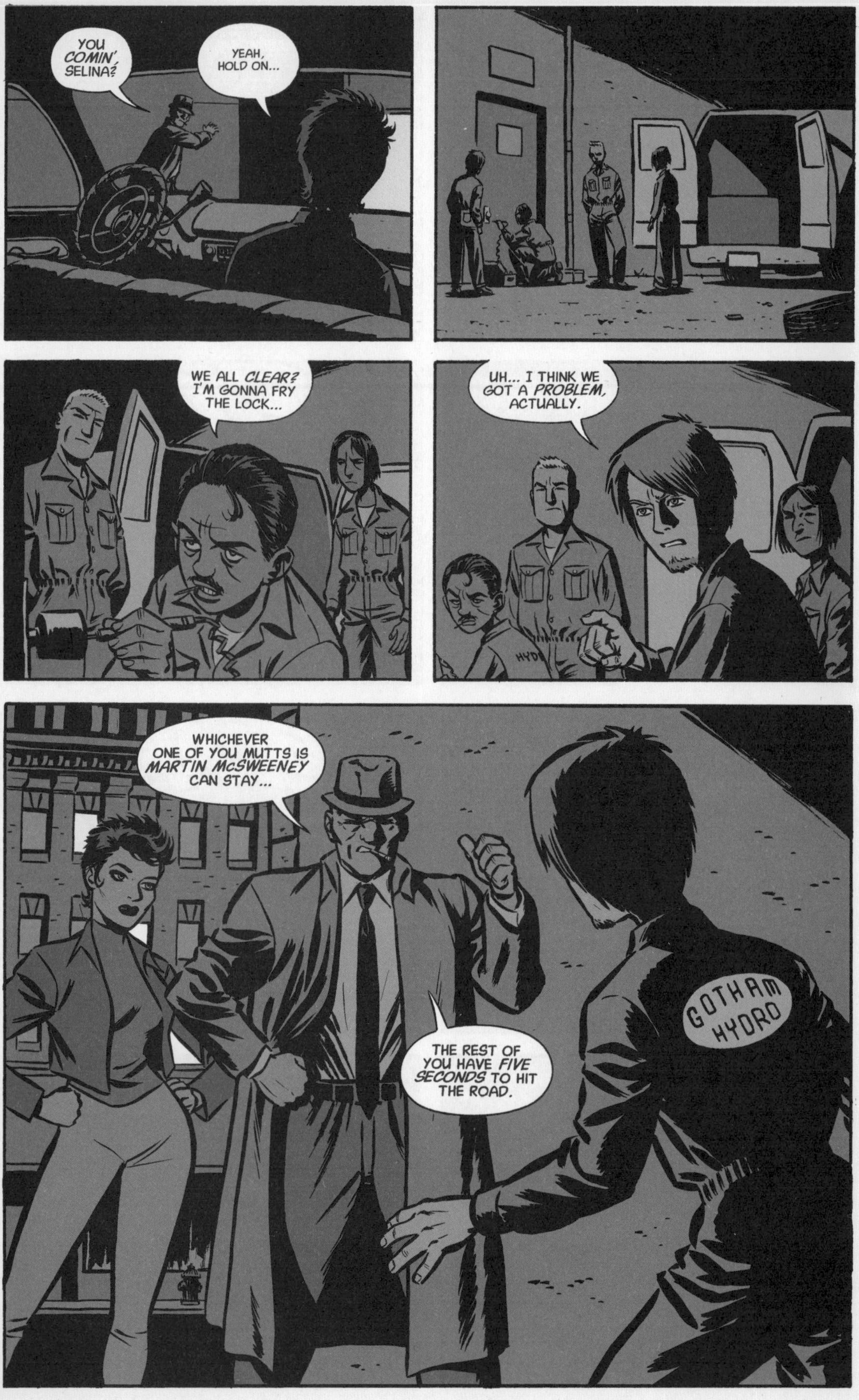
YOU COMIN', SELINA?
YEAH, HOLD ON...
WE ALL CLEAR? I'M GONNA FRY THE LOCK...
UH... I THINK WE GOT A PROBLEM, ACTUALLY.
HYD
WHICHEVER ONE OF YOU MUTTS IS MARTIN McSWEENEY CAN STAY...
THE REST OF YOU HAVE FIVE SECONDS TO HIT THE ROAD.
GOTHAM HYDRO

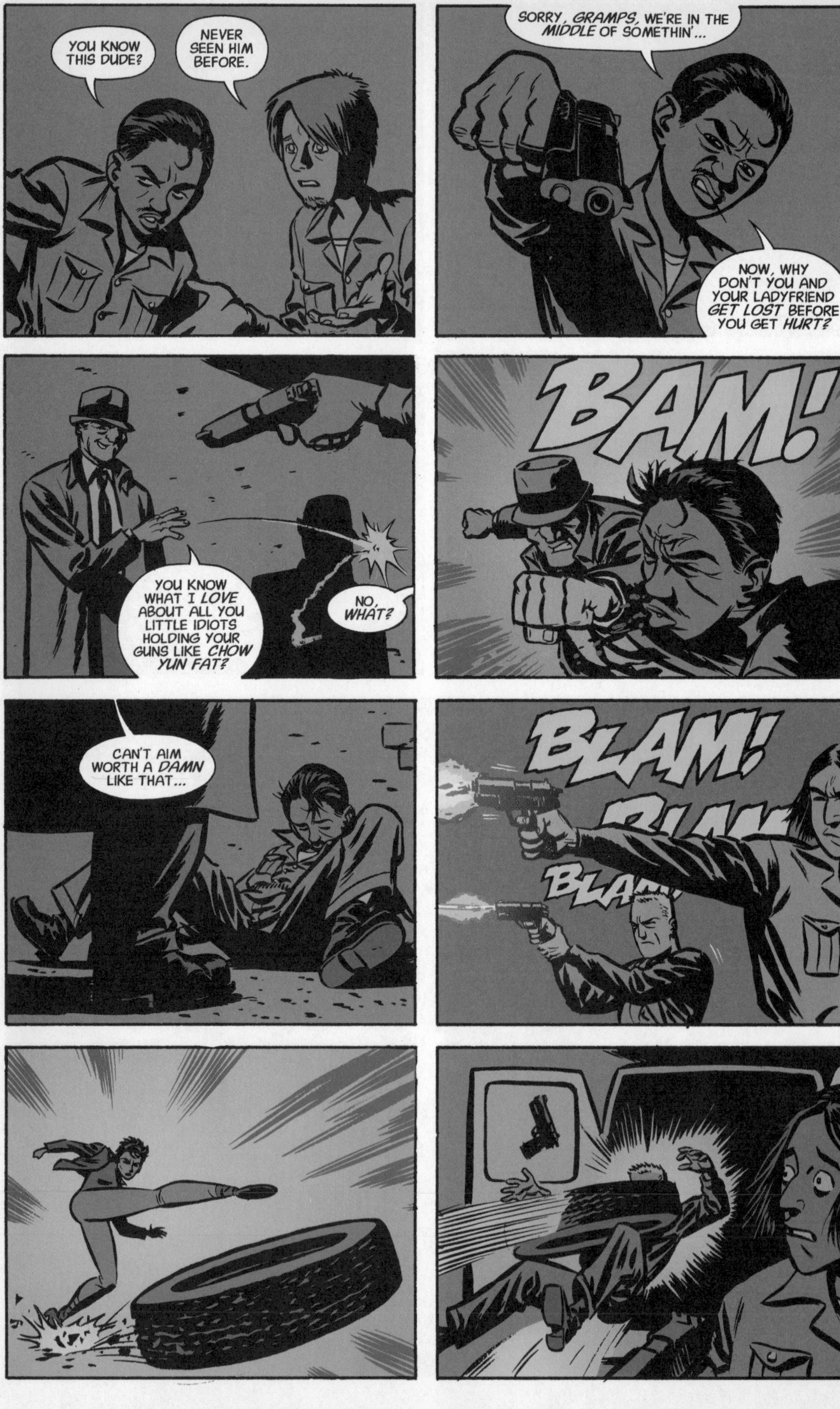
YOU KNOW THIS DUDE?
NEVER SEEN HIM BEFORE.
SORRY, GRAMPS, WE'RE IN THE MIDDLE OF SOMETHIN'...
NOW, WHY DON'T YOU AND YOUR LADYFRIEND GET LOST BEFORE YOU GET HURT?
YOU KNOW WHAT I LOVE ABOUT ALL YOU LITTLE IDIOTS HOLDING YOUR GUNS LIKE CHOW YUN FAT?
NO, WHAT?
BAM!
CAN'T AIM WORTH A DAMN LIKE THAT...
BLAM!

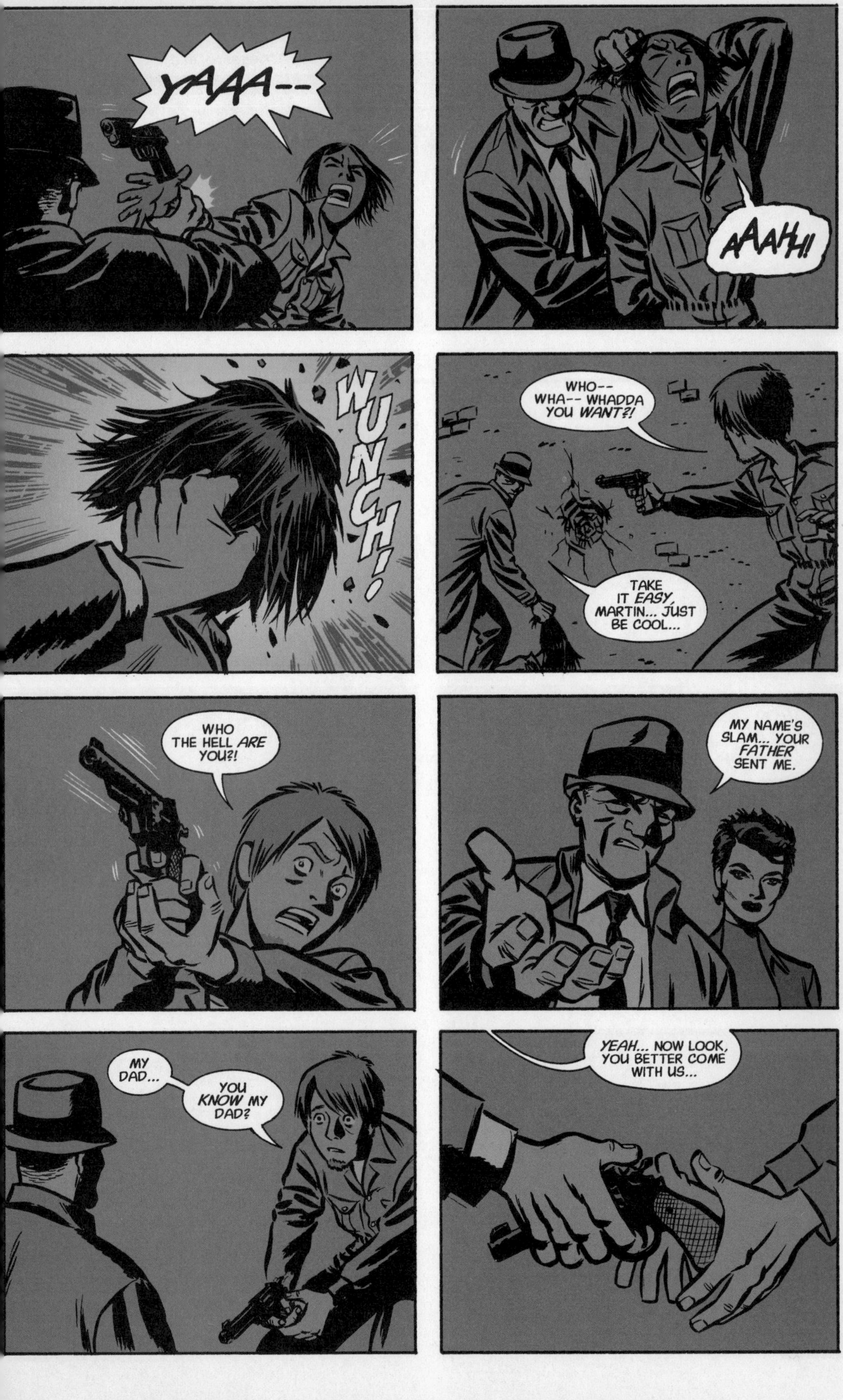

YAAA--
AAAHH!
WUNCH!
WHO-- WHA-- WHADDA YOU WANT?!
TAKE IT EASY, MARTIN... JUST BE COOL...
WHO THE HELL ARE YOU?!
MY NAME'S SLAM... YOUR FATHER SENT ME.
MY DAD...
YOU KNOW MY DAD?
YEAH... NOW LOOK, YOU BETTER COME WITH US...

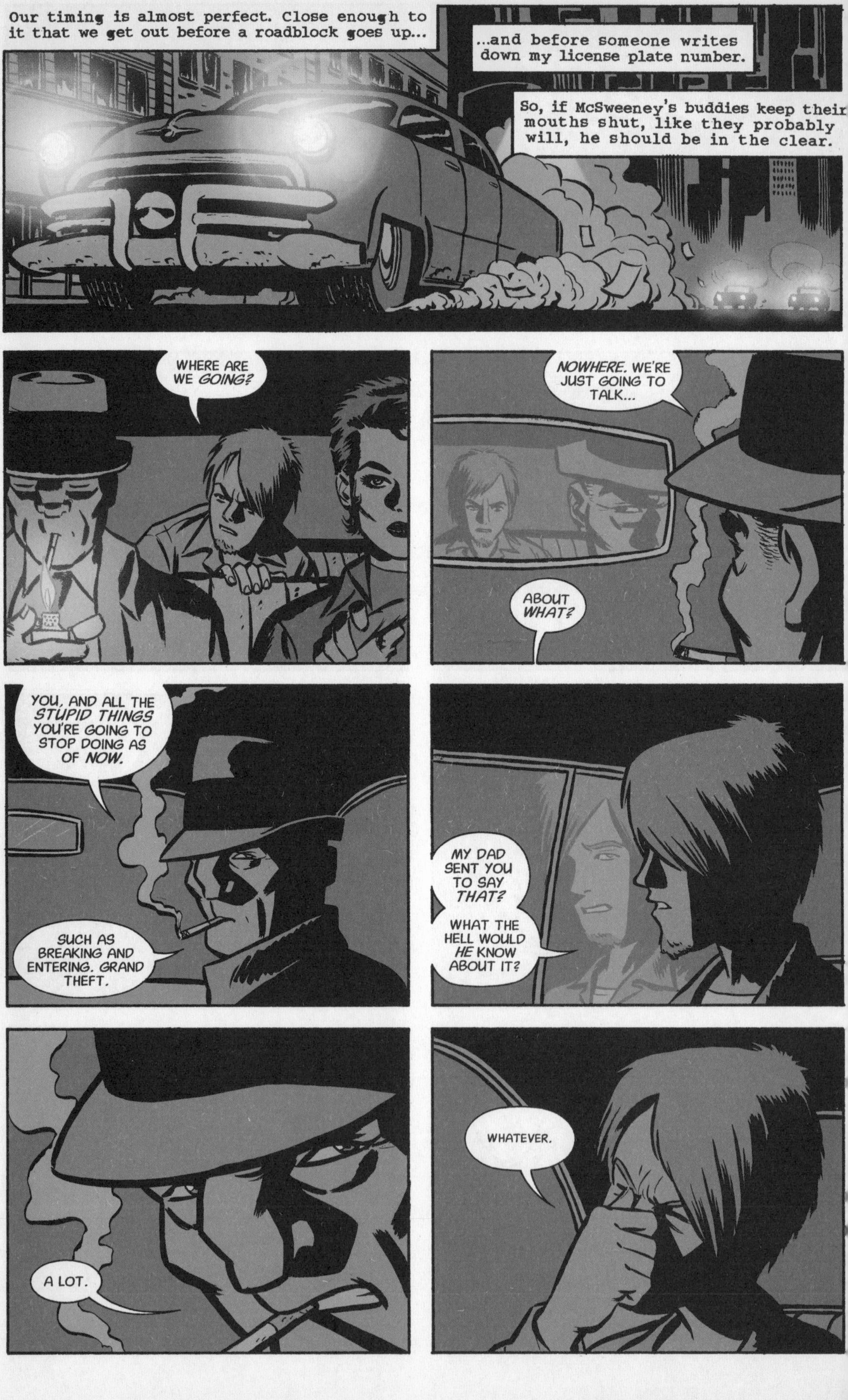
Our timing is almost perfect. Close enough to it that we get out before a roadblock goes up...
...and before someone writes down my license plate number.
So, if McSweeney's buddies keep their mouths shut, like they probably will, he should be in the clear.
WHERE ARE WE GOING?
NOWHERE. WE'RE JUST GOING TO TALK...
ABOUT WHAT?
YOU, AND ALL THE STUPID THINGS YOU'RE GOING TO STOP DOING AS OF NOW.
SUCH AS BREAKING AND ENTERING. GRAND THEFT.
MY DAD SENT YOU TO SAY THAT?
WHAT THE HELL WOULD HE KNOW ABOUT IT?
A LOT.
WHATEVER.

NO, NOT "WHATEVER"-- LOOK, YOUR DAD WAS A *CRUMMY* FATHER. HE *KNOWS* THAT.

BUT HE SEES *YOU* HEADING DOWN THE SAME PATH HE DID... THE DRINKING, THE CRIME...

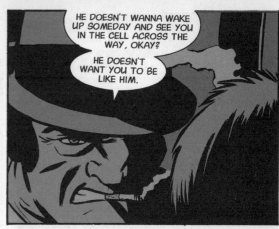

HE DOESN'T WANNA WAKE UP SOMEDAY AND SEE YOU IN THE CELL ACROSS THE WAY, OKAY?

HE DOESN'T WANT YOU TO BE LIKE HIM.

HE SAID HE WANTED TO GIVE YOU THE SECOND CHANCE HE ALWAYS *WISHED* HE HAD, BEFORE IT WAS *TOO LATE* FOR YOU...

...BEFORE YOU SCREWED YOUR LIFE UP *SO BAD* YOU COULD *NEVER GO BACK.*

HE... HE *SAID* THAT?

JUST 'CAUSE HE'S A *LOUSY* DAD DOESN'T MEAN HE'S NOT STILL YOUR *DAD,* KID.

OKAY, HERE YOU GO.

WHAT? WHERE ARE WE?

SKREEK

NOWHERE. NOW GET OUT.

THIS IS WHERE YOUR *SECOND CHANCE* BEGINS.

MOST OF US AREN'T *LUCKY* ENOUGH TO GET ONE. DON'T THROW IT AWAY.

UH... YEAH... I *GUESS.*

SO, WERE YOU FRIENDS WITH HIS DAD OR SOMETHING?

YEAH... SORT OF...

Actually, I helped put his dad, Tommy McSweeney, in prison twelve years ago. He's doing life without the possibility of parole.

And I can't explain why I'm not more forthcoming about this with Selina...

Certainly I trust her, it's just, thinking about the McSweeneys makes me think about other things, too.

Pitiful fathers, wishing they could change the past...

HAPPY FATHER'S DAY!

regardless of all the damage done.

Maybe that's the REAL problem with the modern world...

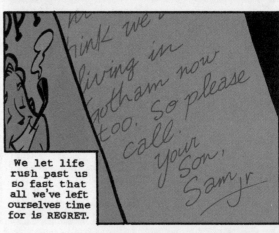

...think we... ...living in ...otham now too. So please call. Your Son, Sam jr

We let life rush past us so fast that all we've left ourselves time for is REGRET.

And God knows there's plenty of that to go around.

YOU'RE IN A WEIRD MOOD TONIGHT...

I'M OKAY... JUST TIRED.

THE END

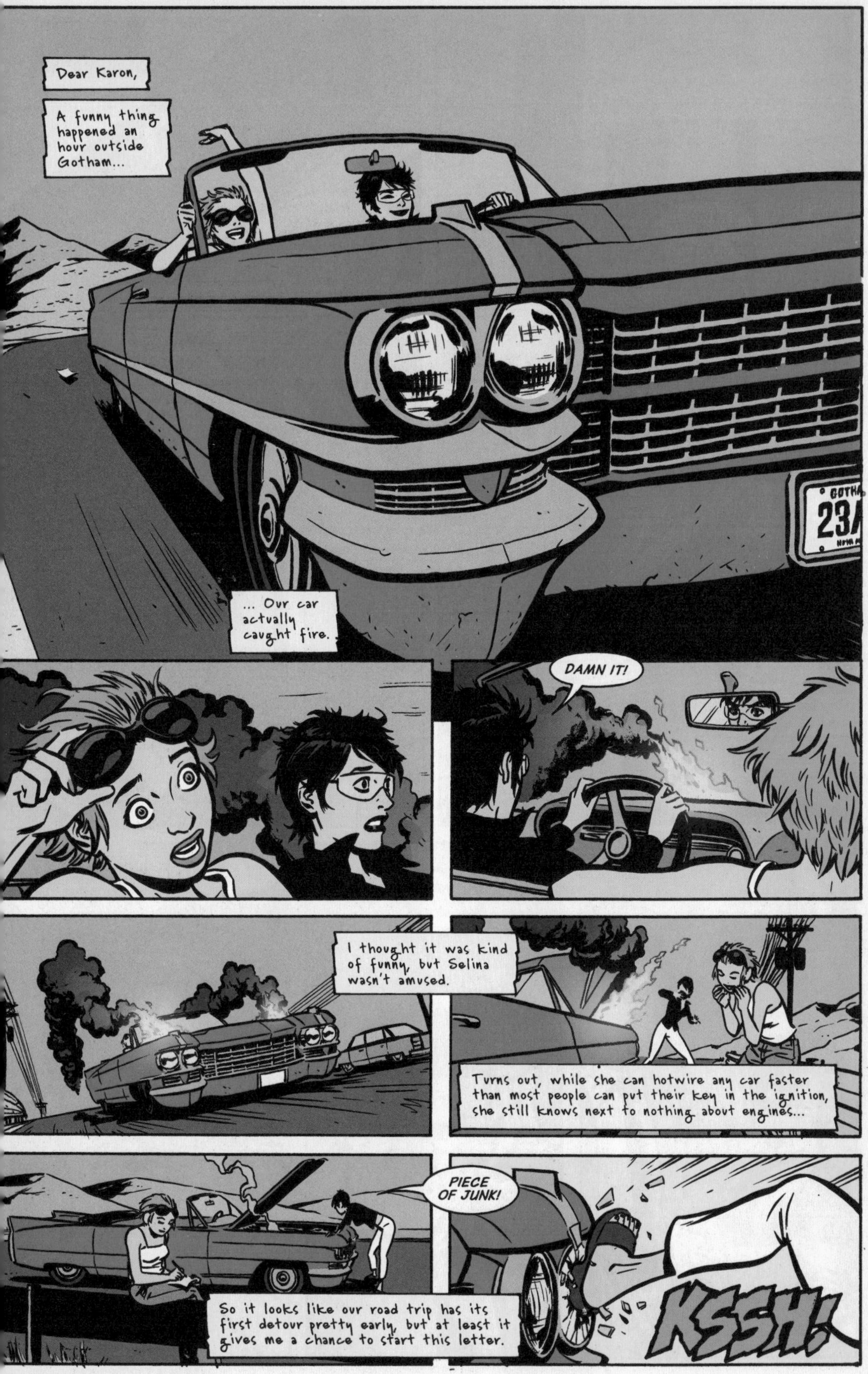
Dear Karon,
A funny thing happened an hour outside Gotham...
... Our car actually caught fire.
DAMN IT!
I thought it was kind of funny, but Selina wasn't amused.
Turns out, while she can hotwire any car faster than most people can put their key in the ignition, she still knows next to nothing about engines...
PIECE OF JUNK!
So it looks like our road trip has its first detour pretty early, but at least it gives me a chance to start this letter.
KSSH!

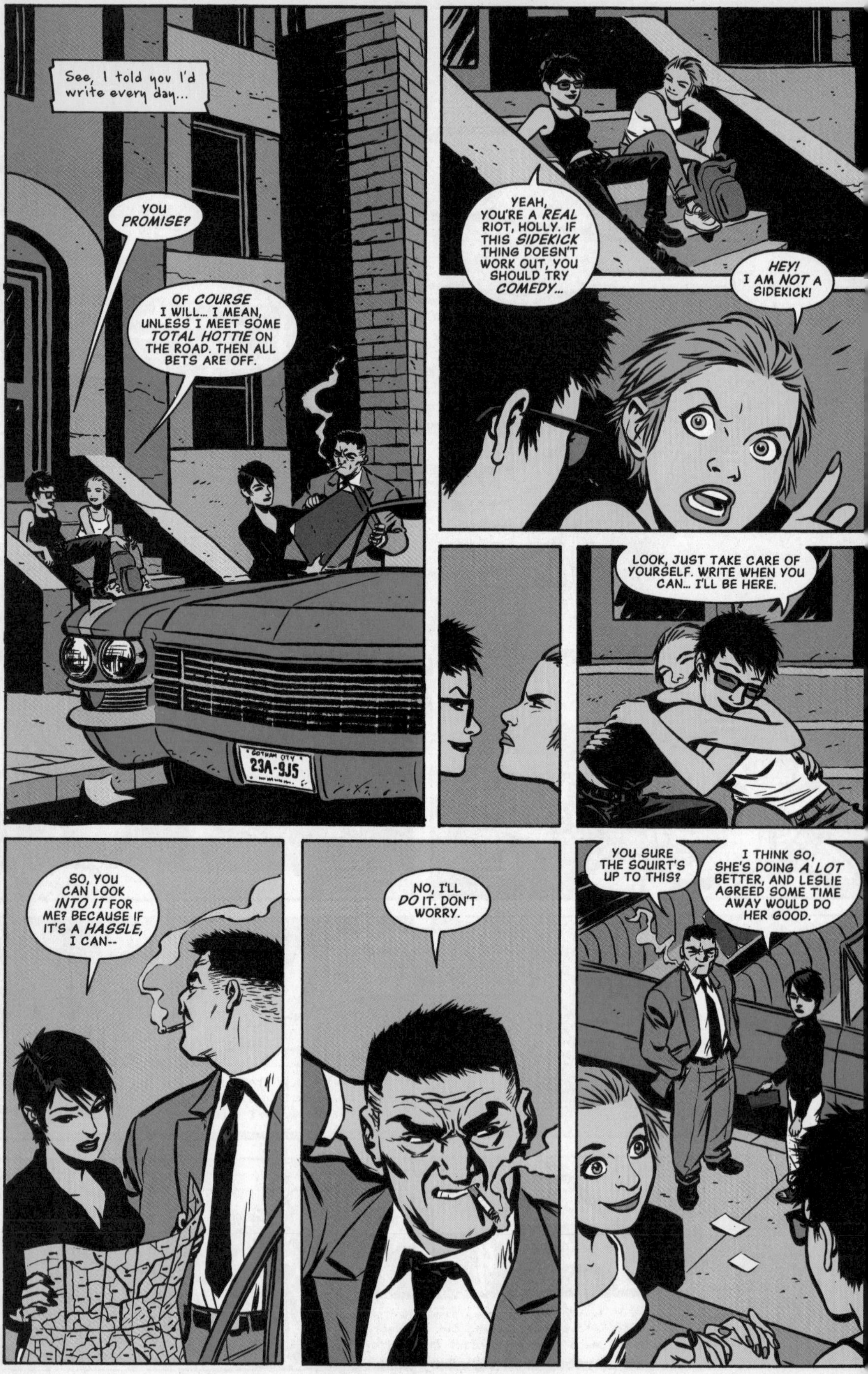
See, I told you I'd write every day...
YOU PROMISE?
OF COURSE I WILL... I MEAN, UNLESS I MEET SOME TOTAL HOTTIE ON THE ROAD. THEN ALL BETS ARE OFF.
GOTHAM CITY
23A-9J5
YEAH, YOU'RE A REAL RIOT, HOLLY. IF THIS SIDEKICK THING DOESN'T WORK OUT, YOU SHOULD TRY COMEDY...
HEY! I AM NOT A SIDEKICK!
LOOK, JUST TAKE CARE OF YOURSELF. WRITE WHEN YOU CAN... I'LL BE HERE.
SO, YOU CAN LOOK INTO IT FOR ME? BECAUSE IF IT'S A HASSLE, I CAN--
NO, I'LL DO IT. DON'T WORRY.
YOU SURE THE SQUIRT'S UP TO THIS?
I THINK SO, SHE'S DOING A LOT BETTER, AND LESLIE AGREED SOME TIME AWAY WOULD DO HER GOOD.

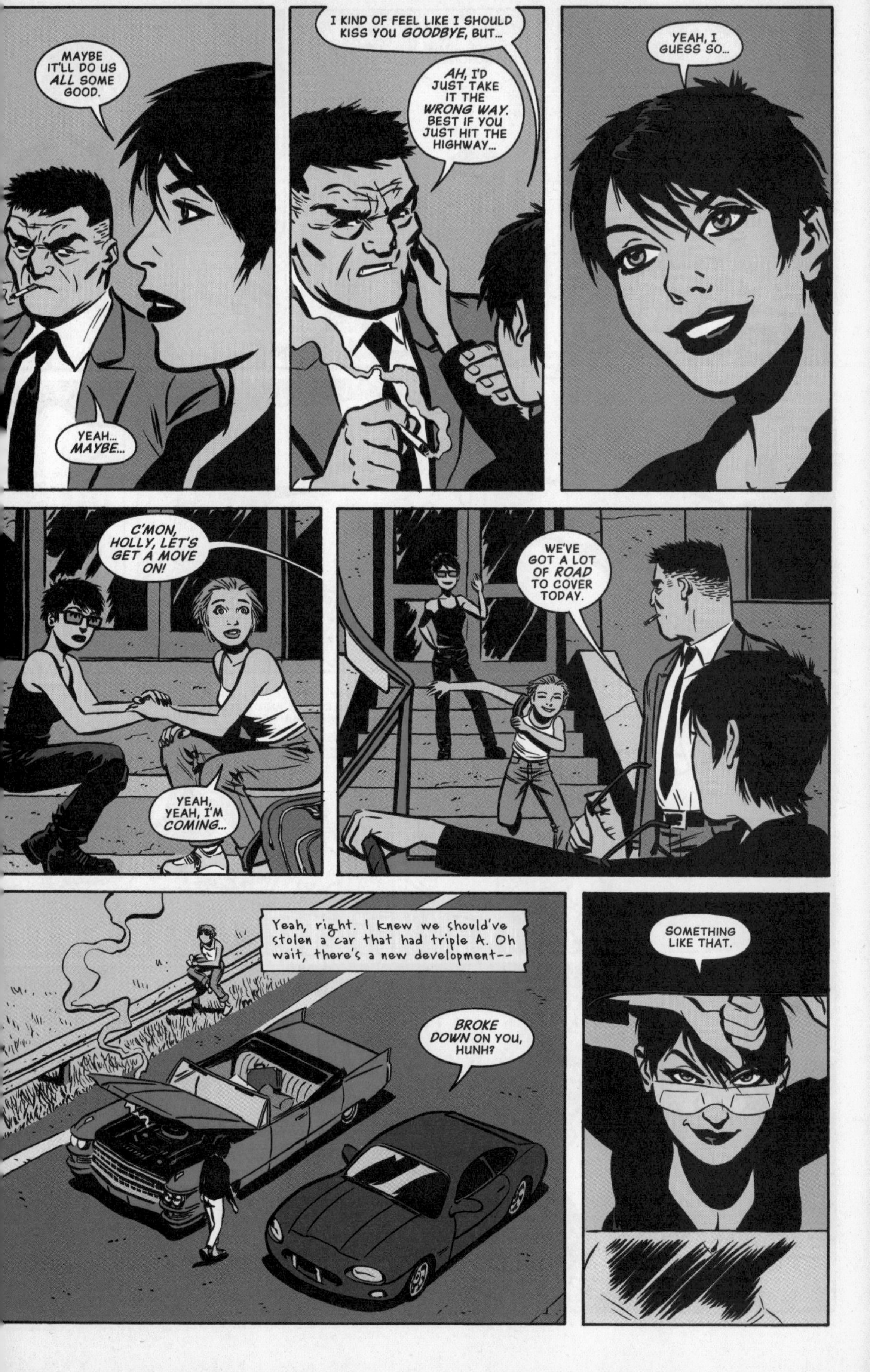
MAYBE IT'LL DO US ALL SOME GOOD.
YEAH... MAYBE...
I KIND OF FEEL LIKE I SHOULD KISS YOU GOODBYE, BUT...
AH, I'D JUST TAKE IT THE WRONG WAY. BEST IF YOU JUST HIT THE HIGHWAY...
YEAH, I GUESS SO...
C'MON, HOLLY, LET'S GET A MOVE ON!
YEAH, YEAH, I'M COMING...
WE'VE GOT A LOT OF ROAD TO COVER TODAY.
Yeah, right. I knew we should've stolen a car that had triple A. Oh wait, there's a new development--
BROKE DOWN ON YOU, HUNH?
SOMETHING LIKE THAT.

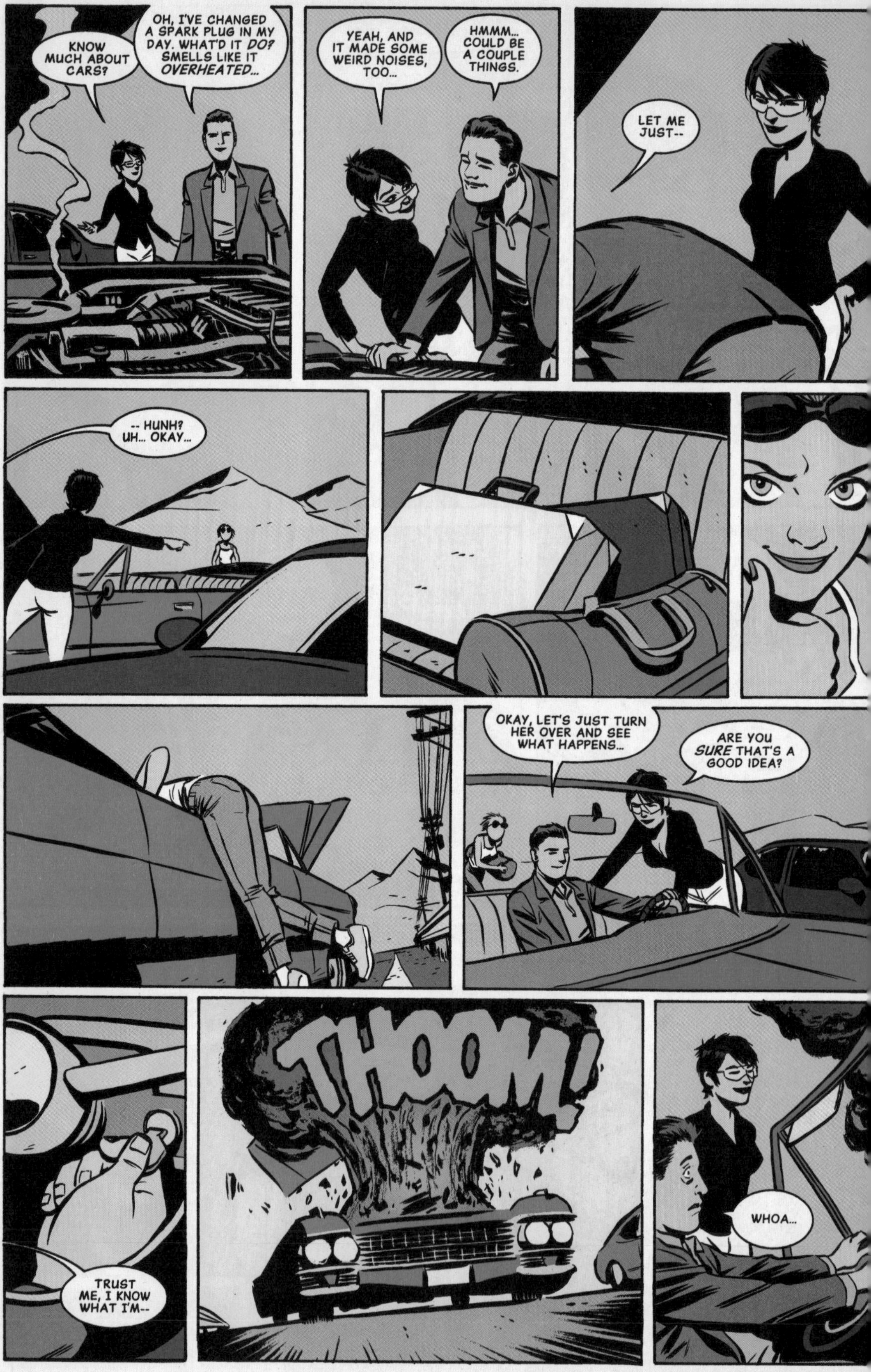

KNOW MUCH ABOUT CARS?
OH, I'VE CHANGED A SPARK PLUG IN MY DAY. WHAT'D IT DO? SMELLS LIKE IT OVERHEATED...
YEAH, AND IT MADE SOME WEIRD NOISES, TOO...
HMMM... COULD BE A COUPLE THINGS.
LET ME JUST--
-- HUNH? UH... OKAY...
OKAY, LET'S JUST TURN HER OVER AND SEE WHAT HAPPENS...
ARE YOU SURE THAT'S A GOOD IDEA?
TRUST ME, I KNOW WHAT I'M--
THOOM!
WHOA...

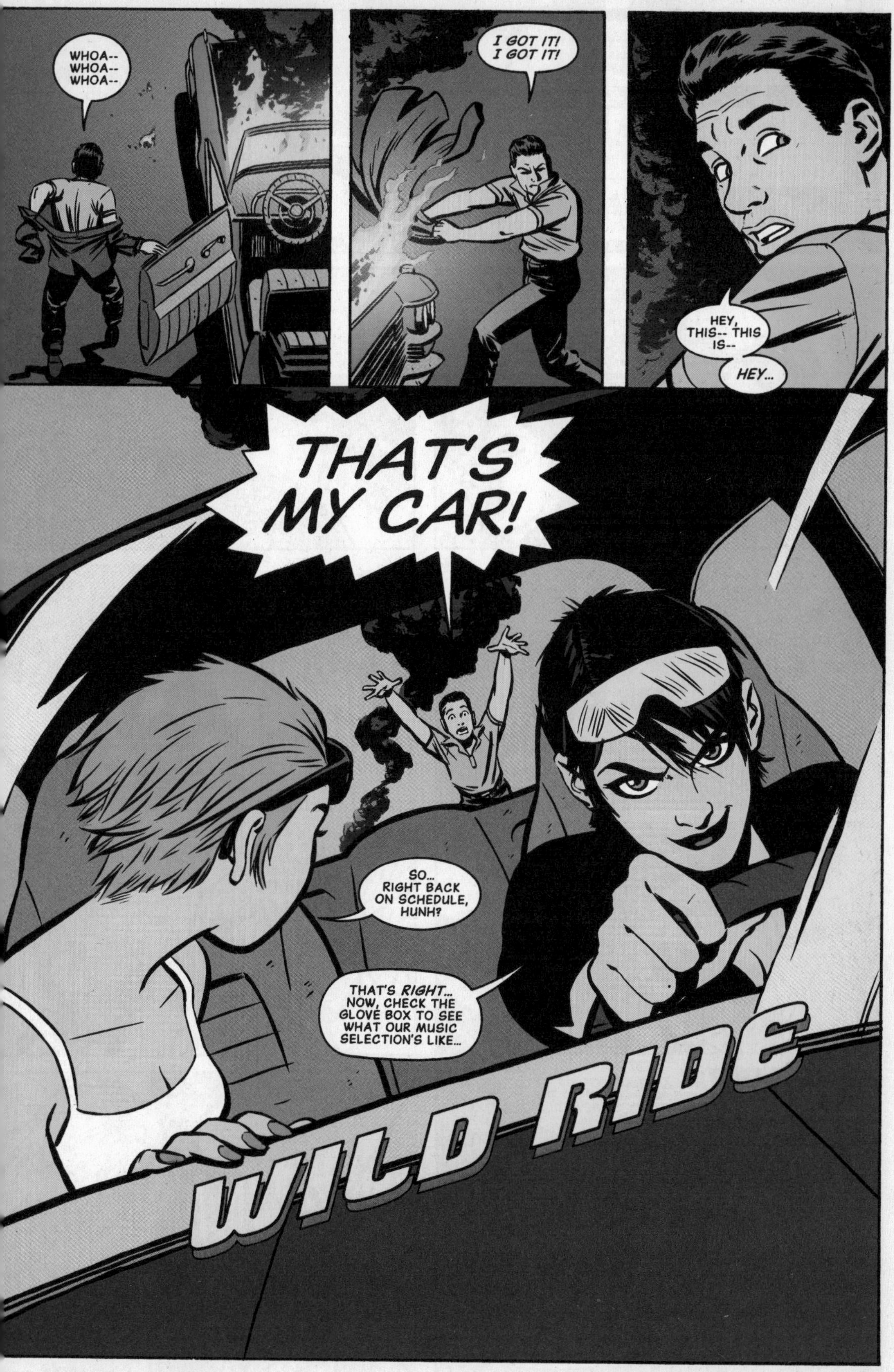
WHOA-- WHOA-- WHOA--
I GOT IT! I GOT IT!
HEY, THIS-- THIS IS--
HEY...
THAT'S MY CAR!
SO... RIGHT BACK ON SCHEDULE, HUNH?
THAT'S RIGHT... NOW, CHECK THE GLOVE BOX TO SEE WHAT OUR MUSIC SELECTION'S LIKE...
WILD RIDE

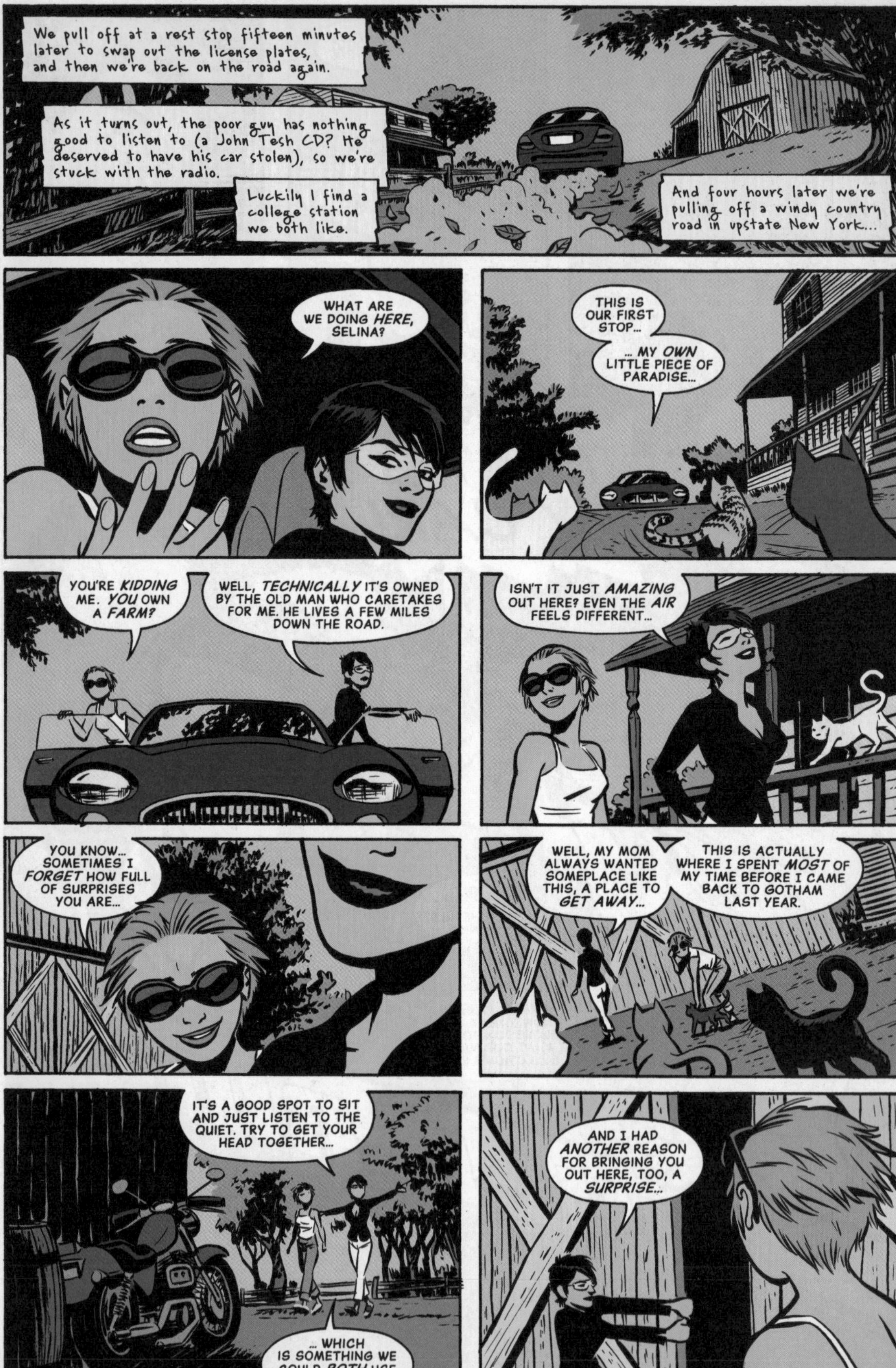

We pull off at a rest stop fifteen minutes later to swap out the license plates, and then we're back on the road again.
As it turns out, the poor guy has nothing good to listen to (a John Tesh CD? He deserved to have his car stolen), so we're stuck with the radio.
Luckily I find a college station we both like.
And four hours later we're pulling off a windy country road in upstate New York...
WHAT ARE WE DOING HERE, SELINA?
THIS IS OUR FIRST STOP...
... MY OWN LITTLE PIECE OF PARADISE...
YOU'RE KIDDING ME. YOU OWN A FARM?
WELL, TECHNICALLY IT'S OWNED BY THE OLD MAN WHO CARETAKES FOR ME. HE LIVES A FEW MILES DOWN THE ROAD.
ISN'T IT JUST AMAZING OUT HERE? EVEN THE AIR FEELS DIFFERENT...
YOU KNOW... SOMETIMES I FORGET HOW FULL OF SURPRISES YOU ARE...
WELL, MY MOM ALWAYS WANTED SOMEPLACE LIKE THIS, A PLACE TO GET AWAY...
THIS IS ACTUALLY WHERE I SPENT MOST OF MY TIME BEFORE I CAME BACK TO GOTHAM LAST YEAR.
IT'S A GOOD SPOT TO SIT AND JUST LISTEN TO THE QUIET. TRY TO GET YOUR HEAD TOGETHER...
... WHICH IS SOMETHING WE COULD BOTH USE ABOUT NOW.
AND I HAD ANOTHER REASON FOR BRINGING YOU OUT HERE, TOO, A SURPRISE...

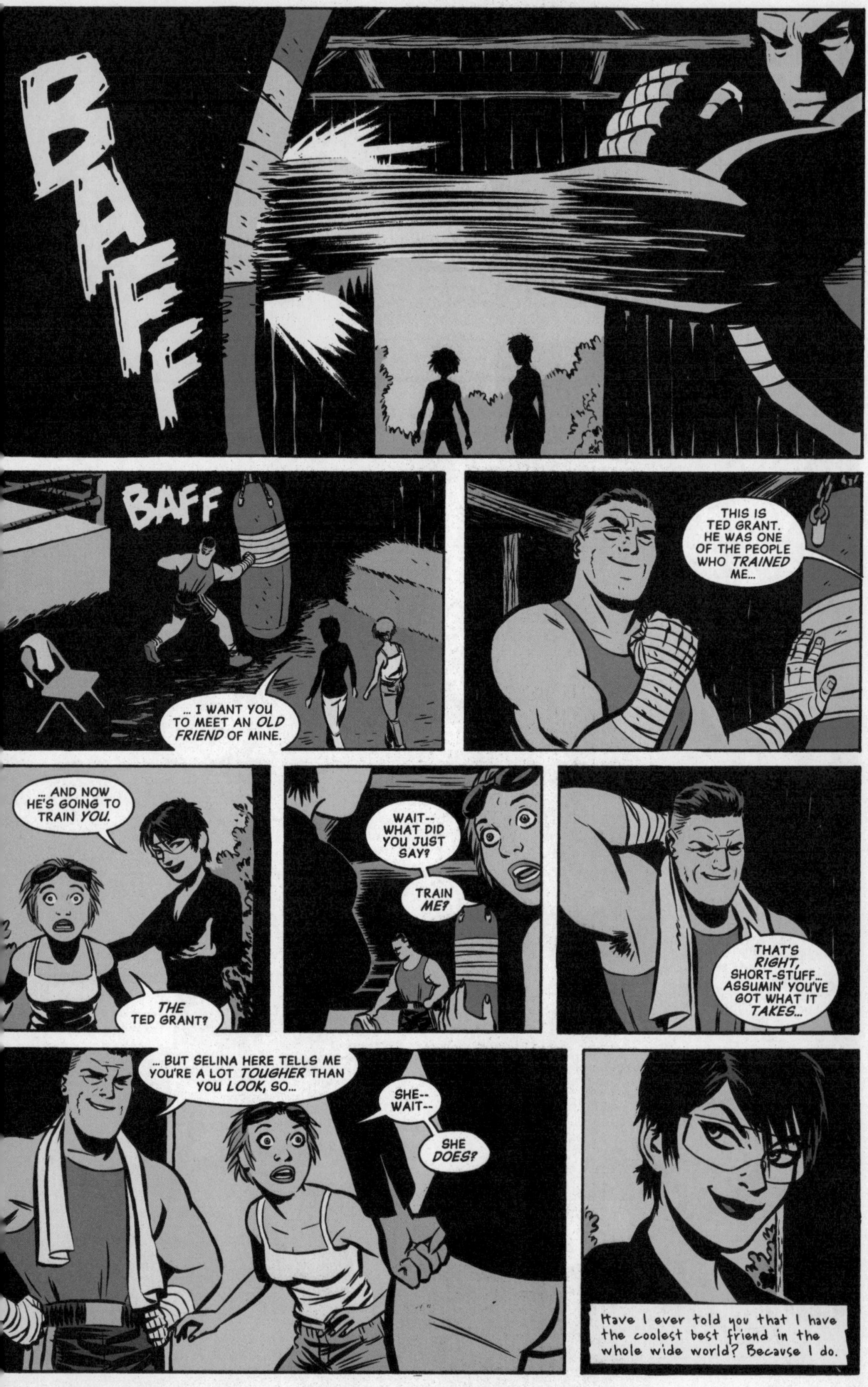
BAFF
BAFF
... I WANT YOU TO MEET AN OLD FRIEND OF MINE.
THIS IS TED GRANT. HE WAS ONE OF THE PEOPLE WHO TRAINED ME...
... AND NOW HE'S GOING TO TRAIN YOU.
THE TED GRANT?
WAIT-- WHAT DID YOU JUST SAY?
TRAIN ME?
THAT'S RIGHT, SHORT-STUFF... ASSUMIN' YOU'VE GOT WHAT IT TAKES...
... BUT SELINA HERE TELLS ME YOU'RE A LOT TOUGHER THAN YOU LOOK, SO...
SHE-- WAIT--
SHE DOES?
Have I ever told you that I have the coolest best friend in the whole wide world? Because I do.

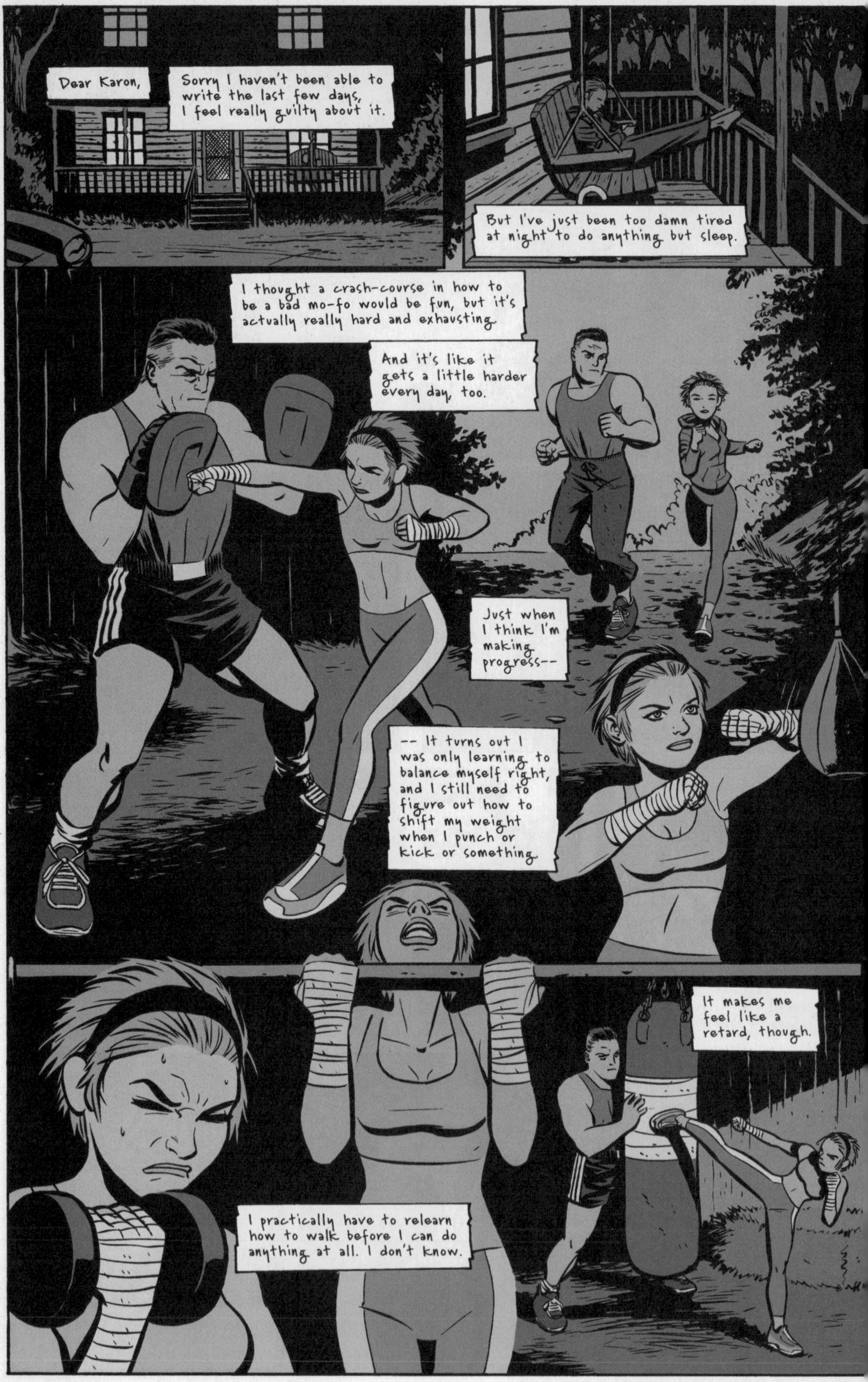

Dear Karon,
Sorry I haven't been able to write the last few days, I feel really guilty about it.
But I've just been too damn tired at night to do anything but sleep.
I thought a crash-course in how to be a bad mo-fo would be fun, but it's actually really hard and exhausting.
And it's like it gets a little harder every day, too.
Just when I think I'm making progress--
-- It turns out I was only learning to balance myself right, and I still need to figure out how to shift my weight when I punch or kick or something.
I practically have to relearn how to walk before I can do anything at all. I don't know.
It makes me feel like a retard, though.

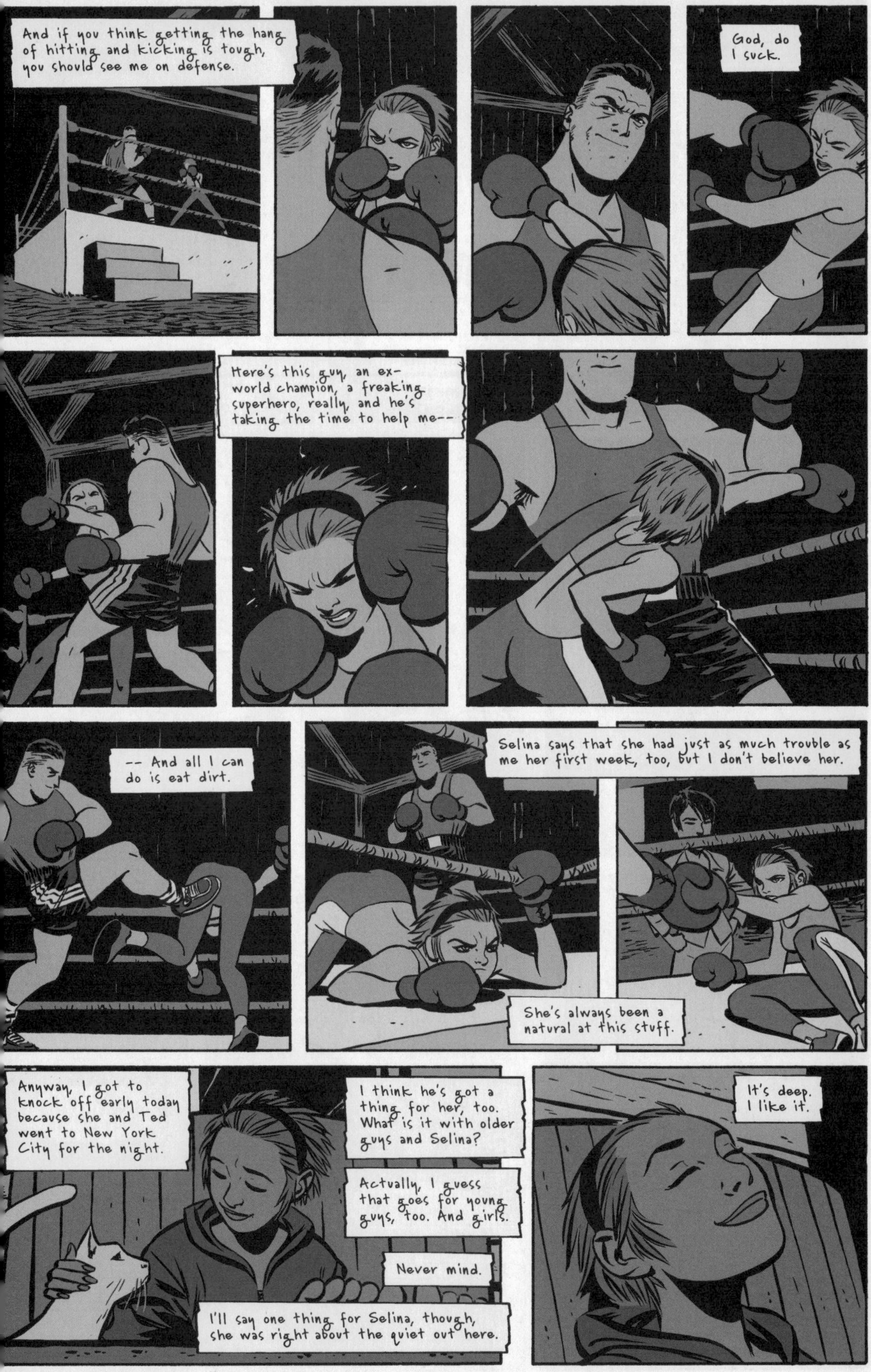
And if you think getting the hang of hitting and kicking is tough, you should see me on defense.
God, do I suck.
Here's this guy, an ex-world champion, a freaking superhero, really, and he's taking the time to help me--
-- And all I can do is eat dirt.
Selina says that she had just as much trouble as me her first week, too, but I don't believe her.
She's always been a natural at this stuff.
Anyway, I got to knock off early today because she and Ted went to New York City for the night.
I think he's got a thing for her, too. What is it with older guys and Selina?
Actually, I guess that goes for young guys, too. And girls.
Never mind.
I'll say one thing for Selina, though, she was right about the quiet out here.
It's deep. I like it.

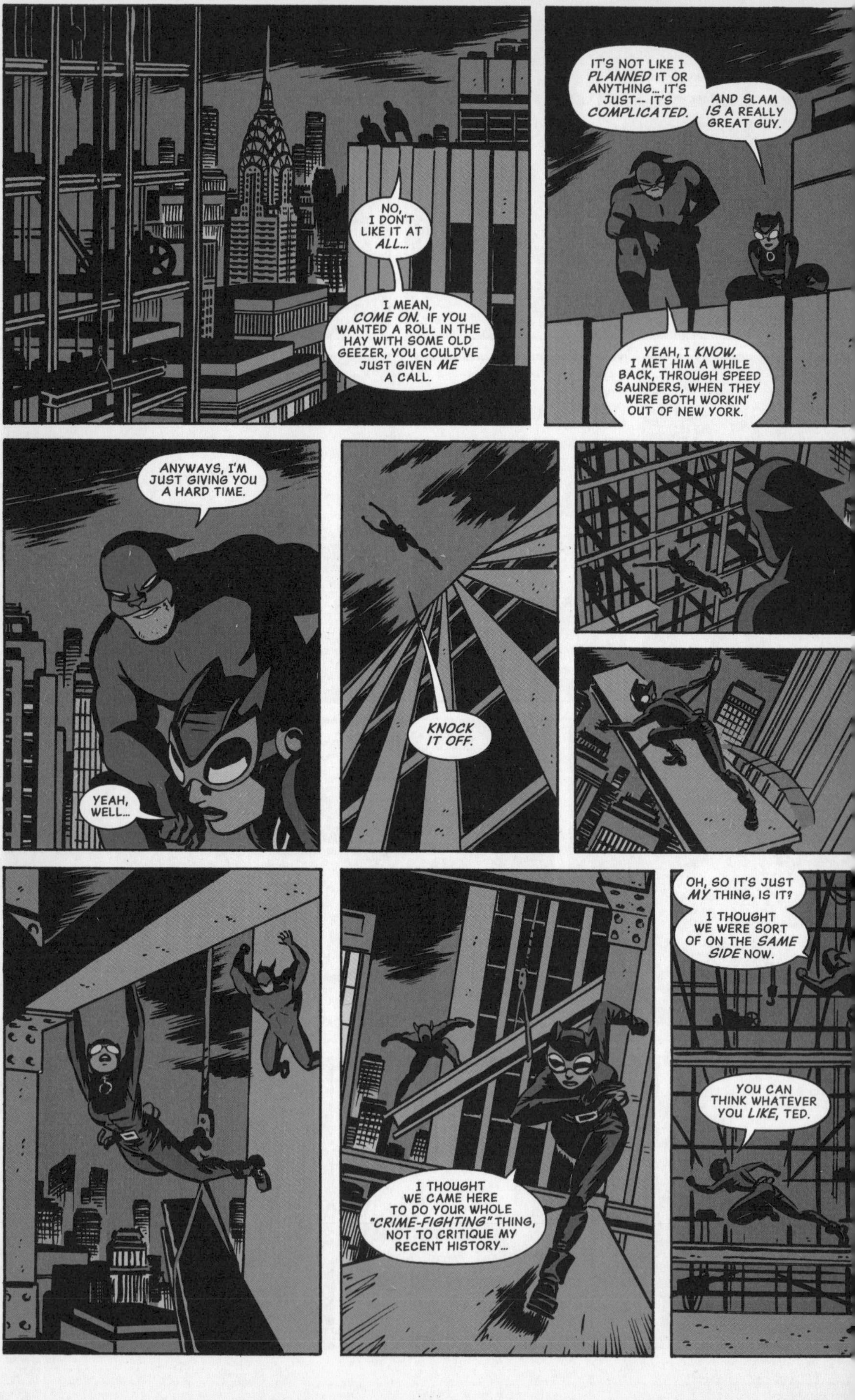
NO, I DON'T LIKE IT AT ALL...
I MEAN, COME ON. IF YOU WANTED A ROLL IN THE HAY WITH SOME OLD GEEZER, YOU COULD'VE JUST GIVEN ME A CALL.
IT'S NOT LIKE I PLANNED IT OR ANYTHING... IT'S JUST-- IT'S COMPLICATED.
AND SLAM IS A REALLY GREAT GUY.
YEAH, I KNOW. I MET HIM A WHILE BACK, THROUGH SPEED SAUNDERS, WHEN THEY WERE BOTH WORKIN' OUT OF NEW YORK.
ANYWAYS, I'M JUST GIVING YOU A HARD TIME.
YEAH, WELL...
KNOCK IT OFF.
I THOUGHT WE CAME HERE TO DO YOUR WHOLE "CRIME-FIGHTING" THING, NOT TO CRITIQUE MY RECENT HISTORY...
OH, SO IT'S JUST MY THING, IS IT?
I THOUGHT WE WERE SORT OF ON THE SAME SIDE NOW.
YOU CAN THINK WHATEVER YOU LIKE, TED.

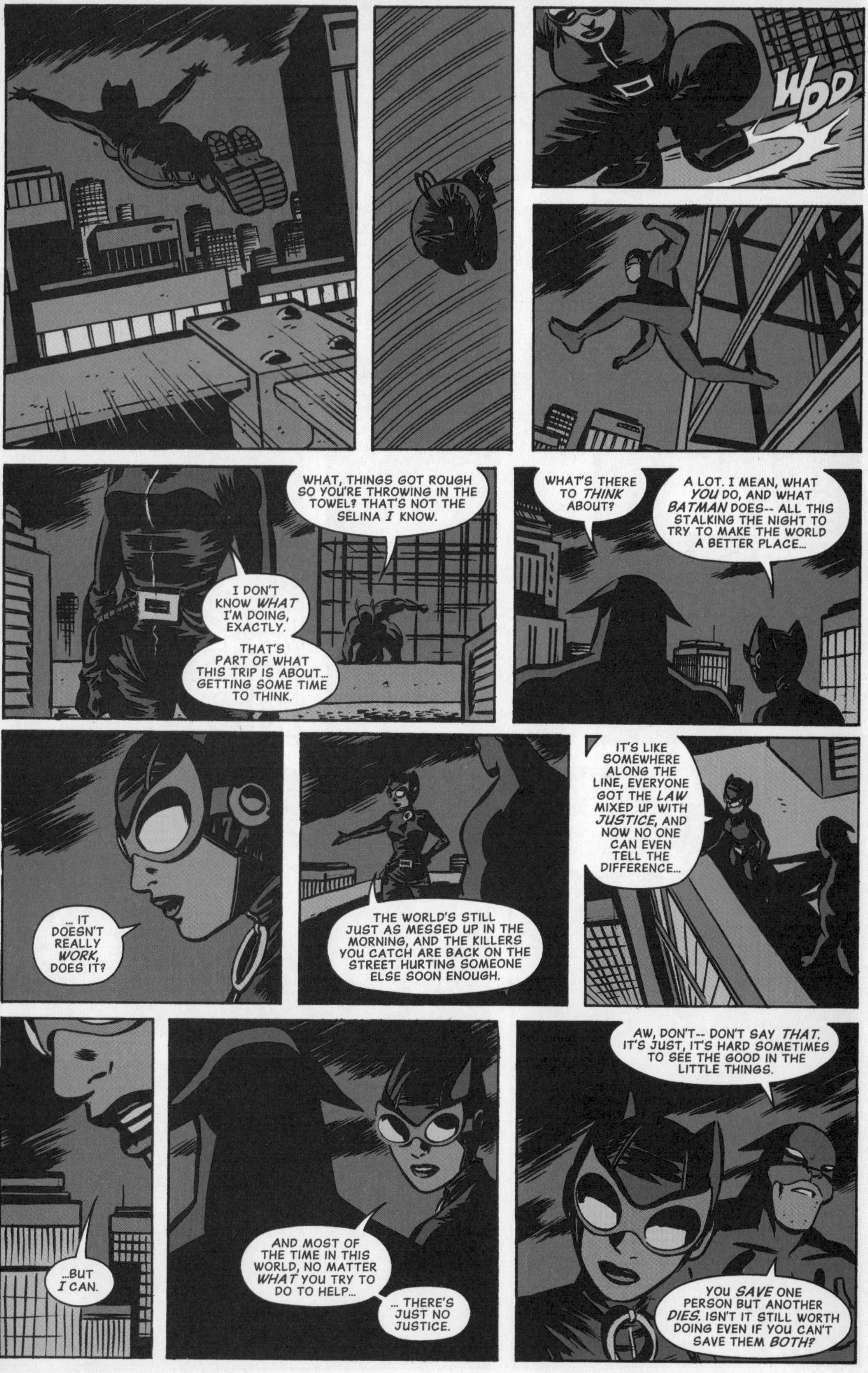
WDD
WHAT, THINGS GOT ROUGH SO YOU'RE THROWING IN THE TOWEL? THAT'S NOT THE SELINA I KNOW.
I DON'T KNOW WHAT I'M DOING, EXACTLY.
THAT'S PART OF WHAT THIS TRIP IS ABOUT... GETTING SOME TIME TO THINK.
WHAT'S THERE TO THINK ABOUT?
A LOT. I MEAN, WHAT YOU DO, AND WHAT BATMAN DOES-- ALL THIS STALKING THE NIGHT TO TRY TO MAKE THE WORLD A BETTER PLACE...
... IT DOESN'T REALLY WORK, DOES IT?
THE WORLD'S STILL JUST AS MESSED UP IN THE MORNING, AND THE KILLERS YOU CATCH ARE BACK ON THE STREET HURTING SOMEONE ELSE SOON ENOUGH.
IT'S LIKE SOMEWHERE ALONG THE LINE, EVERYONE GOT THE LAW MIXED UP WITH JUSTICE, AND NOW NO ONE CAN EVEN TELL THE DIFFERENCE...
...BUT I CAN.
AND MOST OF THE TIME IN THIS WORLD, NO MATTER WHAT YOU TRY TO DO TO HELP...
... THERE'S JUST NO JUSTICE.
AW, DON'T-- DON'T SAY THAT. IT'S JUST, IT'S HARD SOMETIMES TO SEE THE GOOD IN THE LITTLE THINGS.
YOU SAVE ONE PERSON BUT ANOTHER DIES. ISN'T IT STILL WORTH DOING EVEN IF YOU CAN'T SAVE THEM BOTH?

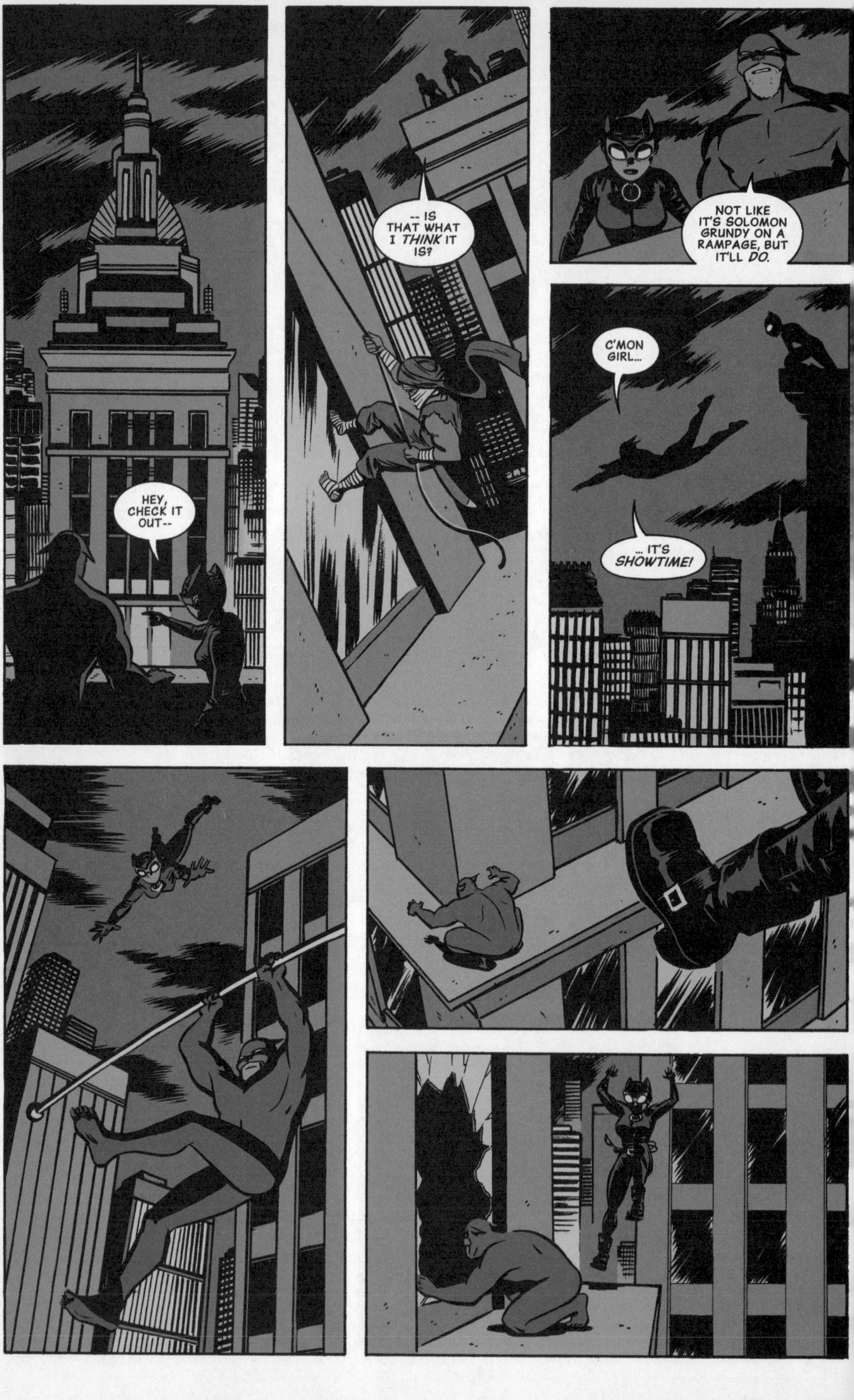
HEY, CHECK IT OUT--
-- IS THAT WHAT I *THINK* IT IS?
NOT LIKE IT'S SOLOMON GRUNDY ON A RAMPAGE, BUT IT'LL *DO*.
C'MON GIRL...
... IT'S *SHOWTIME!*

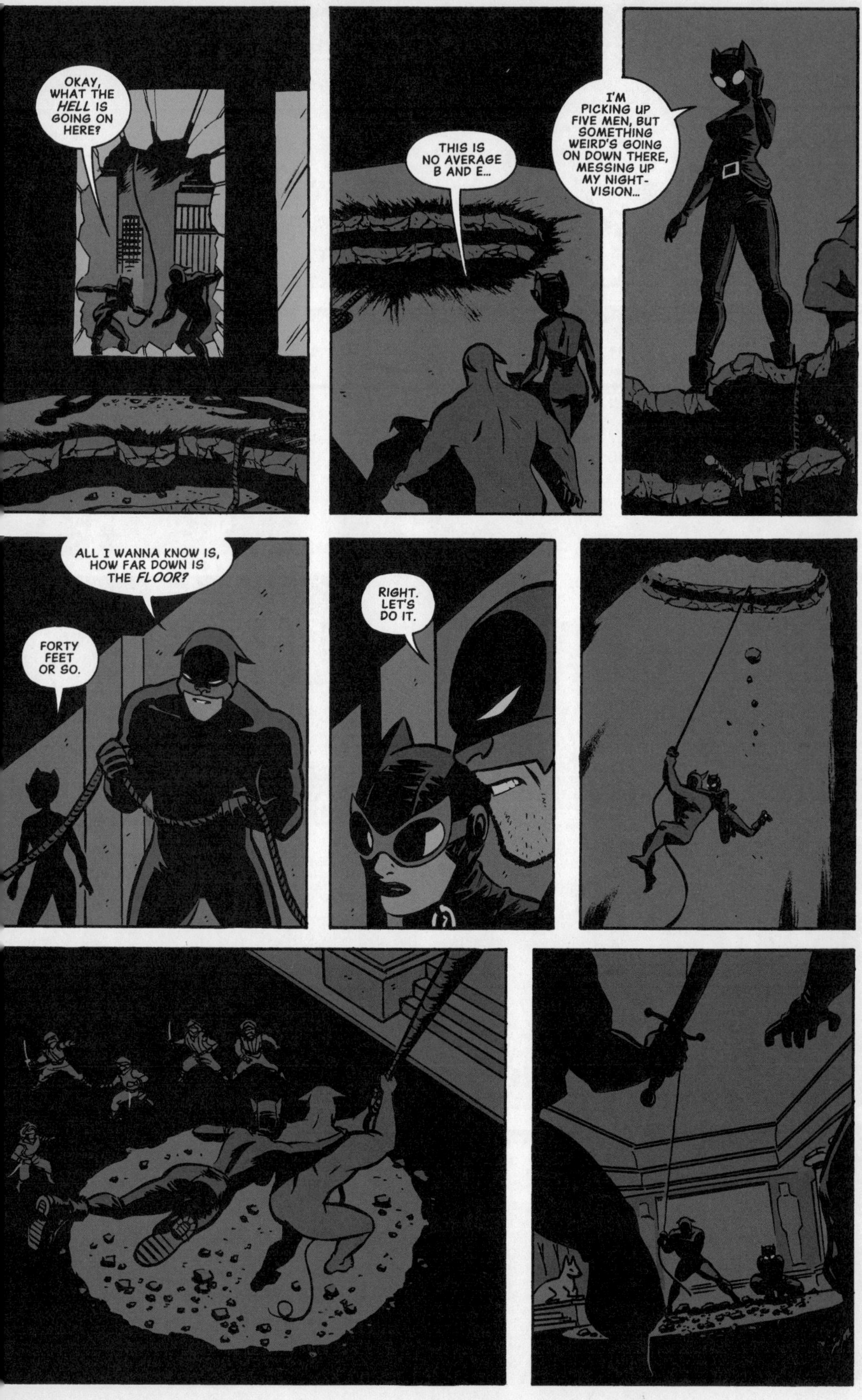
OKAY, WHAT THE *HELL* IS GOING ON HERE?
THIS IS NO AVERAGE B AND E...
I'M PICKING UP FIVE MEN, BUT SOMETHING WEIRD'S GOING ON DOWN THERE, MESSING UP MY NIGHT-VISION...
ALL I WANNA KNOW IS, HOW FAR DOWN IS THE *FLOOR?*
FORTY FEET OR SO.
RIGHT. LET'S DO IT.

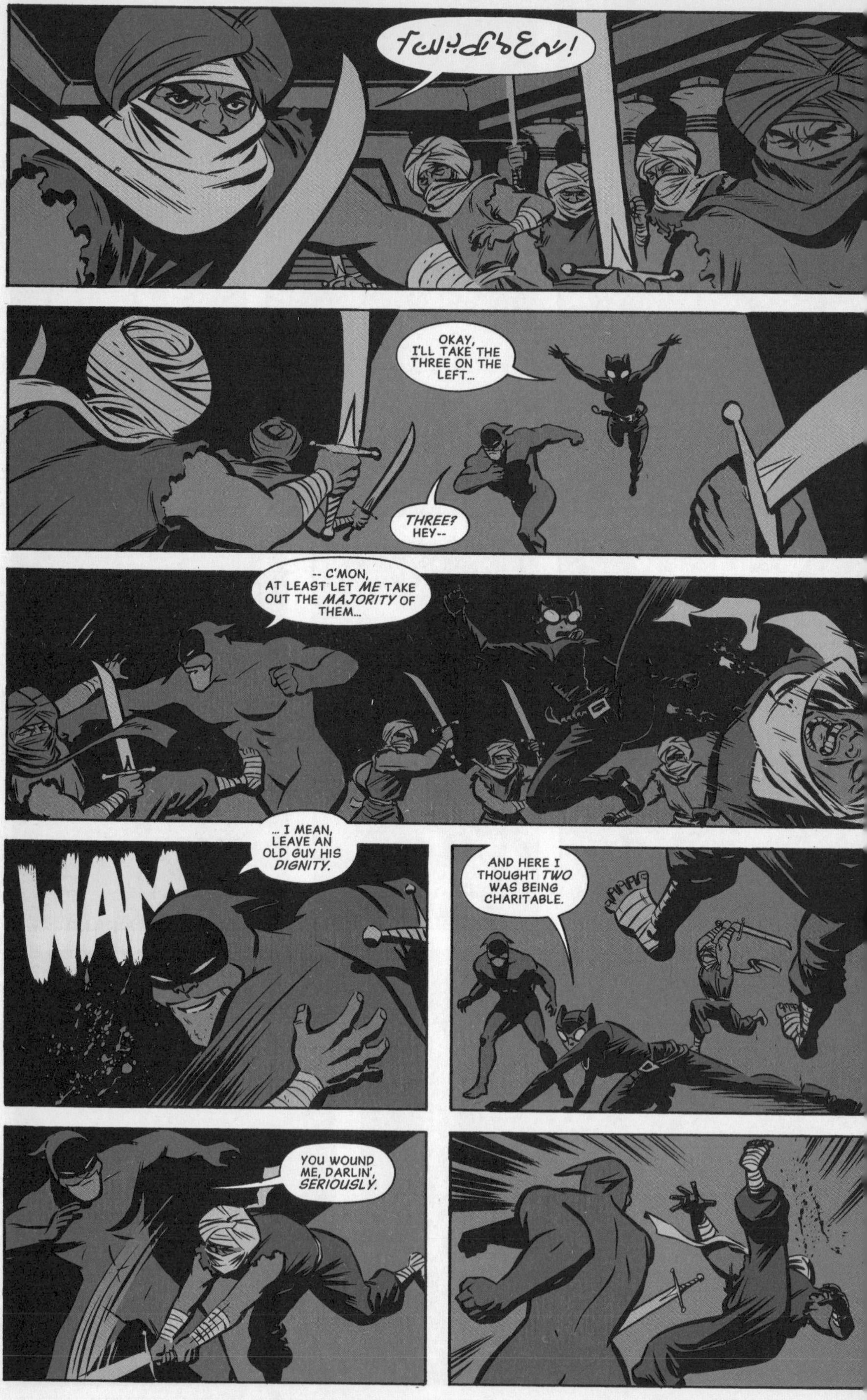
OKAY, I'LL TAKE THE THREE ON THE LEFT...
THREE? HEY--
-- C'MON, AT LEAST LET ME TAKE OUT THE MAJORITY OF THEM...
... I MEAN, LEAVE AN OLD GUY HIS DIGNITY.
WAM
AND HERE I THOUGHT TWO WAS BEING CHARITABLE.
YOU WOUND ME, DARLIN', SERIOUSLY.

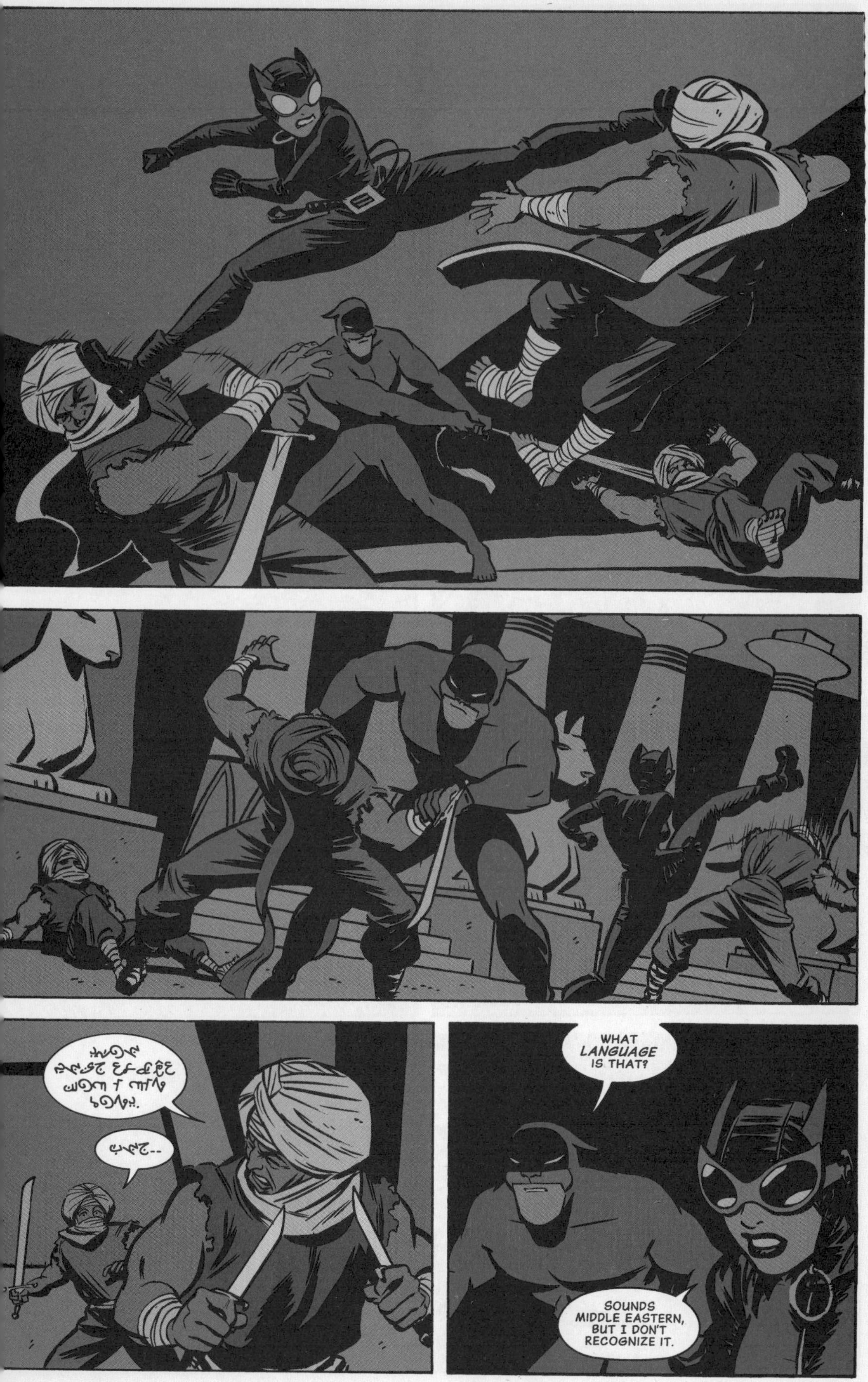
WHAT LANGUAGE IS THAT?
SOUNDS MIDDLE EASTERN, BUT I DON'T RECOGNIZE IT.

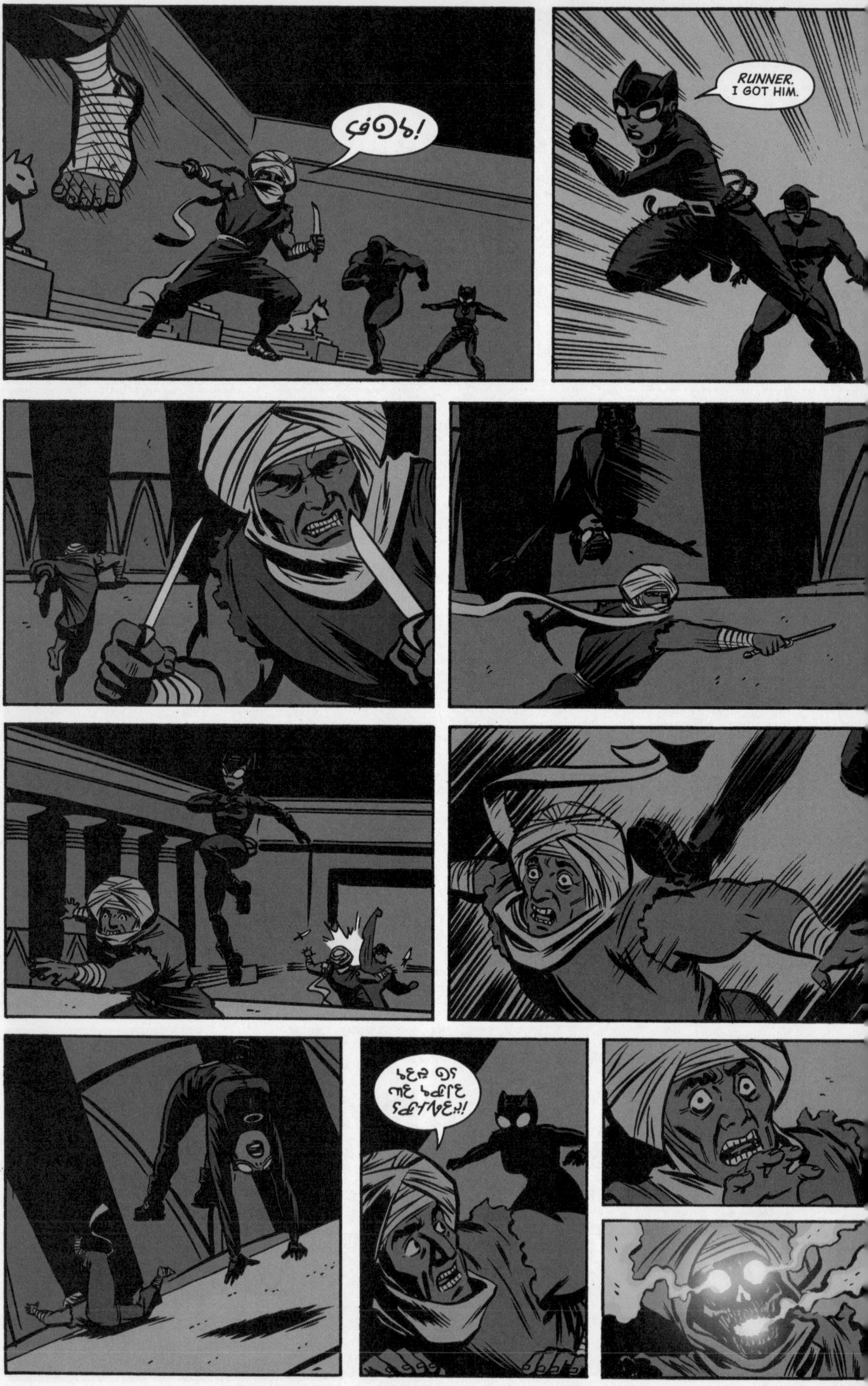
RUNNER.
I GOT HIM.

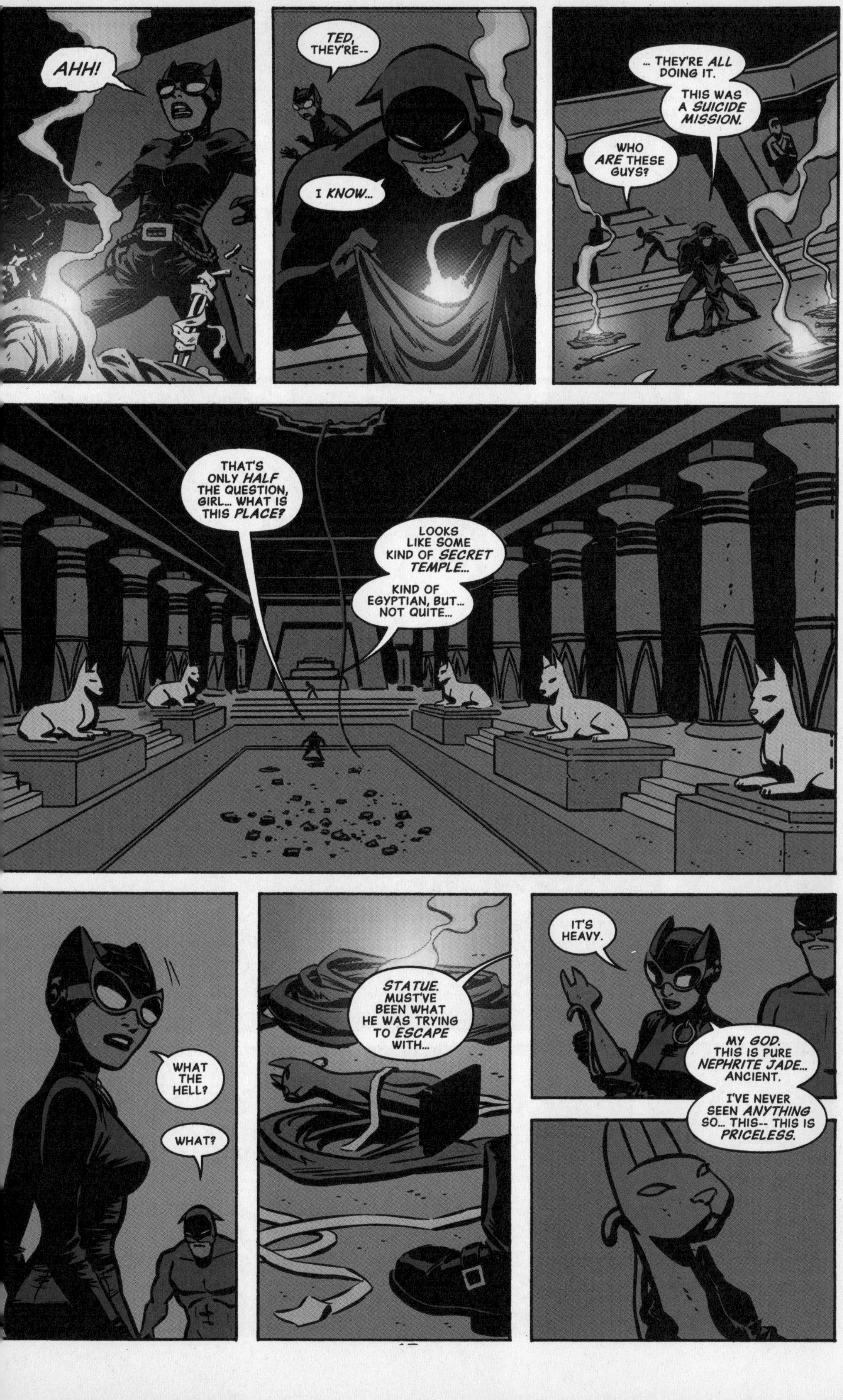
AHH!
TED, THEY'RE--
I KNOW...
... THEY'RE ALL DOING IT.
THIS WAS A SUICIDE MISSION.
WHO ARE THESE GUYS?
THAT'S ONLY HALF THE QUESTION, GIRL... WHAT IS THIS PLACE?
LOOKS LIKE SOME KIND OF SECRET TEMPLE...
KIND OF EGYPTIAN, BUT... NOT QUITE...
WHAT THE HELL?
WHAT?
STATUE. MUST'VE BEEN WHAT HE WAS TRYING TO ESCAPE WITH...
IT'S HEAVY.
MY GOD, THIS IS PURE NEPHRITE JADE... ANCIENT.
I'VE NEVER SEEN ANYTHING SO... THIS-- THIS IS PRICELESS.

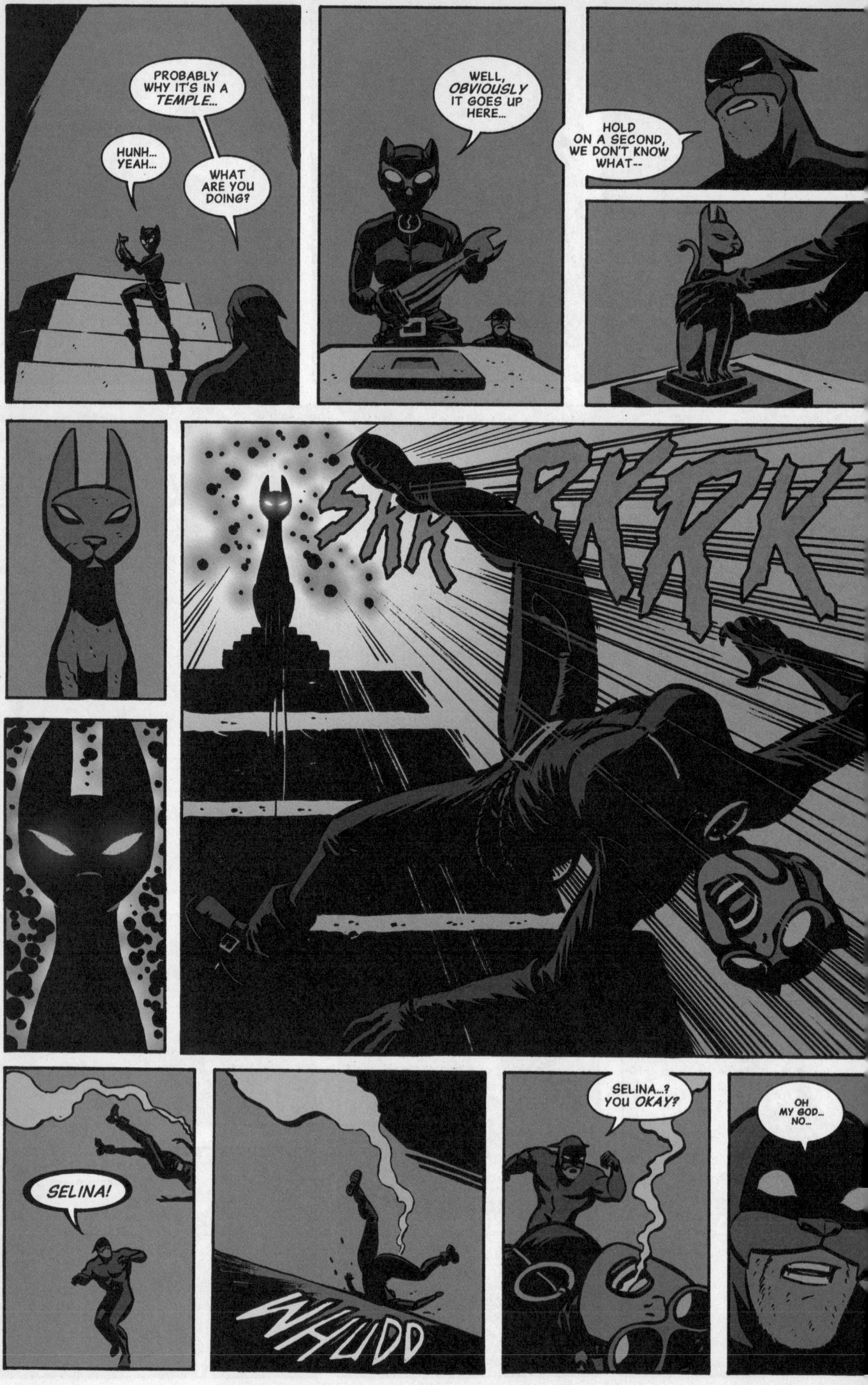
PROBABLY WHY IT'S IN A *TEMPLE*...
HUNH... YEAH...
WHAT ARE YOU DOING?
WELL, *OBVIOUSLY* IT GOES UP HERE...
HOLD ON A SECOND, WE DON'T KNOW WHAT--
SKRRKRKK
SELINA!
WHUDD
SELINA...? YOU *OKAY?*
OH MY GOD... NO...

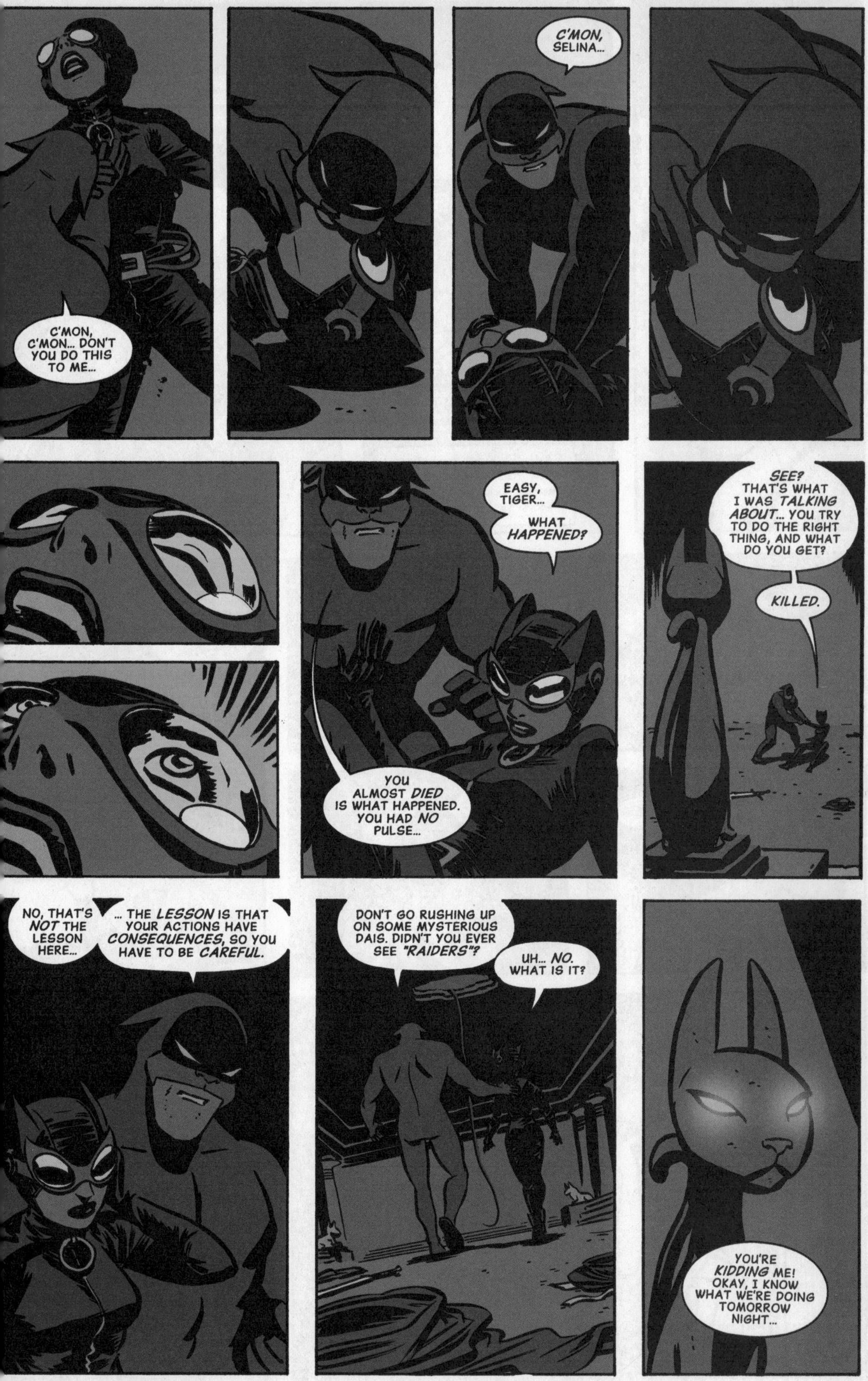
C'MON, C'MON... DON'T YOU DO THIS TO ME...
C'MON, SELINA...
EASY, TIGER...
WHAT HAPPENED?
YOU ALMOST DIED IS WHAT HAPPENED. YOU HAD NO PULSE...
SEE? THAT'S WHAT I WAS TALKING ABOUT... YOU TRY TO DO THE RIGHT THING, AND WHAT DO YOU GET?
KILLED.
NO, THAT'S NOT THE LESSON HERE...
... THE LESSON IS THAT YOUR ACTIONS HAVE CONSEQUENCES, SO YOU HAVE TO BE CAREFUL.
DON'T GO RUSHING UP ON SOME MYSTERIOUS DAIS. DIDN'T YOU EVER SEE "RAIDERS"?
UH... NO. WHAT IS IT?
YOU'RE KIDDING ME! OKAY, I KNOW WHAT WE'RE DOING TOMORROW NIGHT...

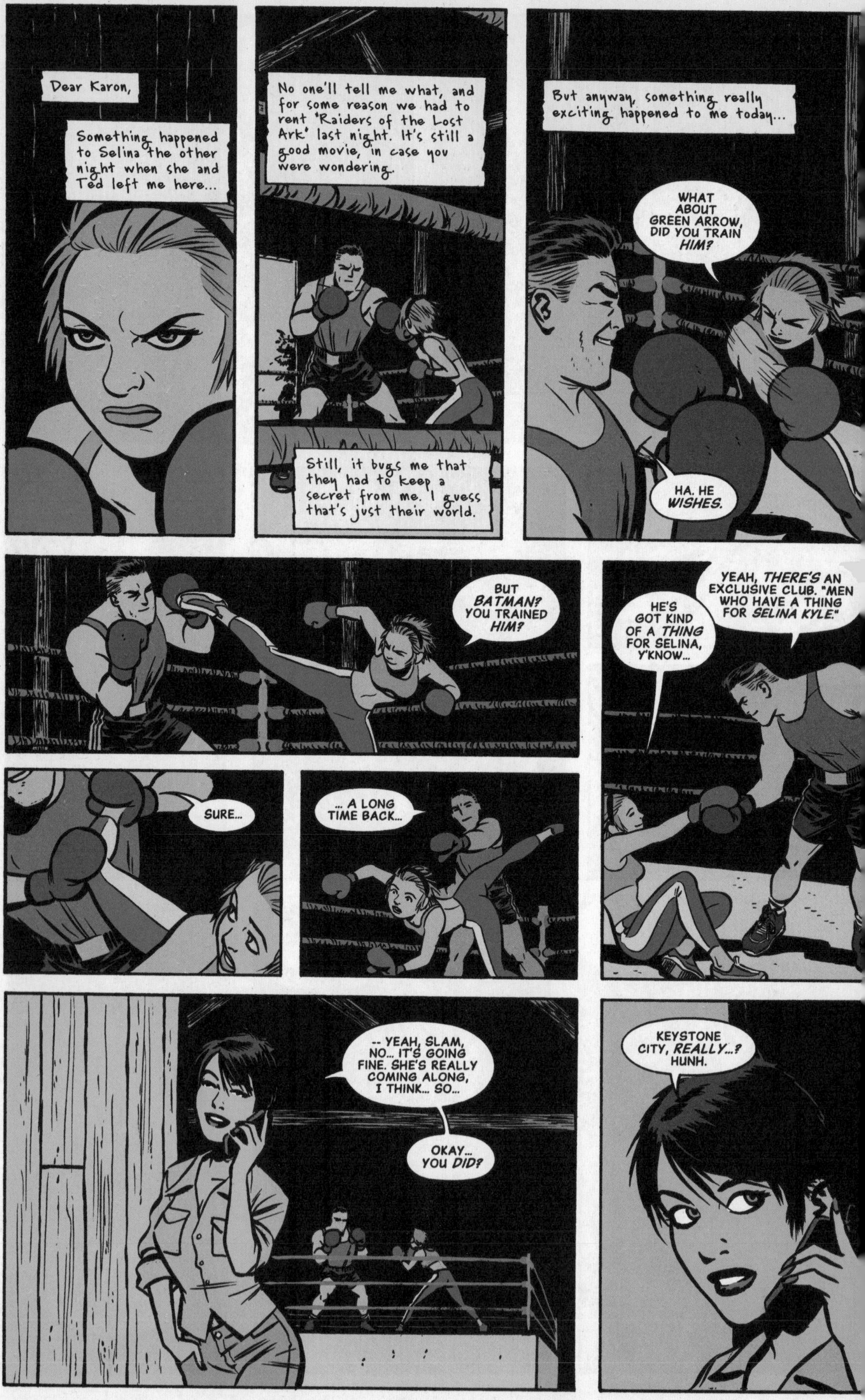
Dear Karon,
Something happened to Selina the other night when she and Ted left me here...
No one'll tell me what, and for some reason we had to rent "Raiders of the Lost Ark" last night. It's still a good movie, in case you were wondering.
Still, it bugs me that they had to keep a secret from me. I guess that's just their world.
But anyway, something really exciting happened to me today...
WHAT ABOUT GREEN ARROW, DID YOU TRAIN HIM?
HA. HE WISHES.
BUT BATMAN? YOU TRAINED HIM?
SURE...
... A LONG TIME BACK...
HE'S GOT KIND OF A THING FOR SELINA, Y'KNOW...
YEAH, THERE'S AN EXCLUSIVE CLUB. "MEN WHO HAVE A THING FOR SELINA KYLE."
-- YEAH, SLAM, NO... IT'S GOING FINE. SHE'S REALLY COMING ALONG, I THINK... SO...
OKAY... YOU DID?
KEYSTONE CITY, REALLY...? HUNH.

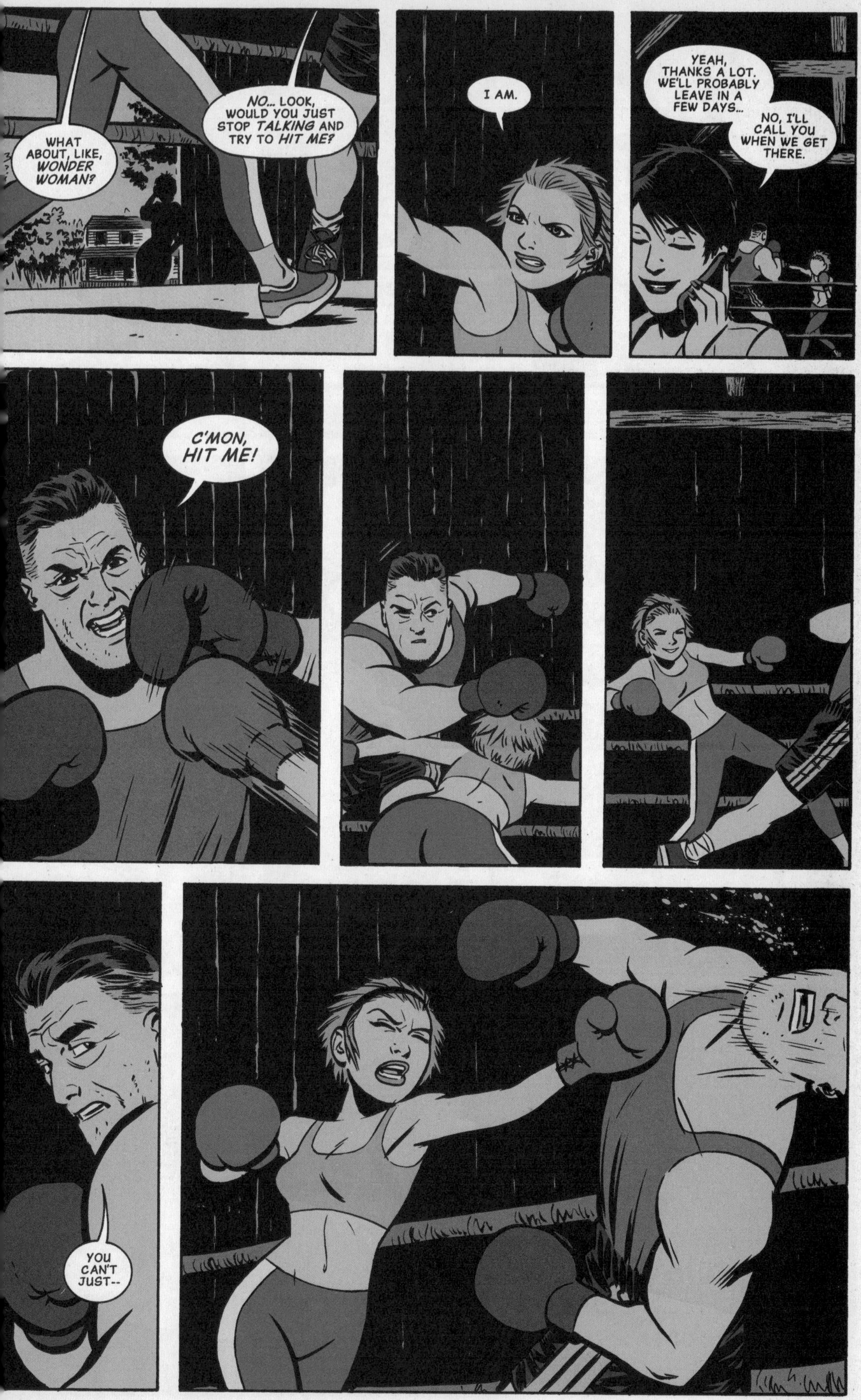
WHAT ABOUT, LIKE, WONDER WOMAN?
NO... LOOK, WOULD YOU JUST STOP TALKING AND TRY TO HIT ME?
I AM.
YEAH, THANKS A LOT. WE'LL PROBABLY LEAVE IN A FEW DAYS...
NO, I'LL CALL YOU WHEN WE GET THERE.
C'MON, HIT ME!
YOU CAN'T JUST--

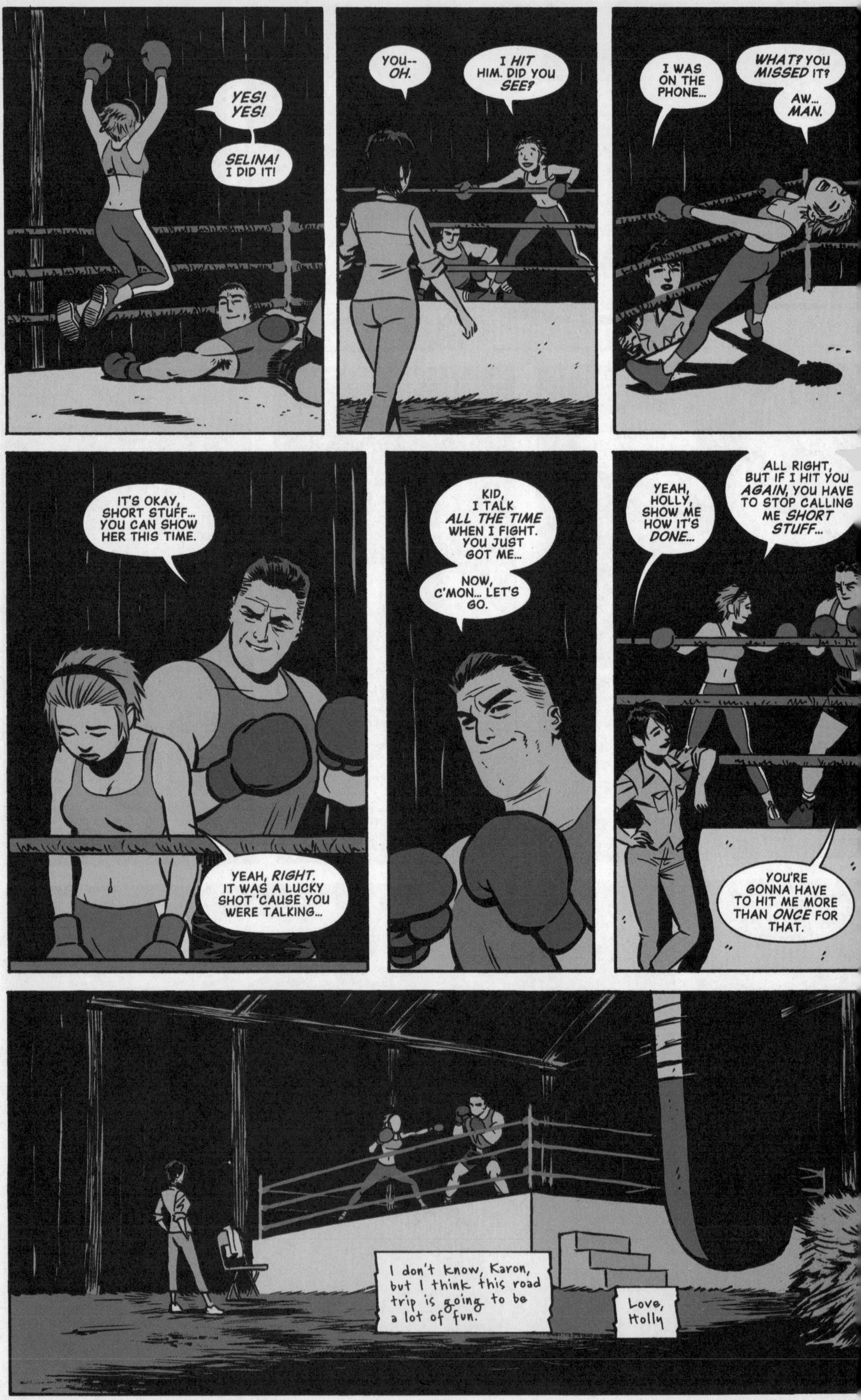
YES! YES!
SELINA! I DID IT!
YOU-- OH.
I HIT HIM. DID YOU SEE?
I WAS ON THE PHONE...
WHAT? YOU MISSED IT?
AW... MAN.
IT'S OKAY, SHORT STUFF... YOU CAN SHOW HER THIS TIME.
YEAH, RIGHT. IT WAS A LUCKY SHOT 'CAUSE YOU WERE TALKING...
KID, I TALK ALL THE TIME WHEN I FIGHT. YOU JUST GOT ME...
NOW, C'MON... LET'S GO.
YEAH, HOLLY, SHOW ME HOW IT'S DONE...
ALL RIGHT, BUT IF I HIT YOU AGAIN, YOU HAVE TO STOP CALLING ME SHORT STUFF...
YOU'RE GONNA HAVE TO HIT ME MORE THAN ONCE FOR THAT.
I don't know, Karon, but I think this road trip is going to be a lot of fun.
Love, Holly

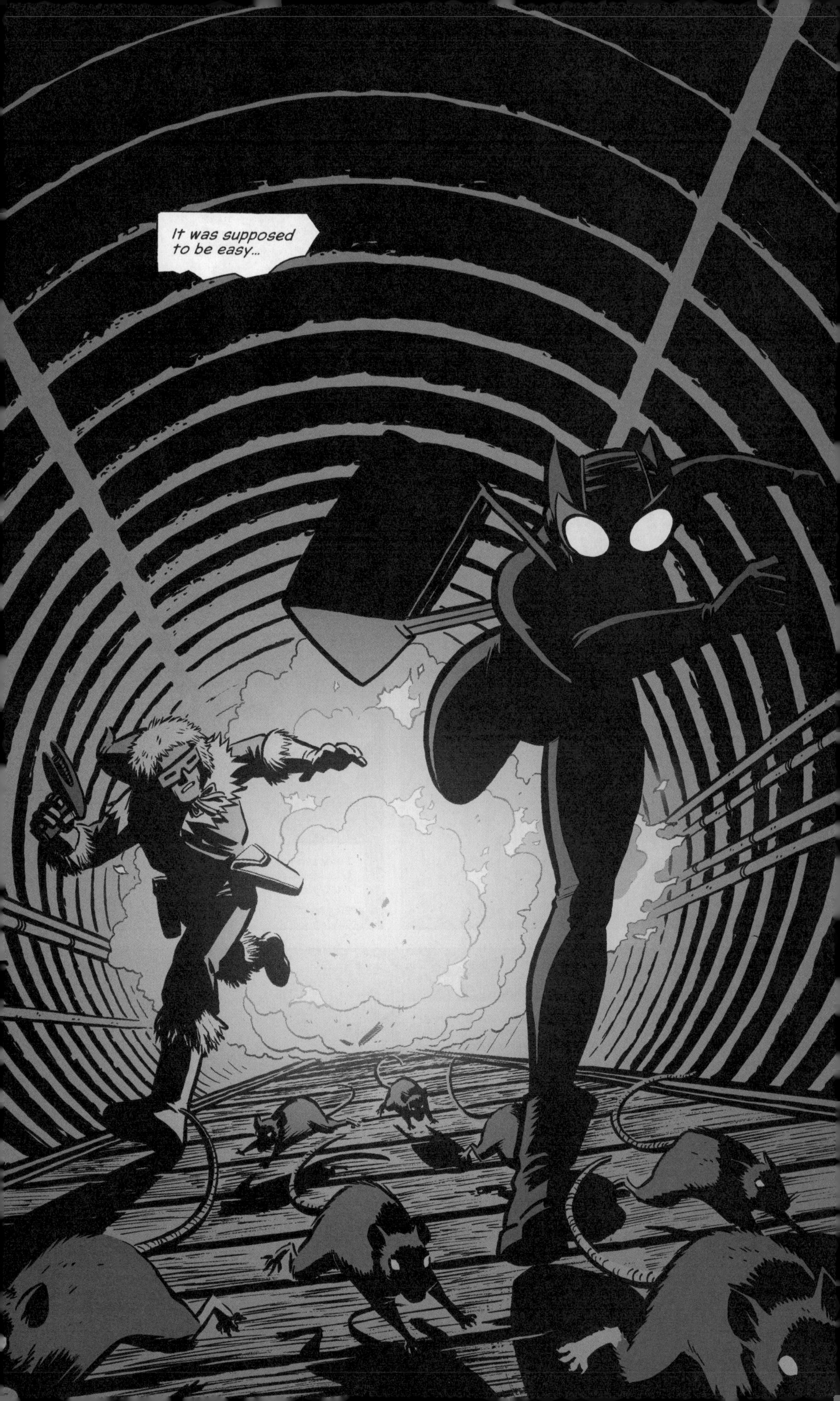
It was supposed to be easy...

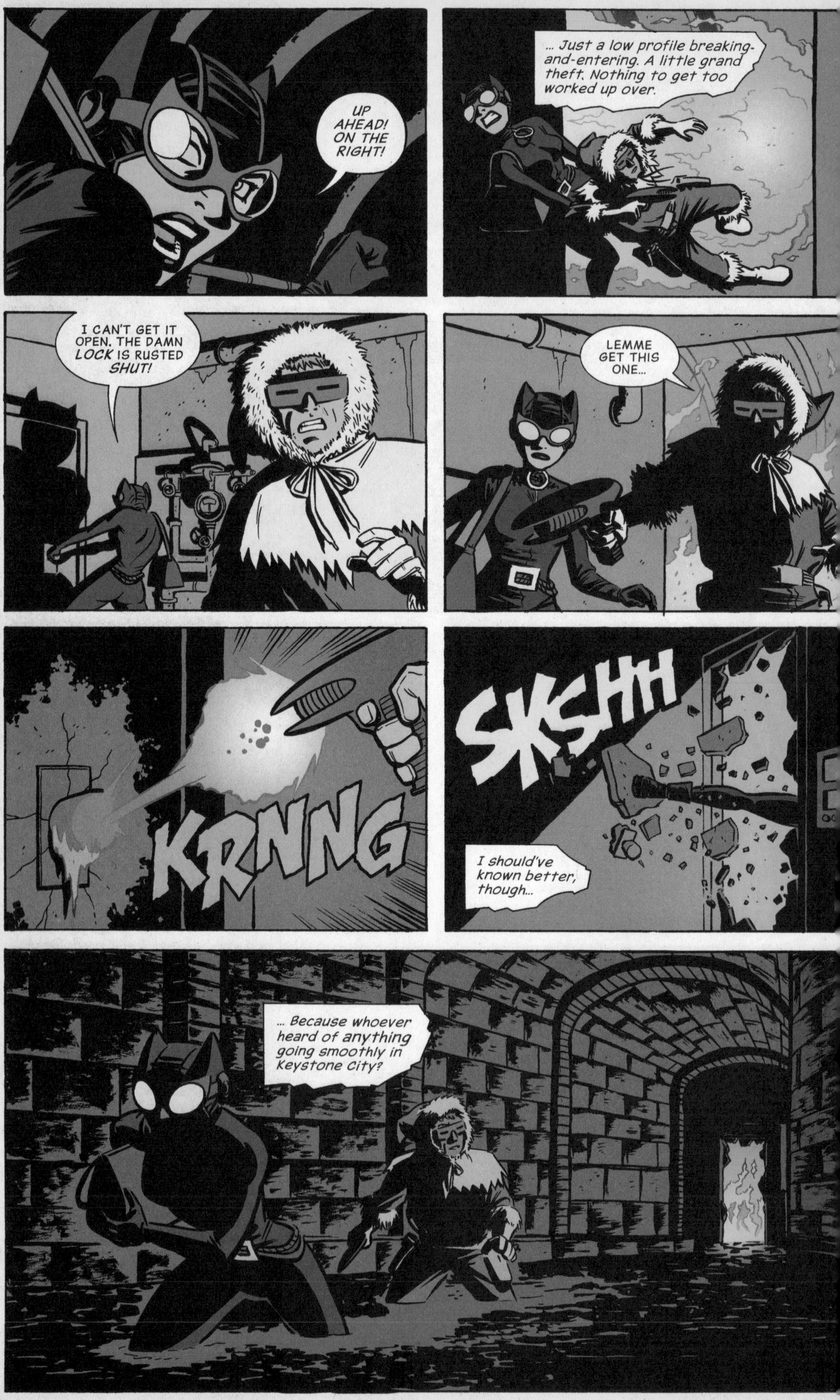

UP AHEAD! ON THE RIGHT!
... Just a low profile breaking-and-entering. A little grand theft. Nothing to get too worked up over.
I CAN'T GET IT OPEN. THE DAMN LOCK IS RUSTED SHUT!
LEMME GET THIS ONE...
KRNNG
SKSHH
I should've known better, though...
... Because whoever heard of anything going smoothly in Keystone City?

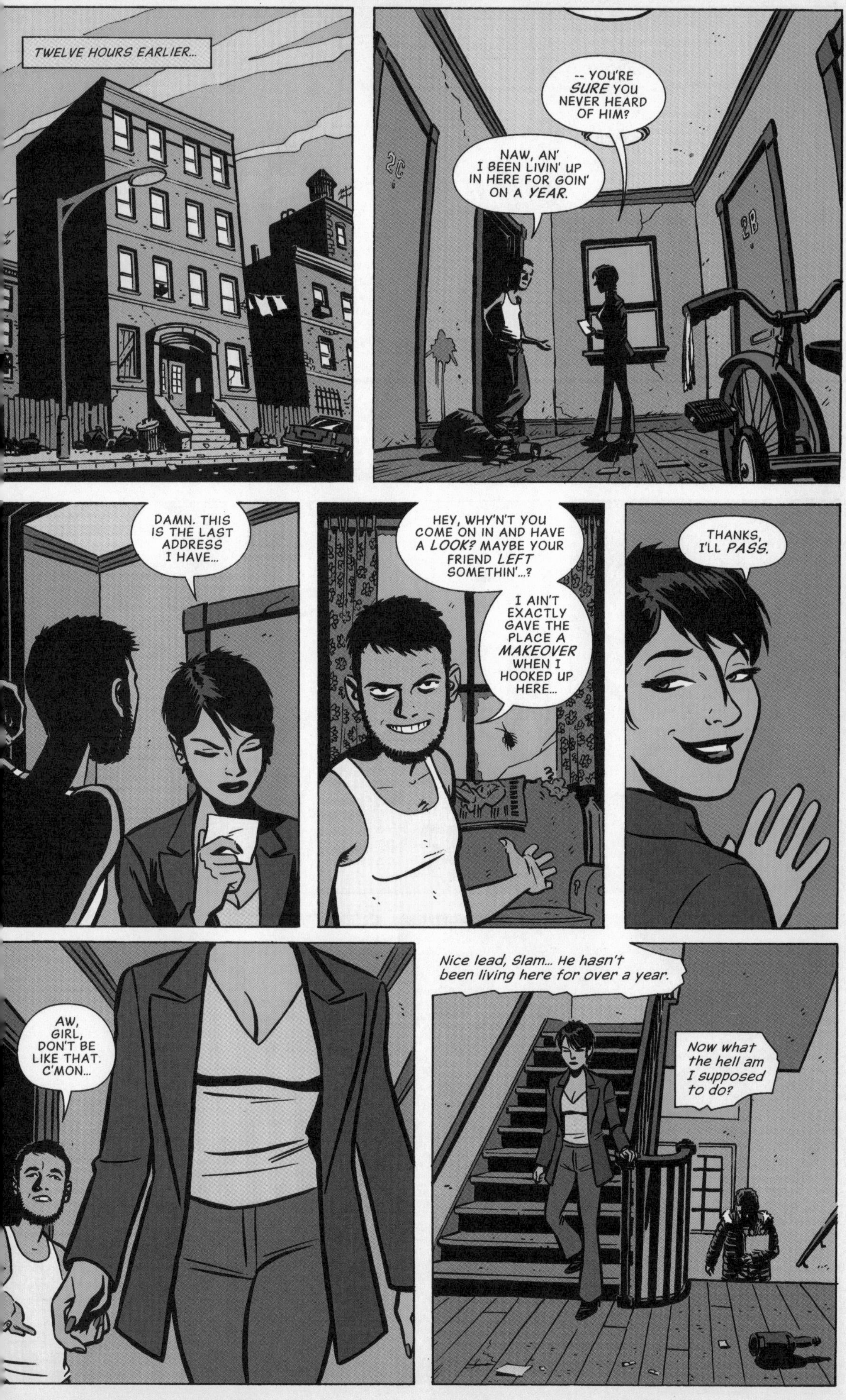
TWELVE HOURS EARLIER...
-- YOU'RE SURE YOU NEVER HEARD OF HIM?
NAW, AN' I BEEN LIVIN' UP IN HERE FOR GOIN' ON A YEAR.
2C
2B
DAMN. THIS IS THE LAST ADDRESS I HAVE...
HEY, WHY'N'T YOU COME ON IN AND HAVE A LOOK? MAYBE YOUR FRIEND LEFT SOMETHIN'...?
I AIN'T EXACTLY GAVE THE PLACE A MAKEOVER WHEN I HOOKED UP HERE...
THANKS, I'LL PASS.
AW, GIRL, DON'T BE LIKE THAT. C'MON...
Nice lead, Slam... He hasn't been living here for over a year.
Now what the hell am I supposed to do?

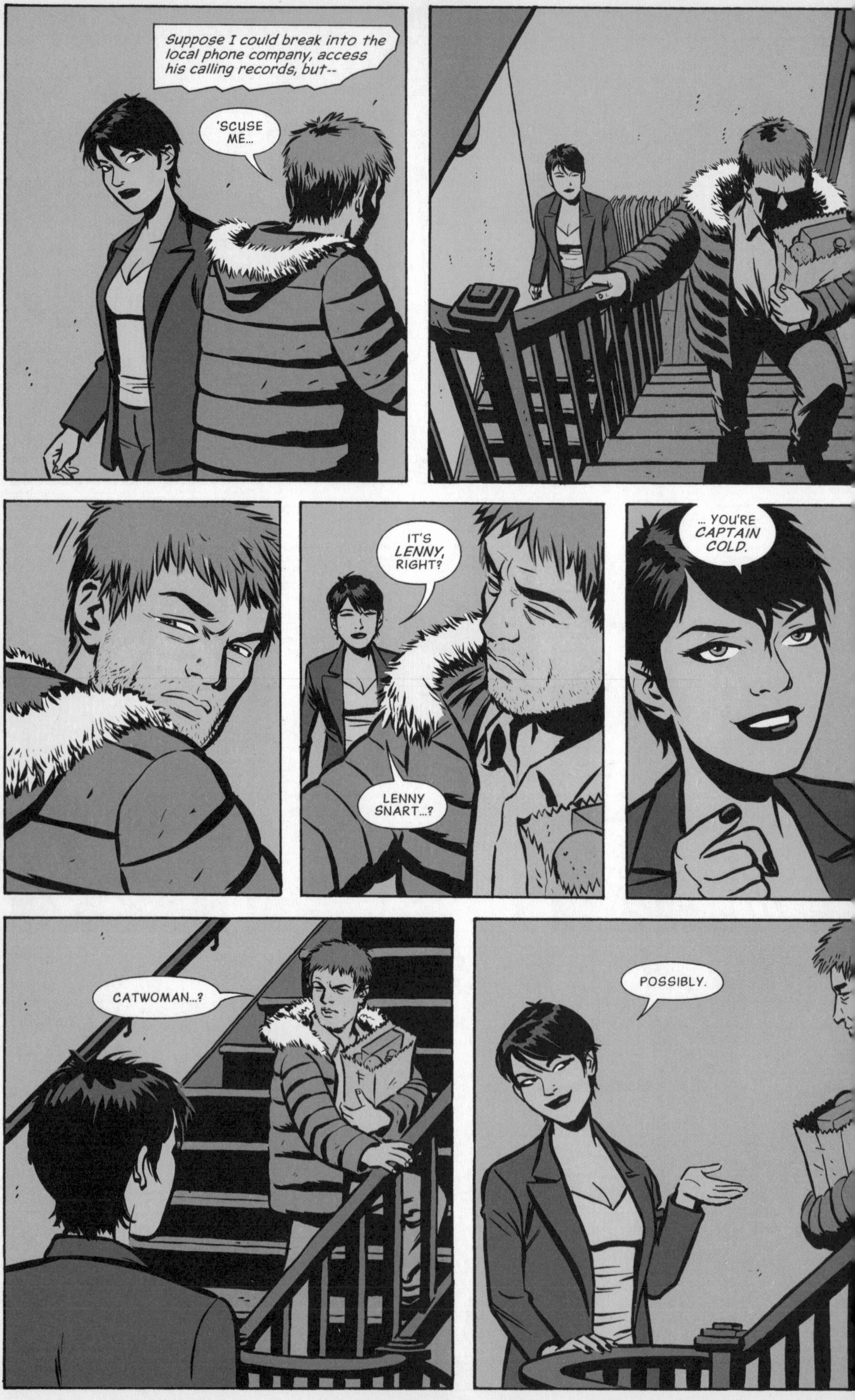

Suppose I could break into the local phone company, access his calling records, but--
'SCUSE ME...
IT'S *LENNY,* RIGHT?
LENNY SNART...?
... YOU'RE *CAPTAIN COLD.*
CATWOMAN...?
POSSIBLY.

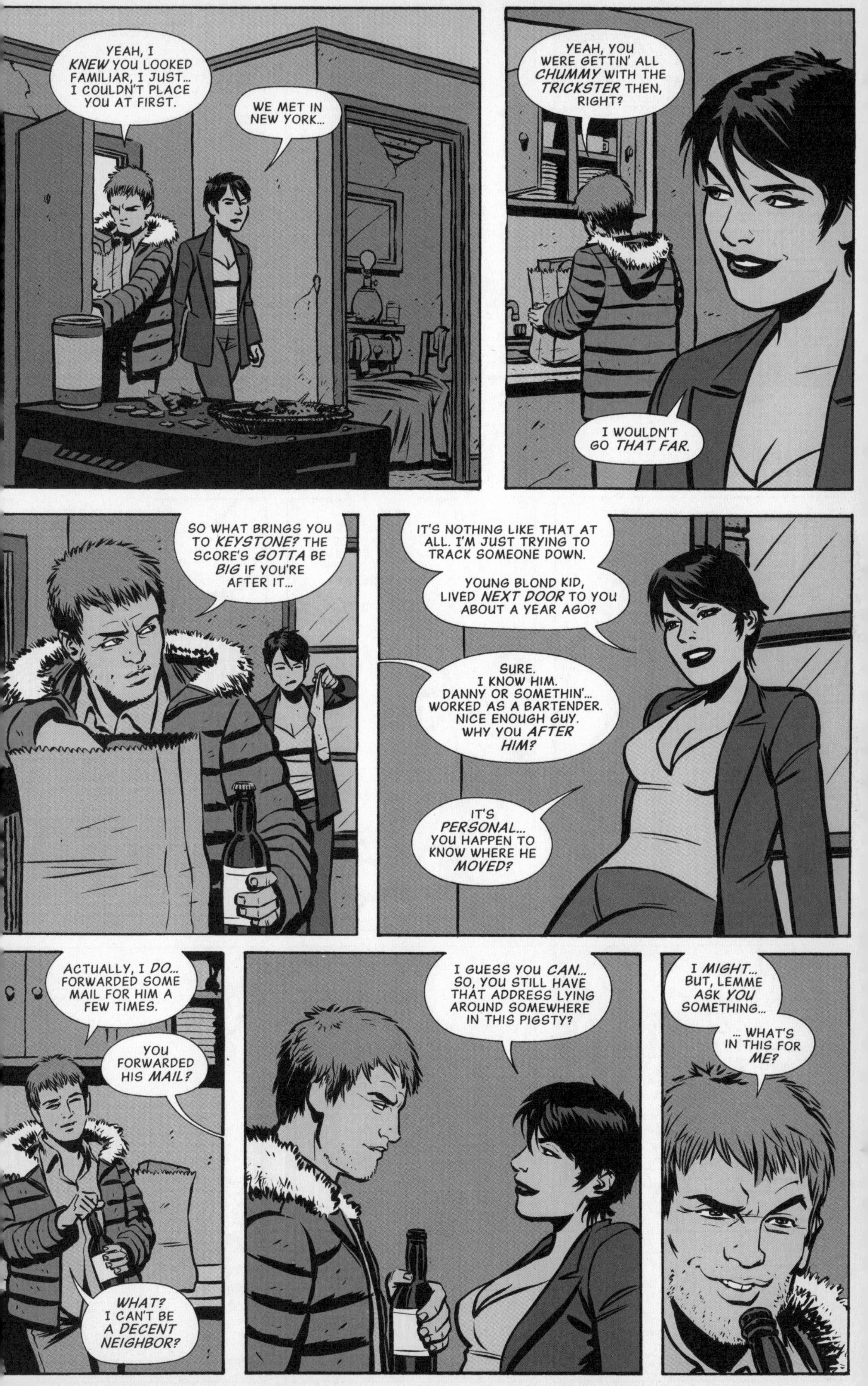

YEAH, I KNEW YOU LOOKED FAMILIAR, I JUST... I COULDN'T PLACE YOU AT FIRST.
WE MET IN NEW YORK...
YEAH, YOU WERE GETTIN' ALL CHUMMY WITH THE TRICKSTER THEN, RIGHT?
I WOULDN'T GO THAT FAR.
SO WHAT BRINGS YOU TO KEYSTONE? THE SCORE'S GOTTA BE BIG IF YOU'RE AFTER IT...
IT'S NOTHING LIKE THAT AT ALL. I'M JUST TRYING TO TRACK SOMEONE DOWN.
YOUNG BLOND KID, LIVED NEXT DOOR TO YOU ABOUT A YEAR AGO?
SURE. I KNOW HIM. DANNY OR SOMETHIN'... WORKED AS A BARTENDER. NICE ENOUGH GUY. WHY YOU AFTER HIM?
IT'S PERSONAL... YOU HAPPEN TO KNOW WHERE HE MOVED?
ACTUALLY, I DO... FORWARDED SOME MAIL FOR HIM A FEW TIMES.
YOU FORWARDED HIS MAIL?
WHAT? I CAN'T BE A DECENT NEIGHBOR?
I GUESS YOU CAN... SO, YOU STILL HAVE THAT ADDRESS LYING AROUND SOMEWHERE IN THIS PIGSTY?
I MIGHT... BUT, LEMME ASK YOU SOMETHING...
... WHAT'S IN THIS FOR ME?

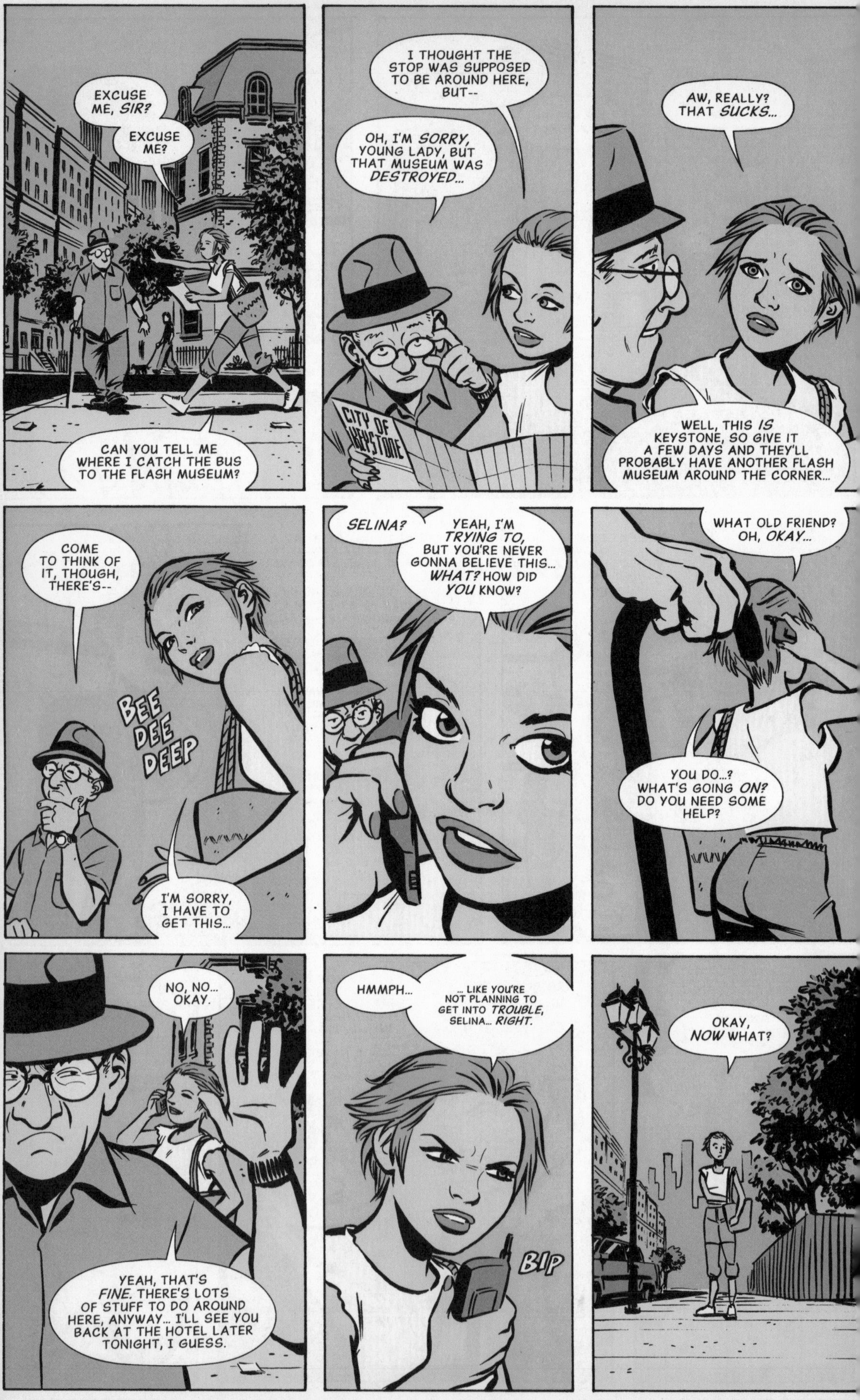
EXCUSE ME, SIR?
EXCUSE ME?
CAN YOU TELL ME WHERE I CATCH THE BUS TO THE FLASH MUSEUM?
I THOUGHT THE STOP WAS SUPPOSED TO BE AROUND HERE, BUT--
OH, I'M SORRY, YOUNG LADY, BUT THAT MUSEUM WAS DESTROYED...
CITY OF KEYSTONE
AW, REALLY? THAT SUCKS...
WELL, THIS IS KEYSTONE, SO GIVE IT A FEW DAYS AND THEY'LL PROBABLY HAVE ANOTHER FLASH MUSEUM AROUND THE CORNER...
COME TO THINK OF IT, THOUGH, THERE'S--
BEE DEE DEEP
I'M SORRY, I HAVE TO GET THIS...
SELINA?
YEAH, I'M TRYING TO, BUT YOU'RE NEVER GONNA BELIEVE THIS... WHAT? HOW DID YOU KNOW?
WHAT OLD FRIEND? OH, OKAY...
YOU DO...? WHAT'S GOING ON? DO YOU NEED SOME HELP?
NO, NO... OKAY.
YEAH, THAT'S FINE. THERE'S LOTS OF STUFF TO DO AROUND HERE, ANYWAY... I'LL SEE YOU BACK AT THE HOTEL LATER TONIGHT, I GUESS.
HMMPH...
... LIKE YOU'RE NOT PLANNING TO GET INTO TROUBLE, SELINA... RIGHT.
BIP
OKAY, NOW WHAT?

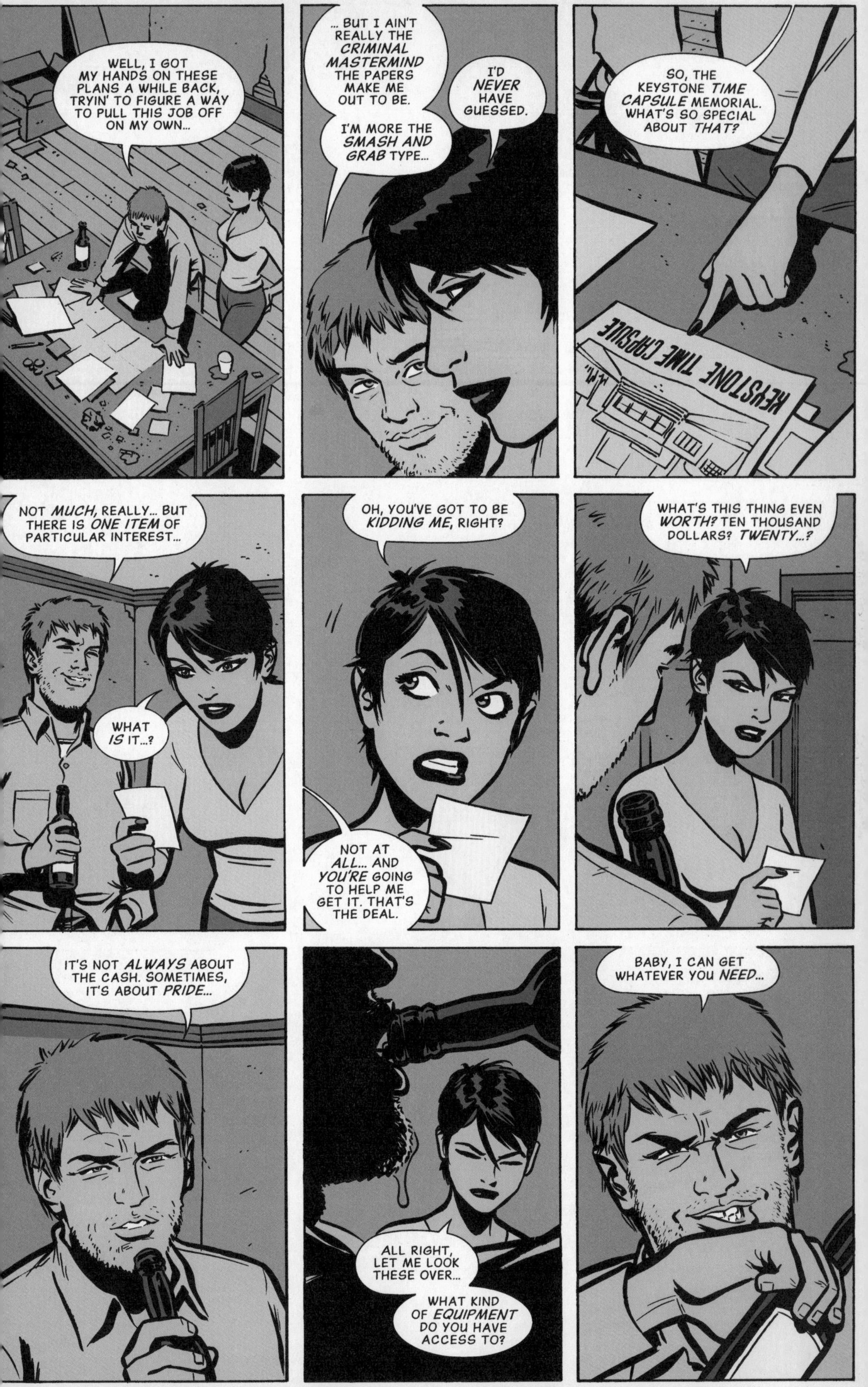

WELL, I GOT MY HANDS ON THESE PLANS A WHILE BACK, TRYIN' TO FIGURE A WAY TO PULL THIS JOB OFF ON MY OWN...
... BUT I AIN'T REALLY THE CRIMINAL MASTERMIND THE PAPERS MAKE ME OUT TO BE.
I'M MORE THE SMASH AND GRAB TYPE...
I'D NEVER HAVE GUESSED.
SO, THE KEYSTONE TIME CAPSULE MEMORIAL. WHAT'S SO SPECIAL ABOUT THAT?
KEYSTONE TIME CAPSULE
NOT MUCH, REALLY... BUT THERE IS ONE ITEM OF PARTICULAR INTEREST...
WHAT IS IT...?
OH, YOU'VE GOT TO BE KIDDING ME, RIGHT?
NOT AT ALL... AND YOU'RE GOING TO HELP ME GET IT. THAT'S THE DEAL.
WHAT'S THIS THING EVEN WORTH? TEN THOUSAND DOLLARS? TWENTY...?
IT'S NOT ALWAYS ABOUT THE CASH. SOMETIMES, IT'S ABOUT PRIDE...
ALL RIGHT, LET ME LOOK THESE OVER...
WHAT KIND OF EQUIPMENT DO YOU HAVE ACCESS TO?
BABY, I CAN GET WHATEVER YOU NEED...

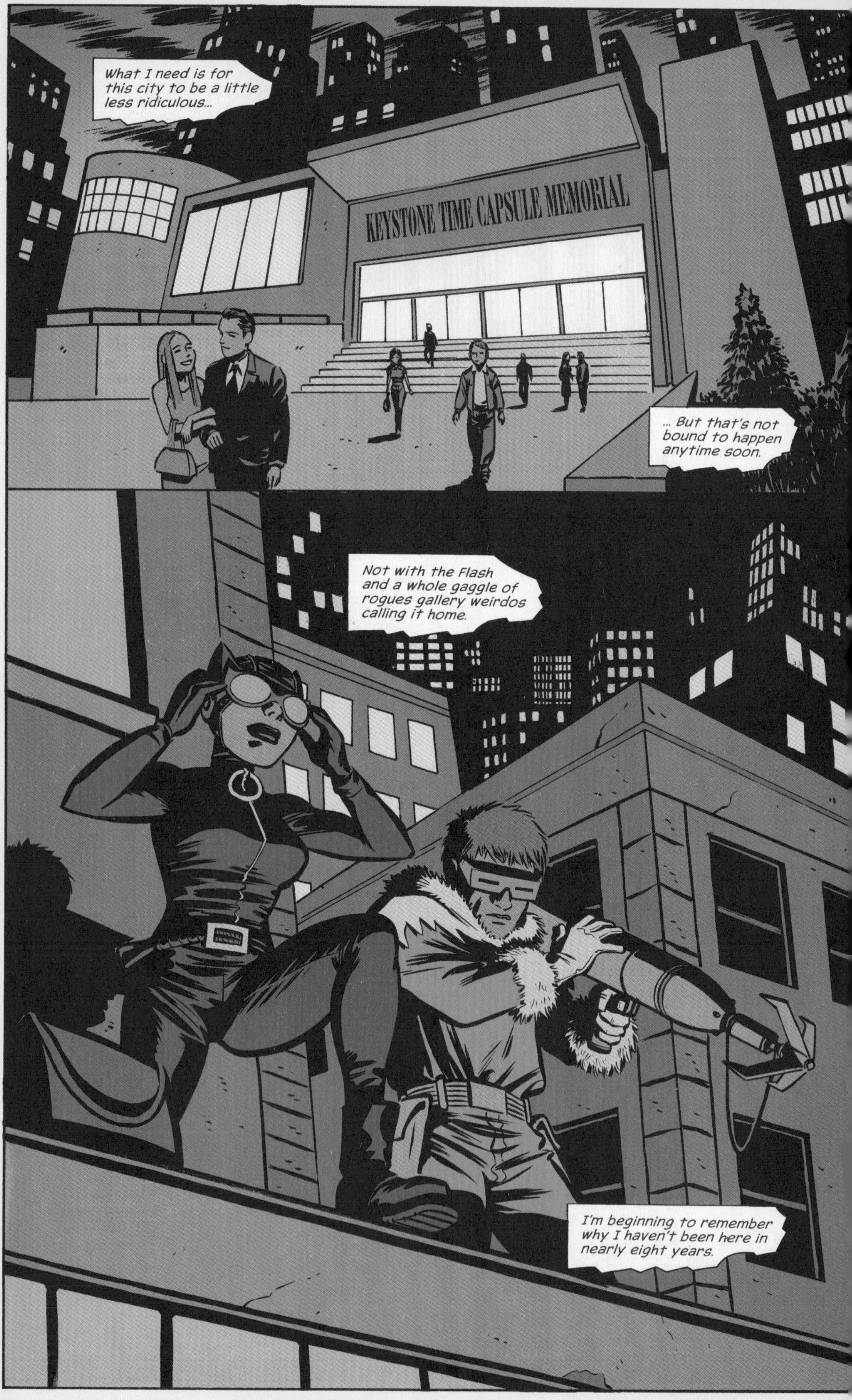
What I need is for this city to be a little less ridiculous...
KEYSTONE TIME CAPSULE MEMORIAL
... But that's not bound to happen anytime soon.
Not with the Flash and a whole gaggle of rogues gallery weirdos calling it home.
I'm beginning to remember why I haven't been here in nearly eight years.

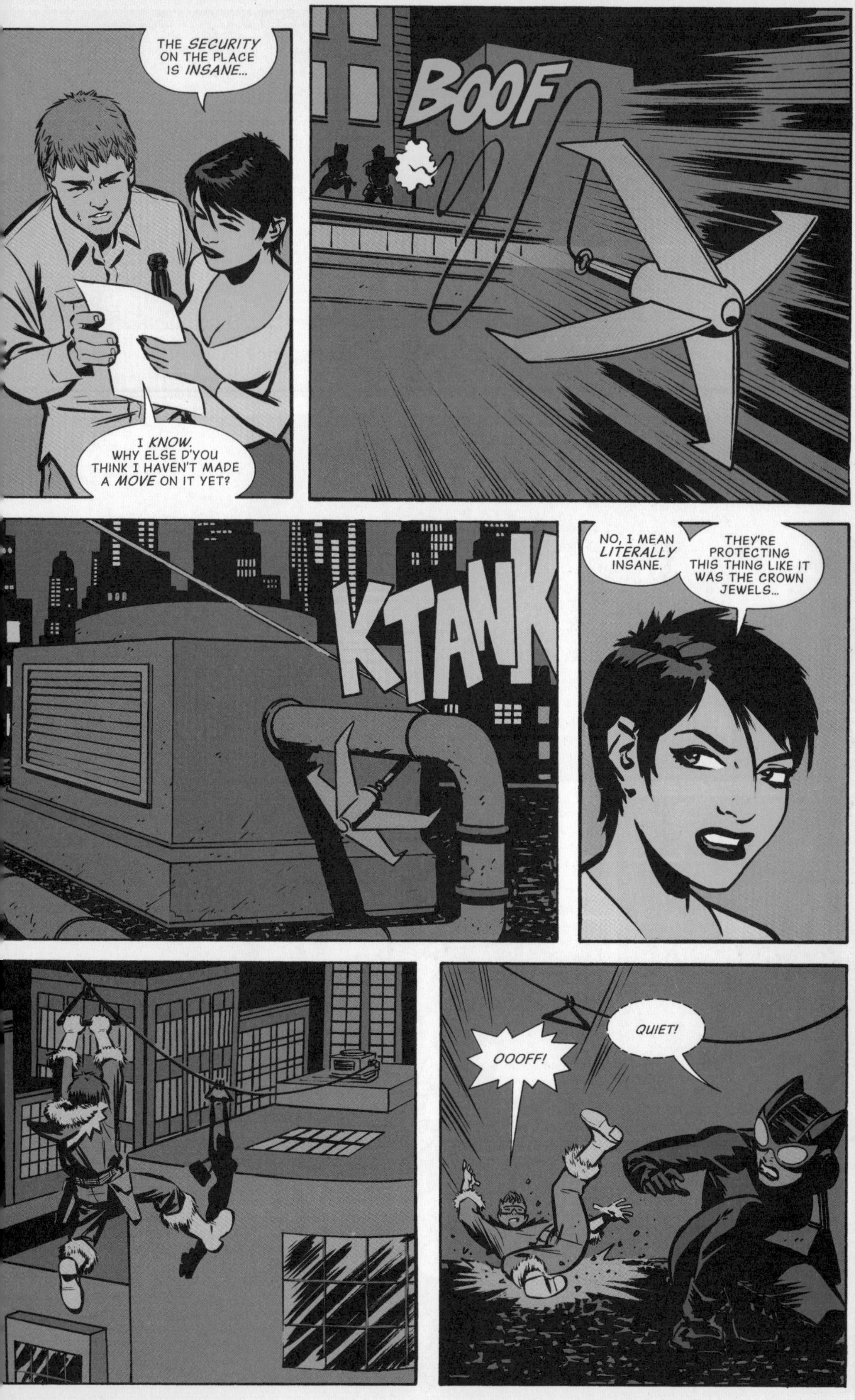
THE SECURITY ON THE PLACE IS INSANE...
I KNOW. WHY ELSE D'YOU THINK I HAVEN'T MADE A MOVE ON IT YET?
BOOF
KTANK
NO, I MEAN LITERALLY INSANE.
THEY'RE PROTECTING THIS THING LIKE IT WAS THE CROWN JEWELS...
OOOFF!
QUIET!

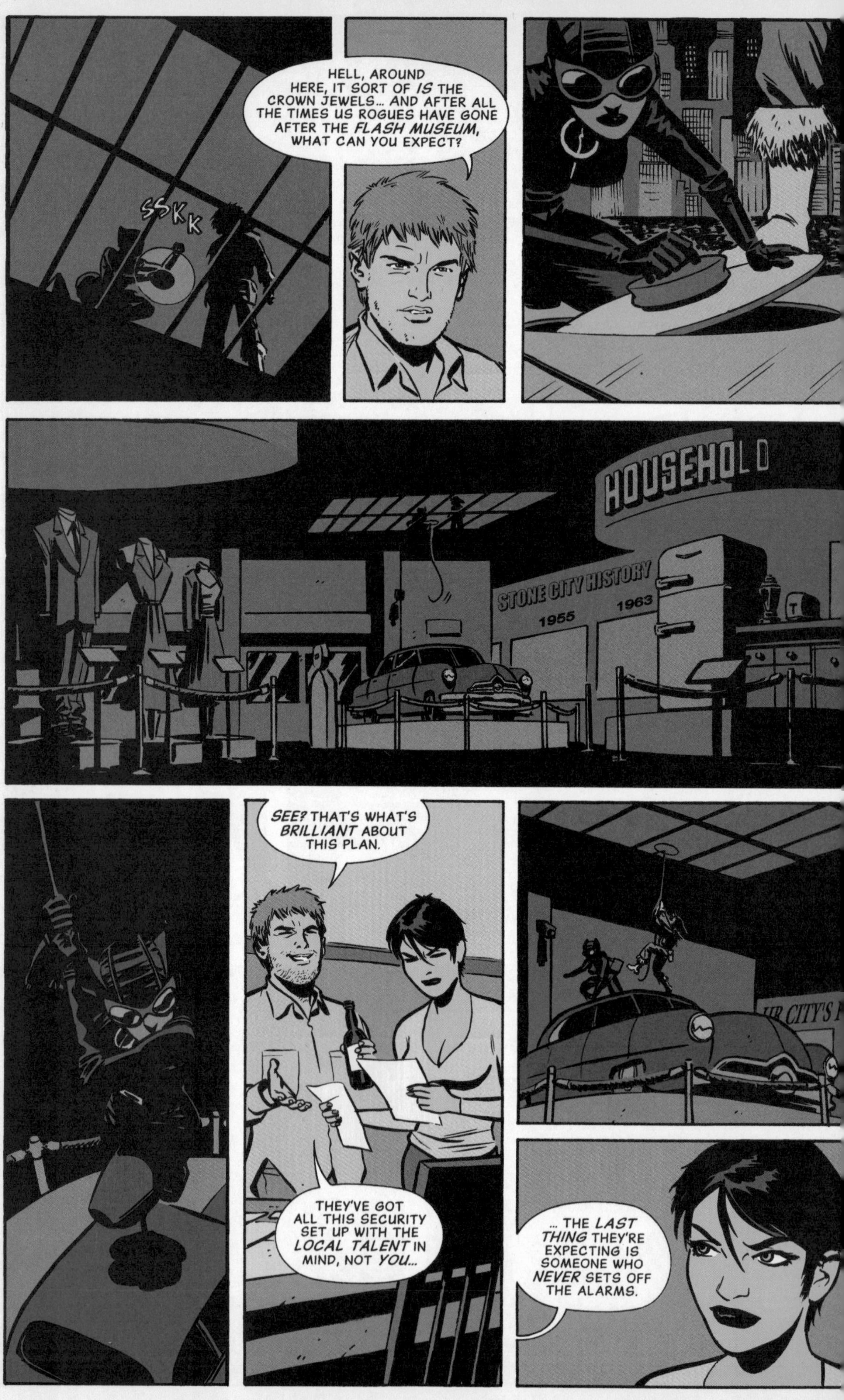
HELL, AROUND HERE, IT SORT OF IS THE CROWN JEWELS... AND AFTER ALL THE TIMES US ROGUES HAVE GONE AFTER THE FLASH MUSEUM, WHAT CAN YOU EXPECT?
SSKK
HOUSEHOLD
STONE CITY HISTORY
1955
1963
SEE? THAT'S WHAT'S BRILLIANT ABOUT THIS PLAN.
THEY'VE GOT ALL THIS SECURITY SET UP WITH THE LOCAL TALENT IN MIND, NOT YOU...
... THE LAST THING THEY'RE EXPECTING IS SOMEONE WHO NEVER SETS OFF THE ALARMS.

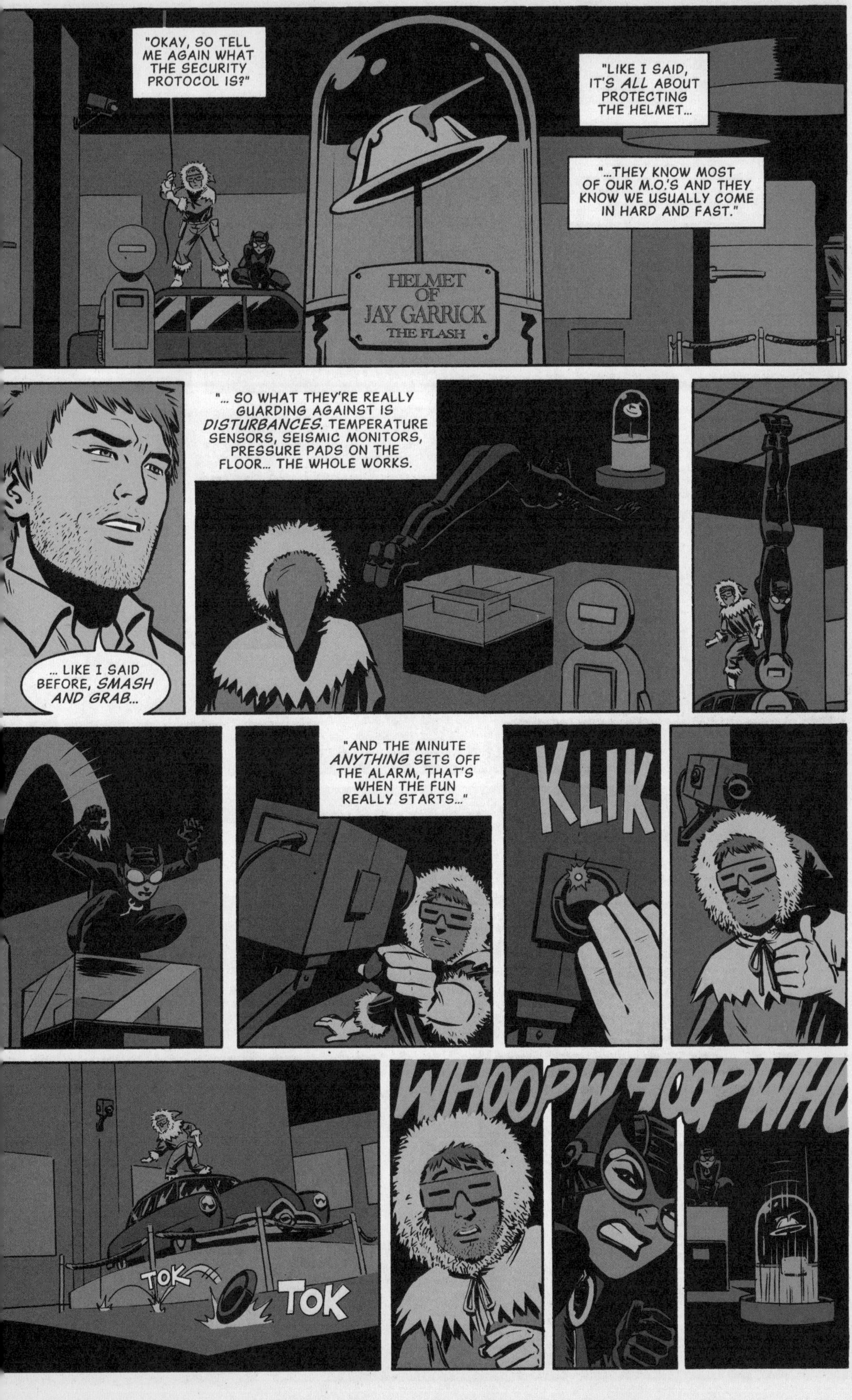
"OKAY, SO TELL ME AGAIN WHAT THE SECURITY PROTOCOL IS?"
"LIKE I SAID, IT'S ALL ABOUT PROTECTING THE HELMET...
"...THEY KNOW MOST OF OUR M.O.'S AND THEY KNOW WE USUALLY COME IN HARD AND FAST."
HELMET OF JAY GARRICK THE FLASH
... LIKE I SAID BEFORE, SMASH AND GRAB...
"... SO WHAT THEY'RE REALLY GUARDING AGAINST IS DISTURBANCES. TEMPERATURE SENSORS, SEISMIC MONITORS, PRESSURE PADS ON THE FLOOR... THE WHOLE WORKS.
"AND THE MINUTE ANYTHING SETS OFF THE ALARM, THAT'S WHEN THE FUN REALLY STARTS..."
KLIK
TOK
TOK
WHOOPWHOOPWHO

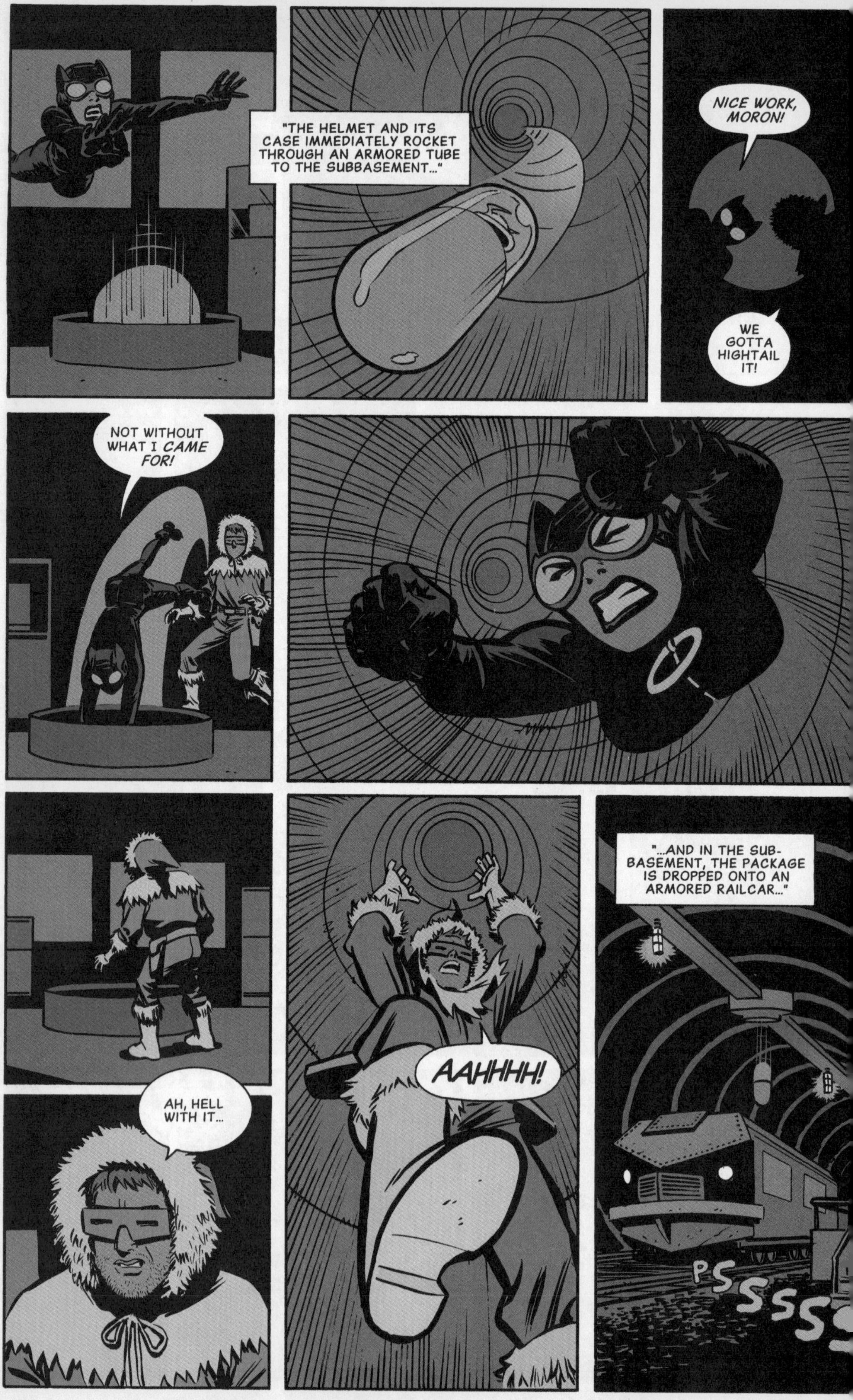
"THE HELMET AND ITS CASE IMMEDIATELY ROCKET THROUGH AN ARMORED TUBE TO THE SUBBASEMENT..."
NICE WORK, MORON!
WE GOTTA HIGHTAIL IT!
NOT WITHOUT WHAT I *CAME* FOR!
AH, HELL WITH IT...
AAHHHH!
"...AND IN THE SUB-BASEMENT, THE PACKAGE IS DROPPED ONTO AN ARMORED RAILCAR..."
PSSSSS

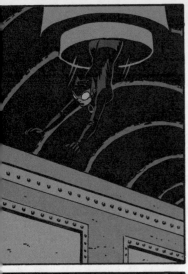

"...WHICH THEN SPEEDS TWO MILES ACROSS TOWN TO A HIGH-SECURITY VAULT."

WPD

THWP

THIS IS CRAZY!

YOU'VE GOT ABOUT ONE MINUTE 'TIL YOU GET TO MEET A FLASH OR TWO...

WE'RE NOT THROUGH YET...

HEY--

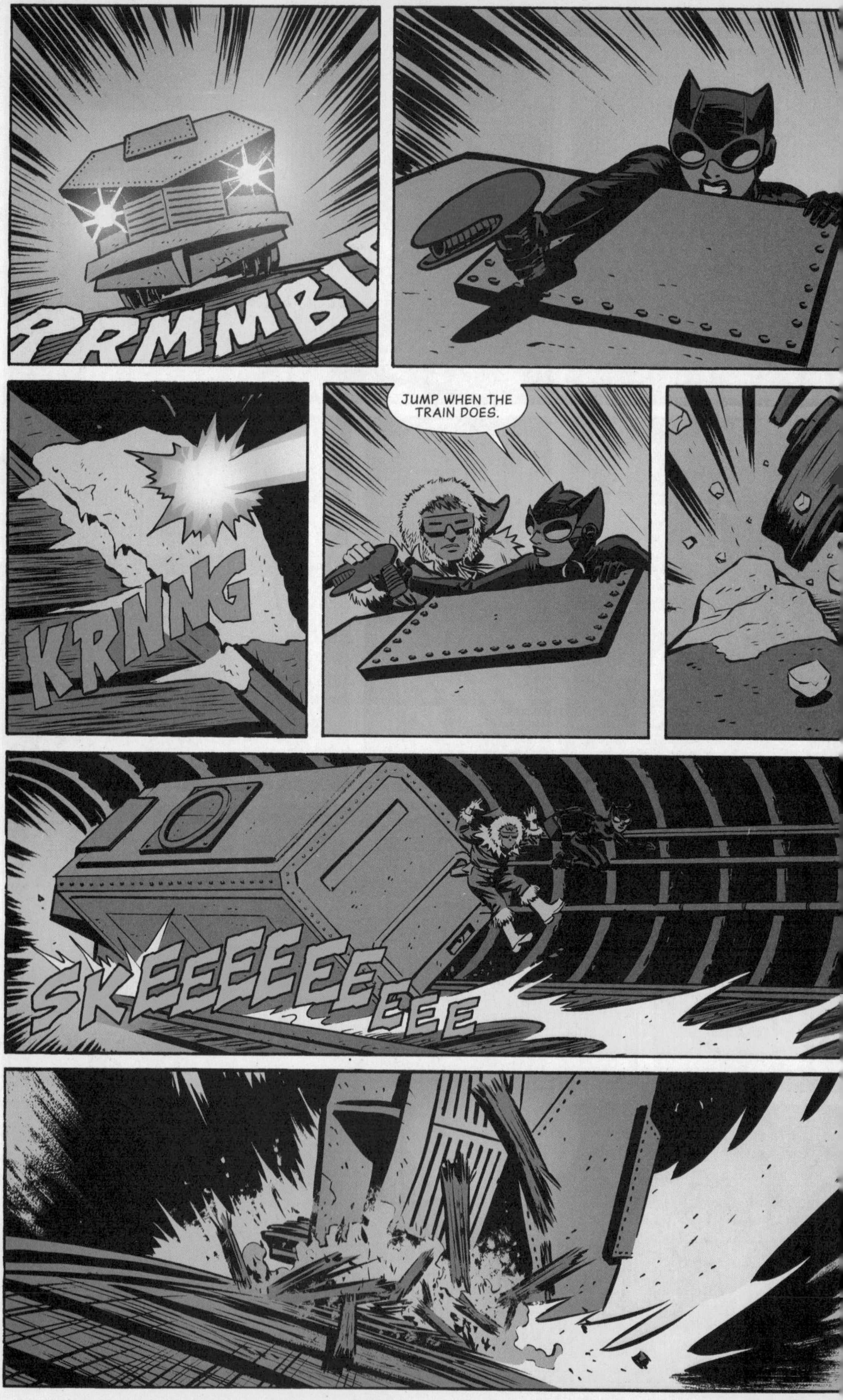

RRMMBL
KRNNG
JUMP WHEN THE TRAIN DOES.
SKEEEEEEEEEE

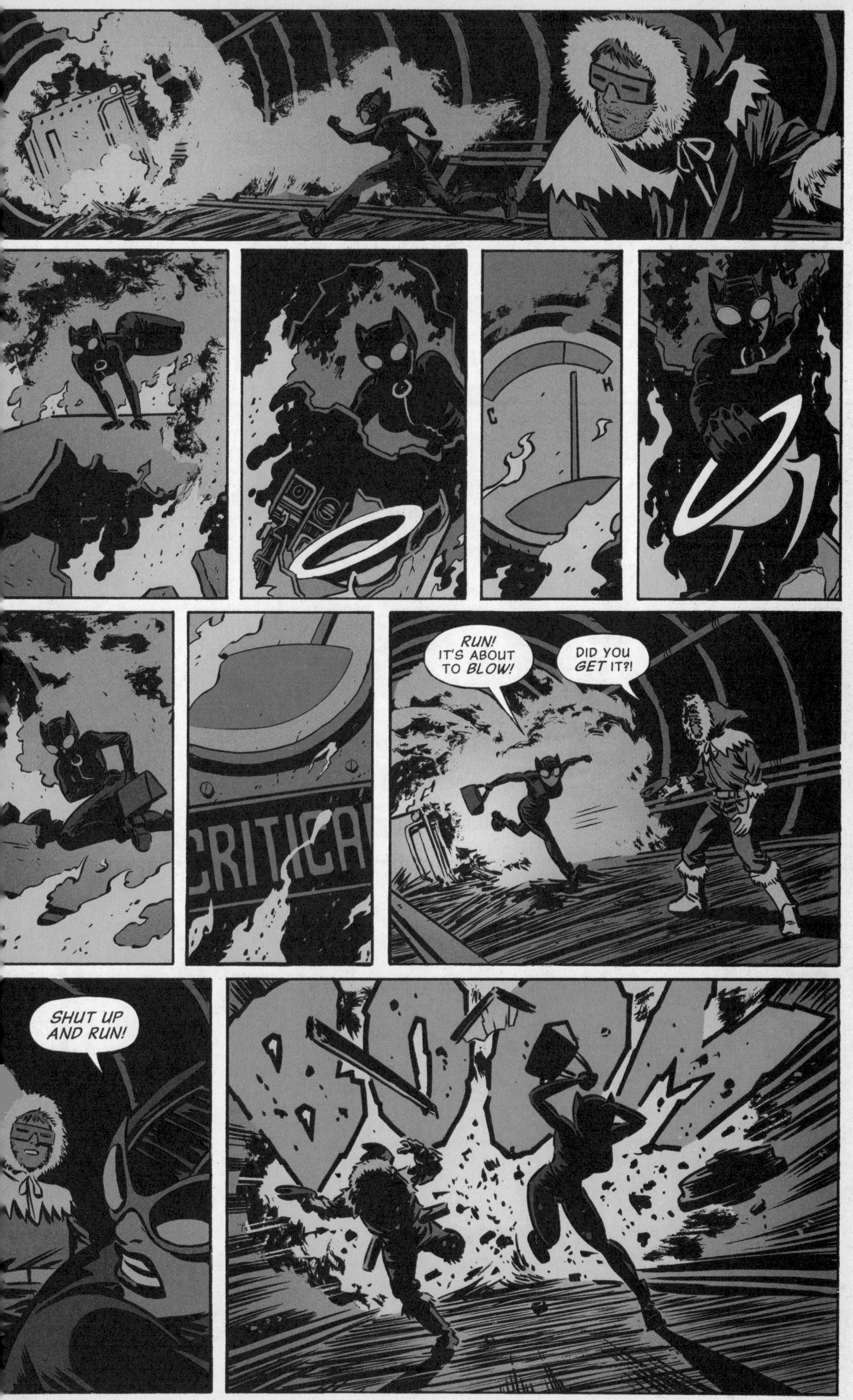
C
H
RUN! IT'S ABOUT TO BLOW!
DID YOU GET IT?!
SHUT UP AND RUN!

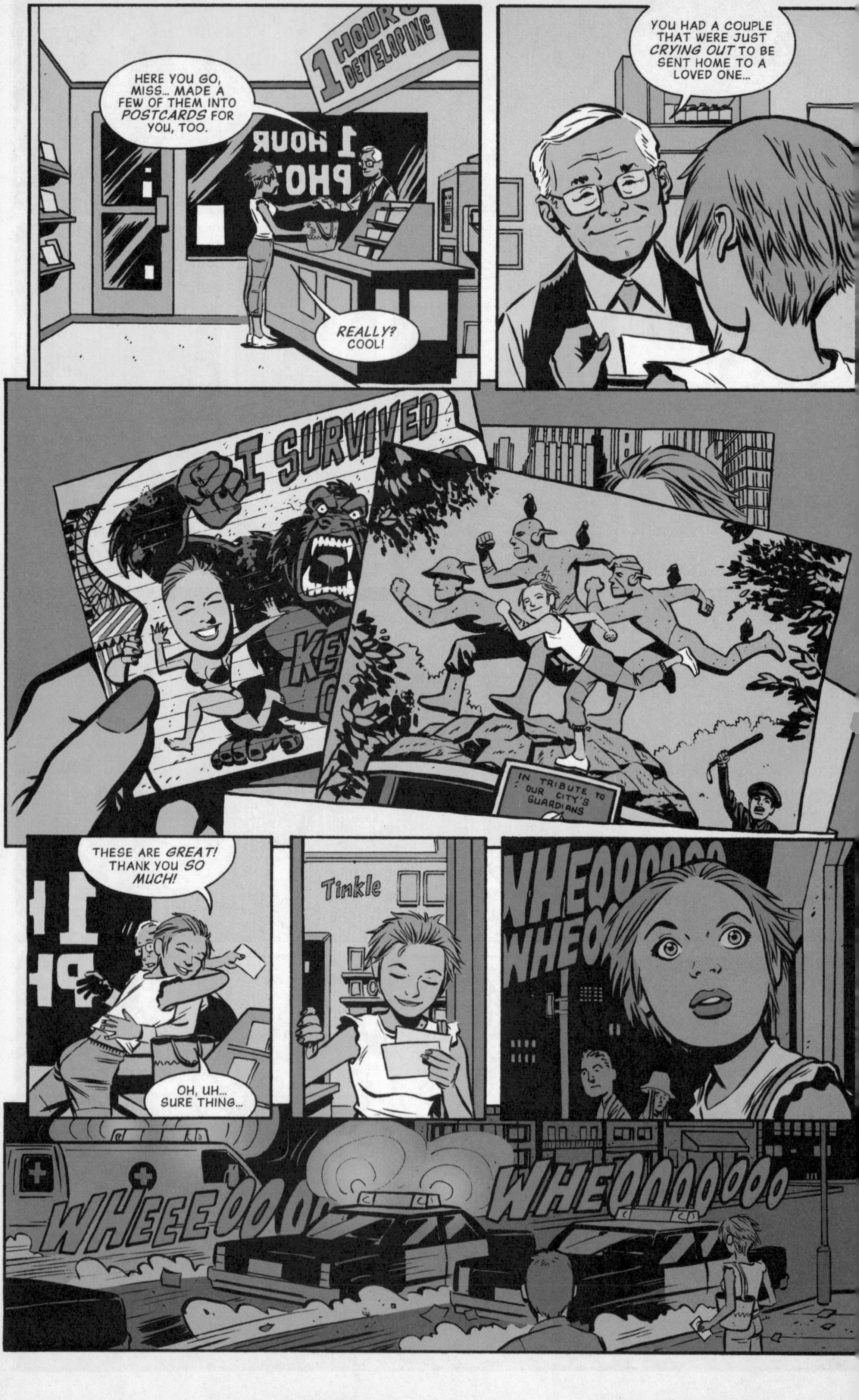
1 HOUR DEVELOPING
HERE YOU GO, MISS... MADE A FEW OF THEM INTO POSTCARDS FOR YOU, TOO.
1 HOUR PHO
REALLY? COOL!
YOU HAD A COUPLE THAT WERE JUST CRYING OUT TO BE SENT HOME TO A LOVED ONE...
I SURVIVED
IN TRIBUTE TO OUR CITY'S GUARDIANS
THESE ARE GREAT! THANK YOU SO MUCH!
OH, UH... SURE THING...
Tinkle
WHEOOOOOO
WHEEEOOOO
WHEOOOOOOO

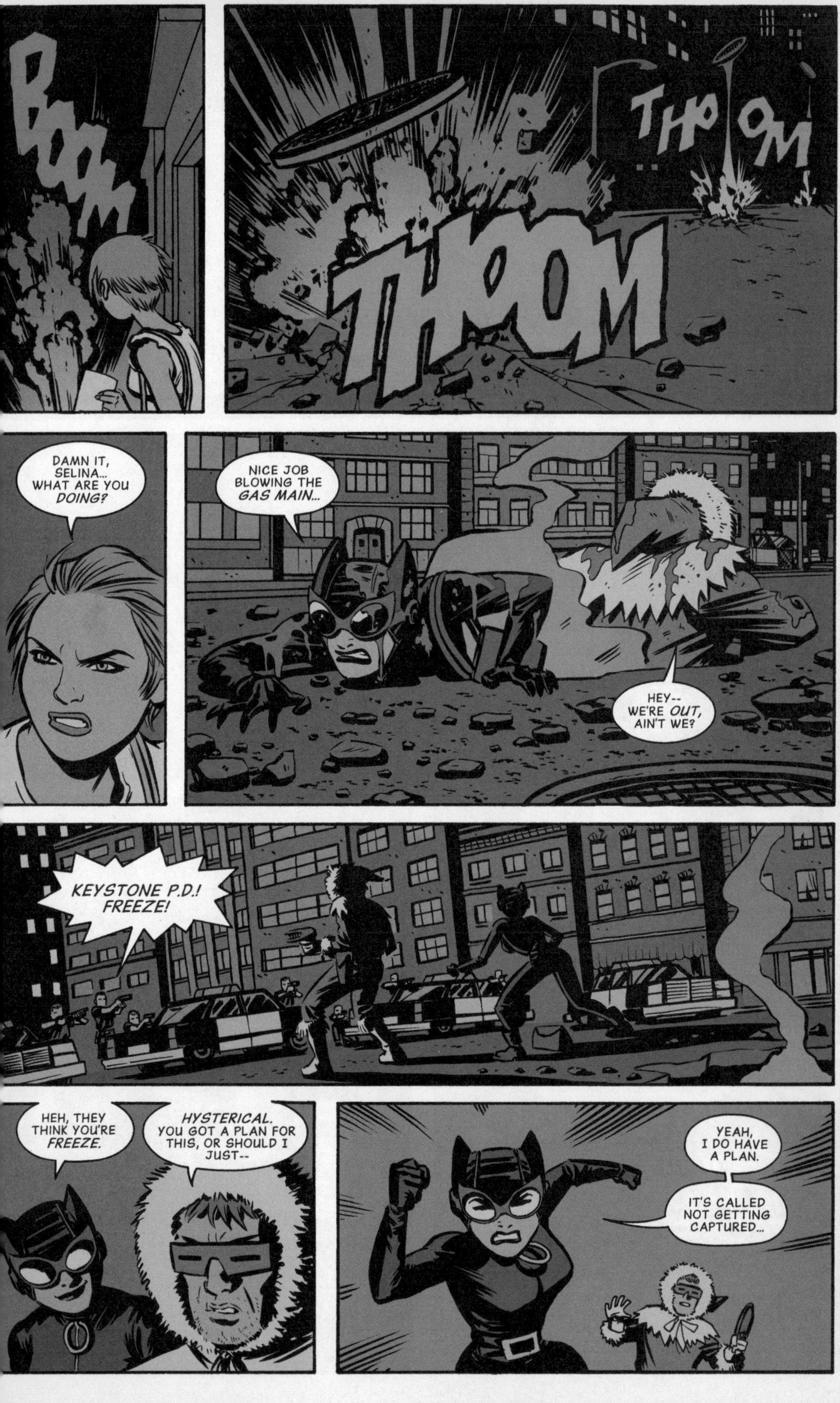
BOOM
THOOM
THOOM
DAMN IT, SELINA... WHAT ARE YOU *DOING?*
NICE JOB BLOWING THE *GAS MAIN...*
HEY-- WE'RE *OUT,* AIN'T WE?
KEYSTONE P.D.! FREEZE!
HEH, THEY THINK YOU'RE *FREEZE.*
HYSTERICAL. YOU GOT A PLAN FOR THIS, OR SHOULD I JUST--
YEAH, I DO HAVE A PLAN.
IT'S CALLED NOT GETTING CAPTURED...

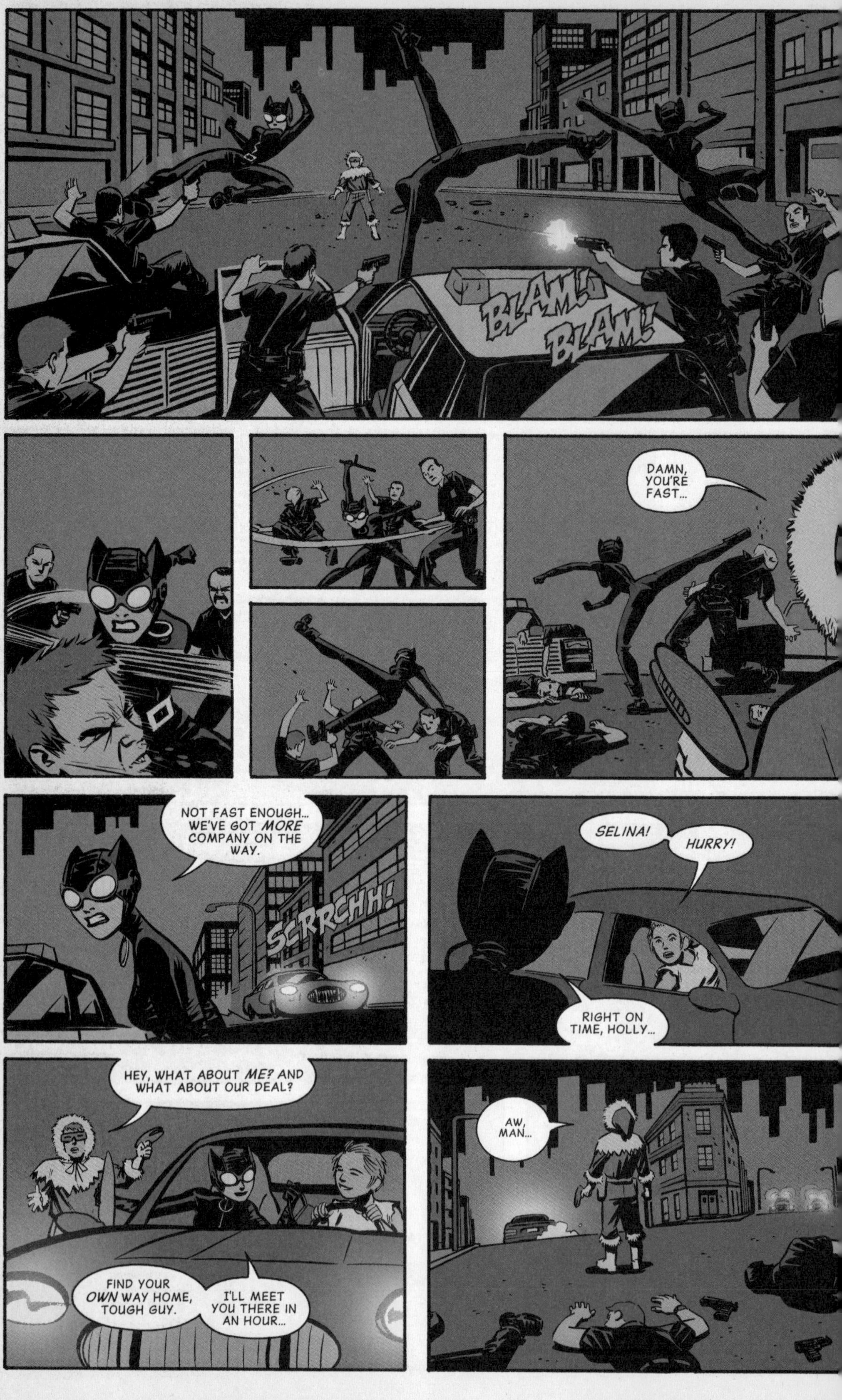
BLAM!
BLAM!
DAMN, YOU'RE FAST...
NOT FAST ENOUGH... WE'VE GOT MORE COMPANY ON THE WAY.
SCRRCHH!
SELINA!
HURRY!
RIGHT ON TIME, HOLLY...
HEY, WHAT ABOUT ME? AND WHAT ABOUT OUR DEAL?
FIND YOUR OWN WAY HOME, TOUGH GUY.
I'LL MEET YOU THERE IN AN HOUR...
AW, MAN...

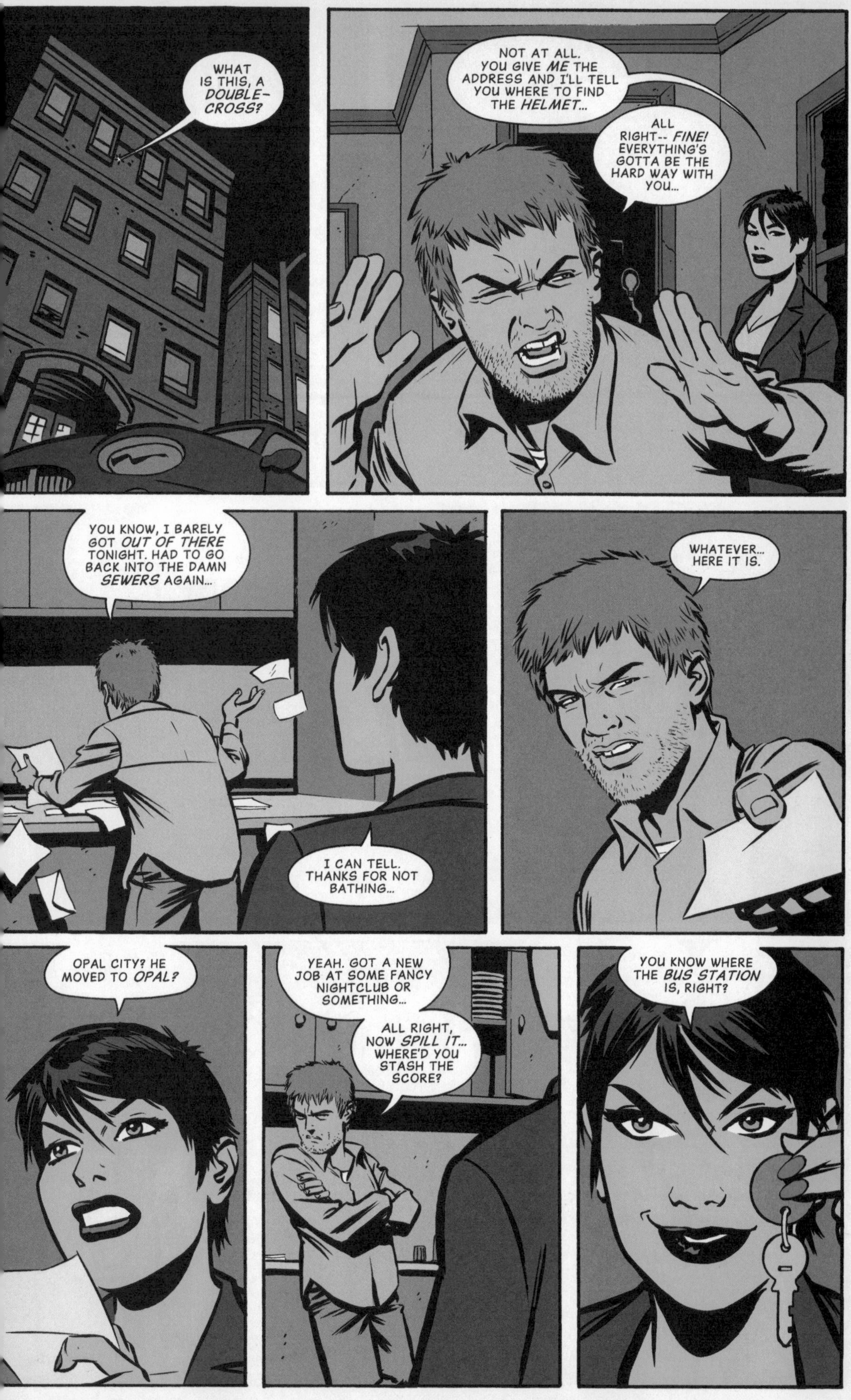
WHAT IS THIS, A DOUBLE-CROSS?
NOT AT ALL. YOU GIVE ME THE ADDRESS AND I'LL TELL YOU WHERE TO FIND THE HELMET...
ALL RIGHT-- FINE! EVERYTHING'S GOTTA BE THE HARD WAY WITH YOU...
YOU KNOW, I BARELY GOT OUT OF THERE TONIGHT. HAD TO GO BACK INTO THE DAMN SEWERS AGAIN...
I CAN TELL. THANKS FOR NOT BATHING...
WHATEVER... HERE IT IS.
OPAL CITY? HE MOVED TO OPAL?
YEAH. GOT A NEW JOB AT SOME FANCY NIGHTCLUB OR SOMETHING...
ALL RIGHT, NOW SPILL IT... WHERE'D YOU STASH THE SCORE?
YOU KNOW WHERE THE BUS STATION IS, RIGHT?

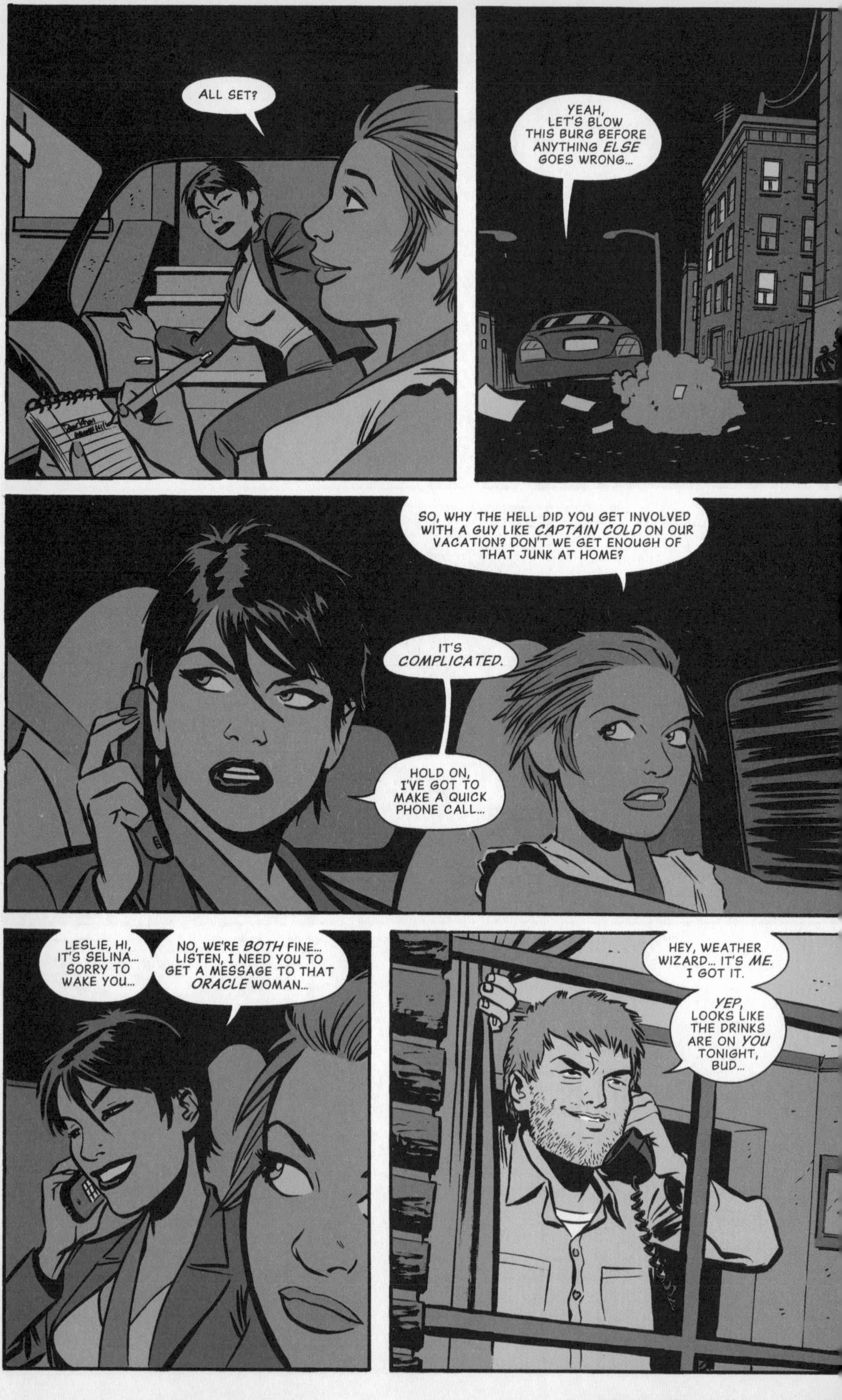
ALL SET?
YEAH, LET'S BLOW THIS BURG BEFORE ANYTHING ELSE GOES WRONG...
SO, WHY THE HELL DID YOU GET INVOLVED WITH A GUY LIKE CAPTAIN COLD ON OUR VACATION? DON'T WE GET ENOUGH OF THAT JUNK AT HOME?
IT'S COMPLICATED.
HOLD ON, I'VE GOT TO MAKE A QUICK PHONE CALL...
LESLIE, HI, IT'S SELINA... SORRY TO WAKE YOU...
NO, WE'RE BOTH FINE... LISTEN, I NEED YOU TO GET A MESSAGE TO THAT ORACLE WOMAN...
HEY, WEATHER WIZARD... IT'S ME. I GOT IT.
YEP, LOOKS LIKE THE DRINKS ARE ON YOU TONIGHT, BUD...

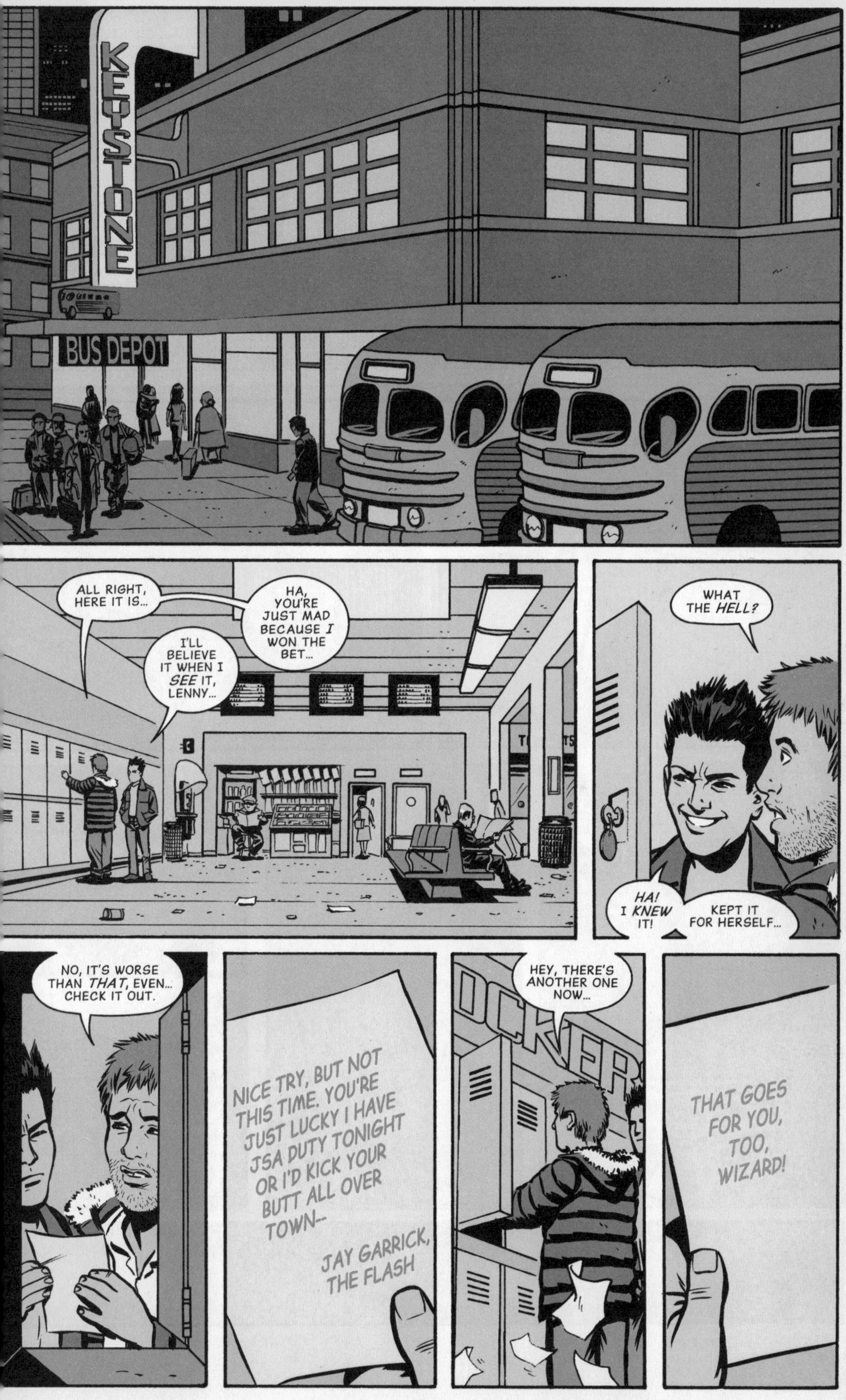
KEYSTONE
BUS DEPOT
ALL RIGHT, HERE IT IS...
HA, YOU'RE JUST MAD BECAUSE *I* WON THE BET...
I'LL BELIEVE IT WHEN I *SEE* IT, LENNY...
WHAT THE *HELL?*
HA! I *KNEW* IT!
KEPT IT FOR HERSELF...
NO, IT'S WORSE THAN *THAT*, EVEN... CHECK IT OUT.
NICE TRY, BUT NOT THIS TIME. YOU'RE JUST LUCKY I HAVE JSA DUTY TONIGHT OR I'D KICK YOUR BUTT ALL OVER TOWN--
JAY GARRICK, THE FLASH
HEY, THERE'S ANOTHER ONE NOW...
THAT GOES FOR YOU, TOO, WIZARD!

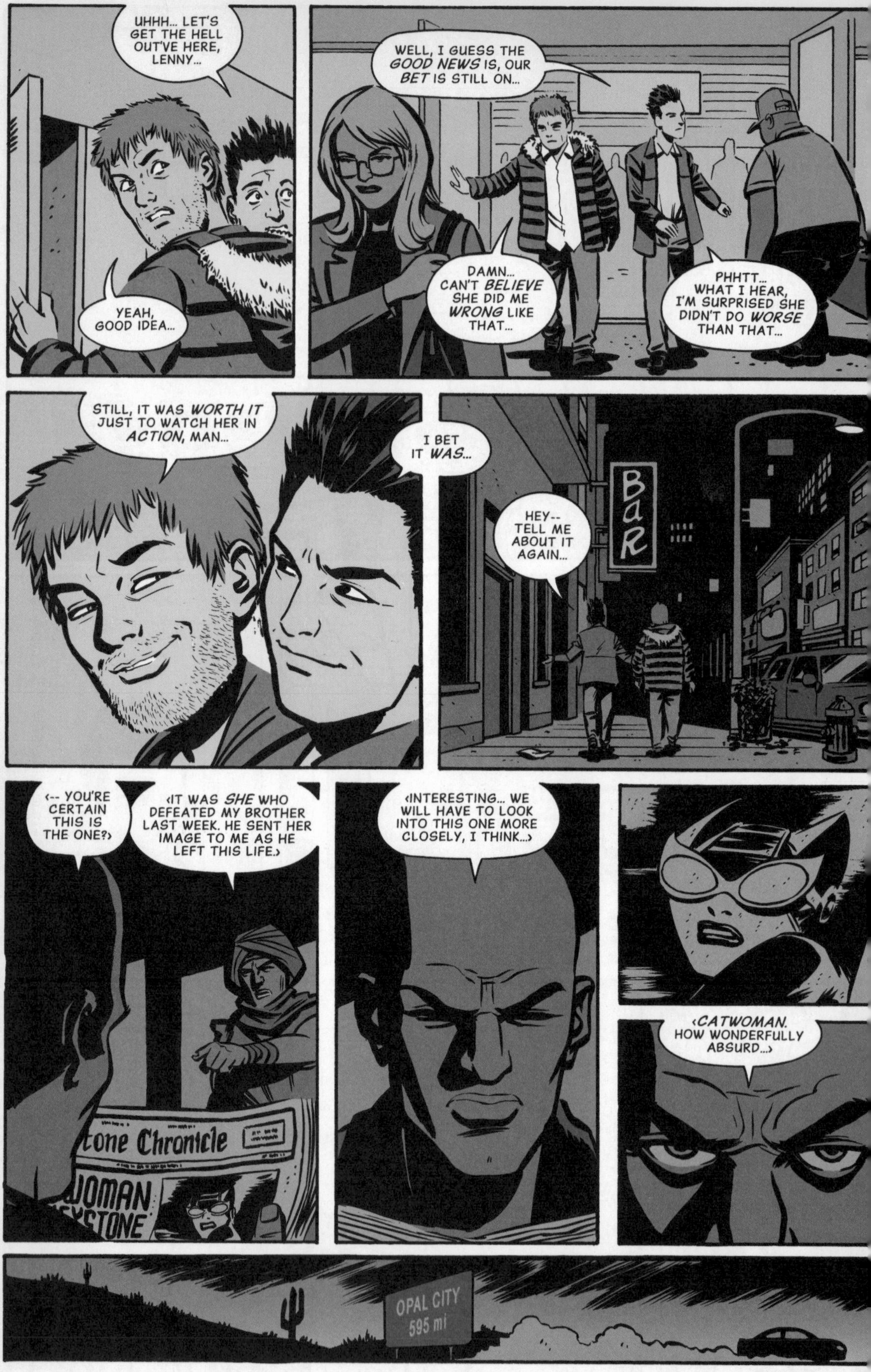
UHHH... LET'S GET THE HELL OUT'VE HERE, LENNY...
YEAH, GOOD IDEA...
WELL, I GUESS THE GOOD NEWS IS, OUR BET IS STILL ON...
DAMN... CAN'T BELIEVE SHE DID ME WRONG LIKE THAT...
PHHTT... WHAT I HEAR, I'M SURPRISED SHE DIDN'T DO WORSE THAN THAT...
STILL, IT WAS WORTH IT JUST TO WATCH HER IN ACTION, MAN...
I BET IT WAS...
BaR
HEY-- TELL ME ABOUT IT AGAIN...
‹-- YOU'RE CERTAIN THIS IS THE ONE?›
‹IT WAS SHE WHO DEFEATED MY BROTHER LAST WEEK. HE SENT HER IMAGE TO ME AS HE LEFT THIS LIFE.›
tone Chronicle
OMAN
STONE
‹INTERESTING... WE WILL HAVE TO LOOK INTO THIS ONE MORE CLOSELY, I THINK...›
‹CATWOMAN. HOW WONDERFULLY ABSURD...›
OPAL CITY
595 mi

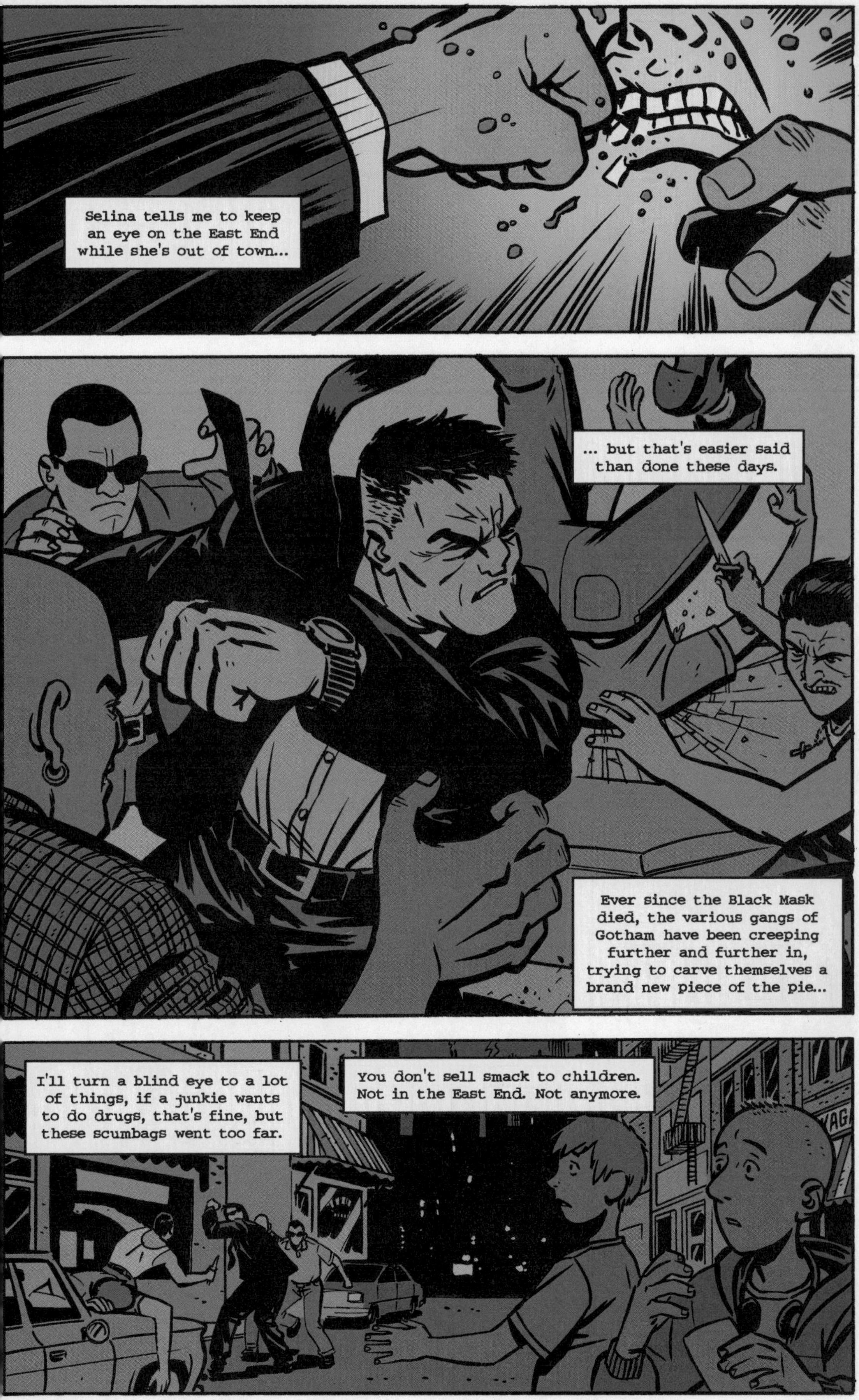
Selina tells me to keep an eye on the East End while she's out of town...
... but that's easier said than done these days.
Ever since the Black Mask died, the various gangs of Gotham have been creeping further and further in, trying to carve themselves a brand new piece of the pie...
I'll turn a blind eye to a lot of things, if a junkie wants to do drugs, that's fine, but these scumbags went too far.
You don't sell smack to children. Not in the East End. Not anymore.

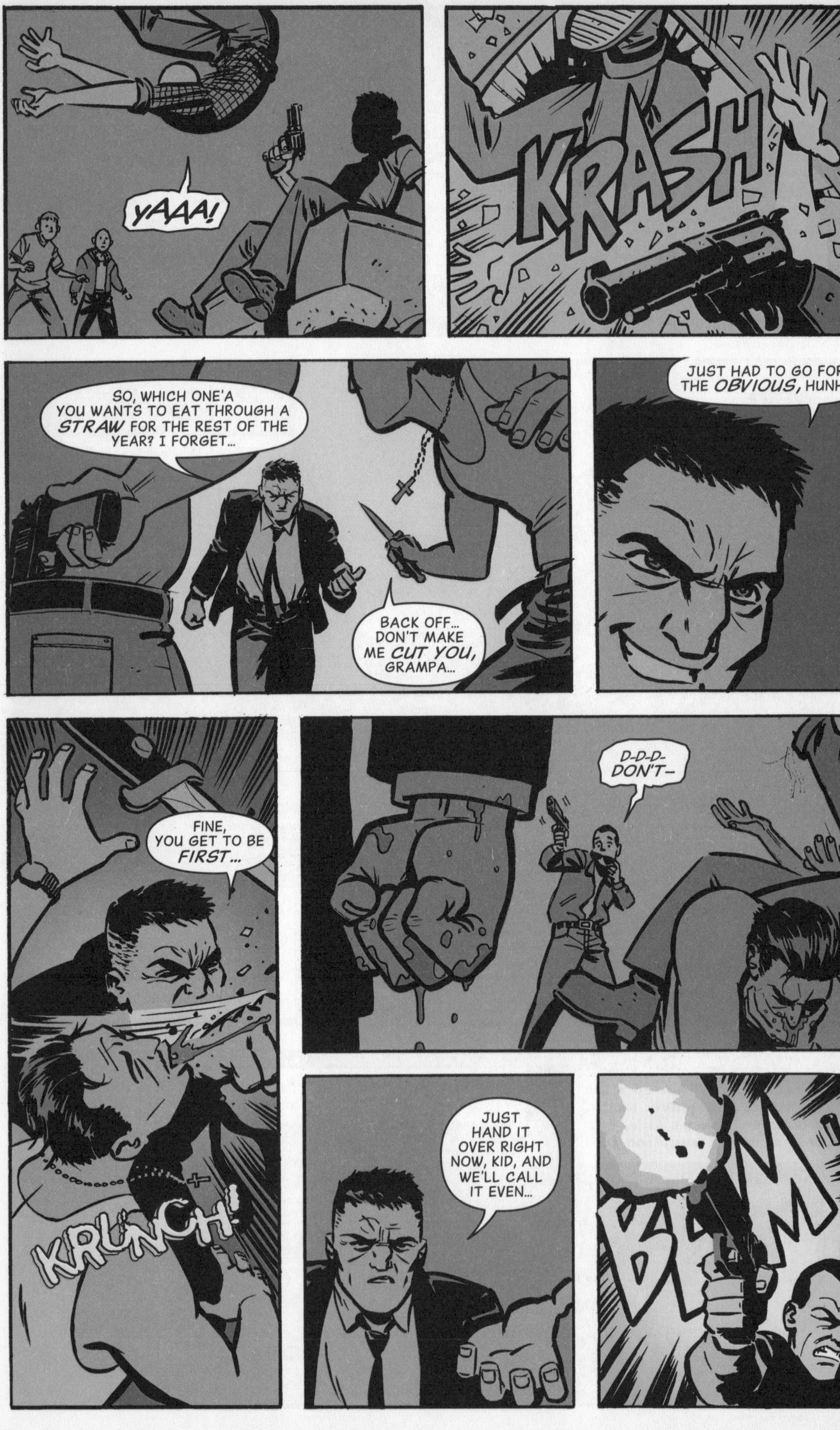
YAAA!
KRASH
SO, WHICH ONE'A YOU WANTS TO EAT THROUGH A STRAW FOR THE REST OF THE YEAR? I FORGET...
BACK OFF... DON'T MAKE ME CUT YOU, GRAMPA...
JUST HAD TO GO FOR THE OBVIOUS, HUNH?
FINE, YOU GET TO BE FIRST...
KRUNCH!
D-D-D-DON'T-
JUST HAND IT OVER RIGHT NOW, KID, AND WE'LL CALL IT EVEN...
BLAM

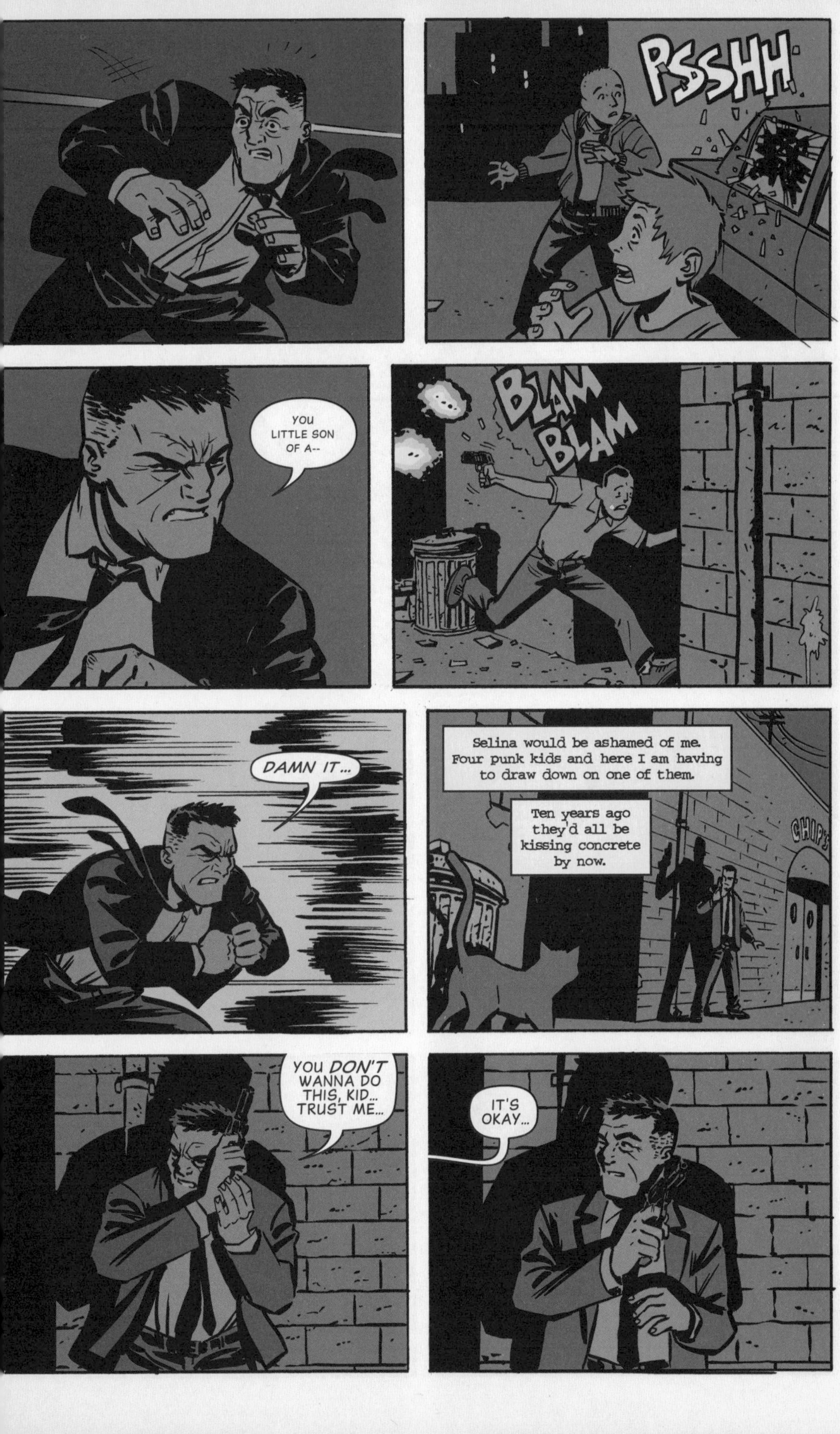
PSSHH
YOU LITTLE SON OF A--
BLAM BLAM
DAMN IT...
Selina would be ashamed of me. Four punk kids and here I am having to draw down on one of them.
Ten years ago they'd all be kissing concrete by now.
CHIP'S
YOU DON'T WANNA DO THIS, KID... TRUST ME...
IT'S OKAY...

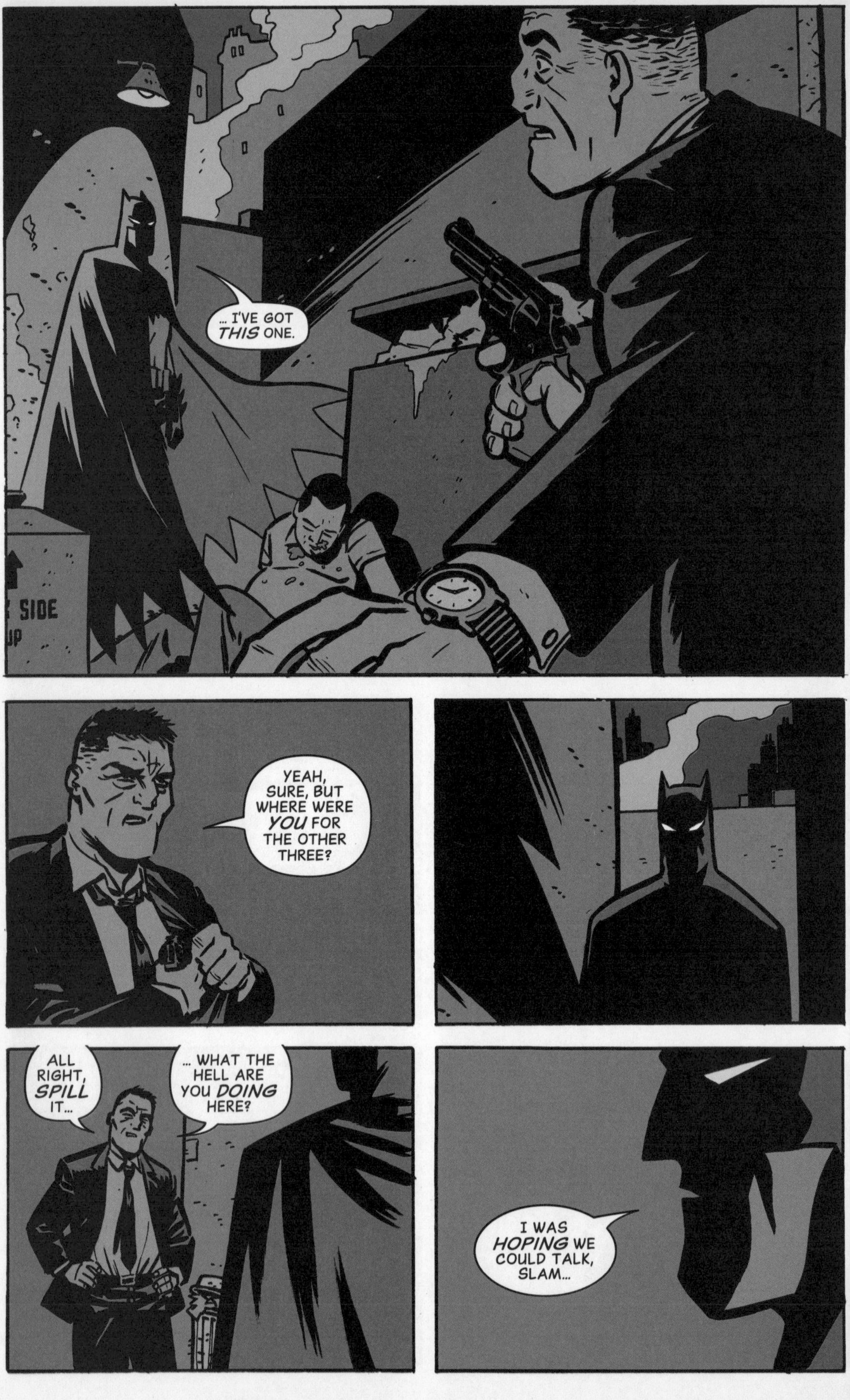
... I'VE GOT THIS ONE.
SIDE
UP
YEAH, SURE, BUT WHERE WERE YOU FOR THE OTHER THREE?
ALL RIGHT, SPILL IT...
... WHAT THE HELL ARE YOU DOING HERE?
I WAS HOPING WE COULD TALK, SLAM...

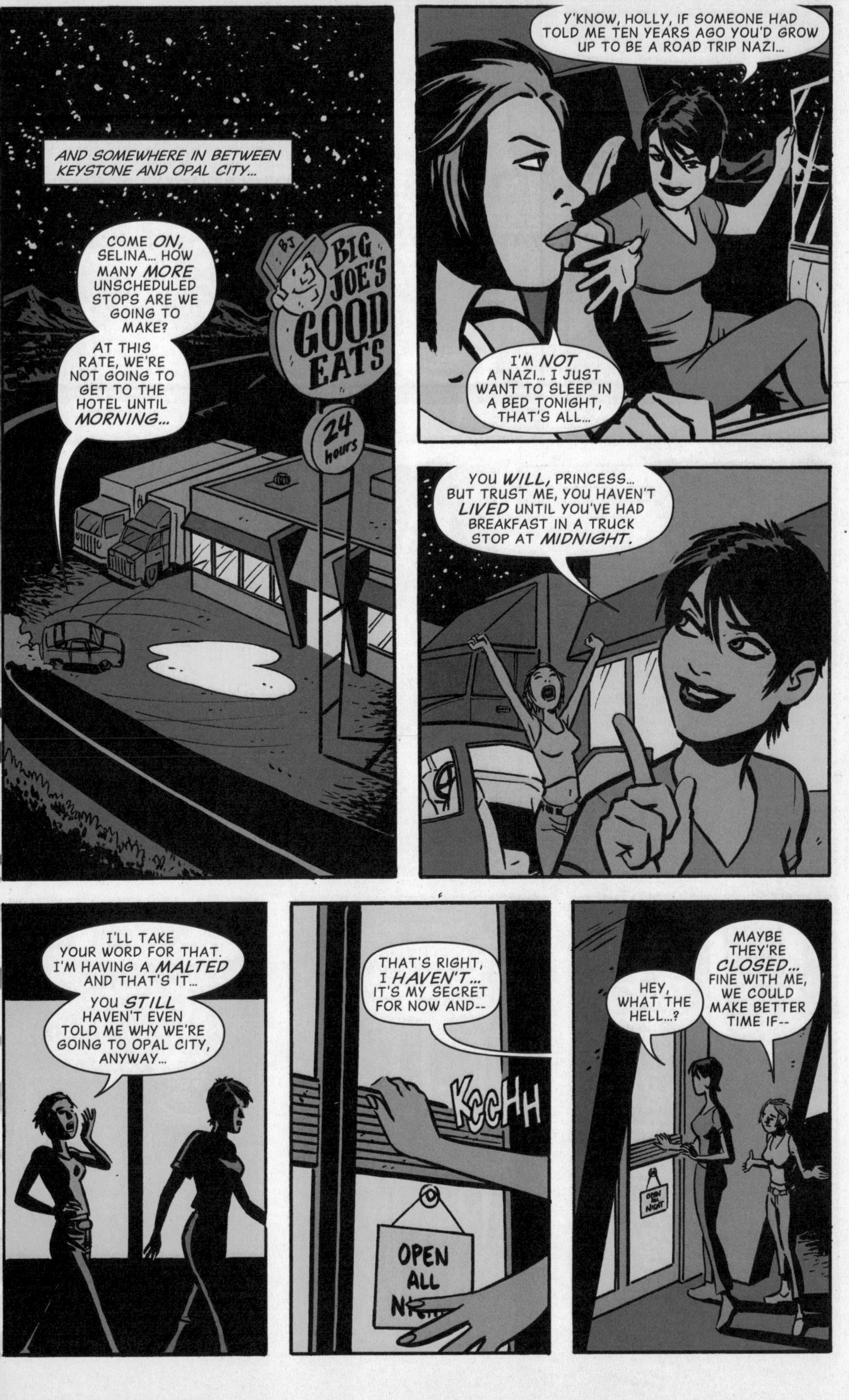
AND SOMEWHERE IN BETWEEN KEYSTONE AND OPAL CITY...
COME ON, SELINA... HOW MANY MORE UNSCHEDULED STOPS ARE WE GOING TO MAKE?
AT THIS RATE, WE'RE NOT GOING TO GET TO THE HOTEL UNTIL MORNING...
BJ
BIG JOE'S GOOD EATS
24 hours
Y'KNOW, HOLLY, IF SOMEONE HAD TOLD ME TEN YEARS AGO YOU'D GROW UP TO BE A ROAD TRIP NAZI...
I'M NOT A NAZI... I JUST WANT TO SLEEP IN A BED TONIGHT, THAT'S ALL...
YOU WILL, PRINCESS... BUT TRUST ME, YOU HAVEN'T LIVED UNTIL YOU'VE HAD BREAKFAST IN A TRUCK STOP AT MIDNIGHT.
I'LL TAKE YOUR WORD FOR THAT. I'M HAVING A MALTED AND THAT'S IT...
YOU STILL HAVEN'T EVEN TOLD ME WHY WE'RE GOING TO OPAL CITY, ANYWAY...
THAT'S RIGHT, I HAVEN'T... IT'S MY SECRET FOR NOW AND--
KCCHH
OPEN ALL
HEY, WHAT THE HELL...?
MAYBE THEY'RE CLOSED... FINE WITH ME, WE COULD MAKE BETTER TIME IF--

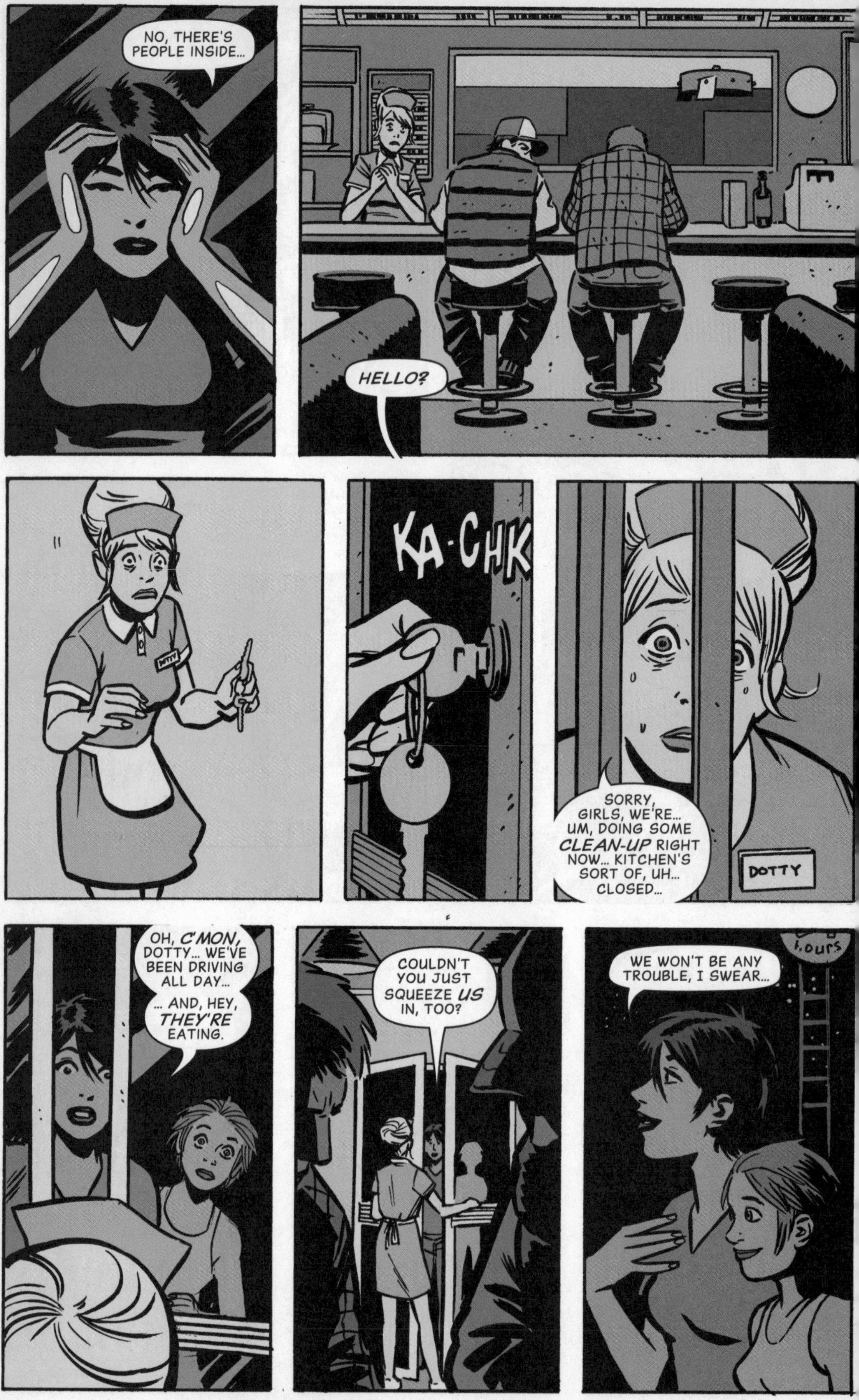
NO, THERE'S PEOPLE INSIDE...
HELLO?
KA-CHK
SORRY, GIRLS, WE'RE... UM, DOING SOME CLEAN-UP RIGHT NOW... KITCHEN'S SORT OF, UH... CLOSED...
DOTTY
OH, C'MON, DOTTY... WE'VE BEEN DRIVING ALL DAY...
... AND, HEY, THEY'RE EATING.
COULDN'T YOU JUST SQUEEZE US IN, TOO?
WE WON'T BE ANY TROUBLE, I SWEAR...

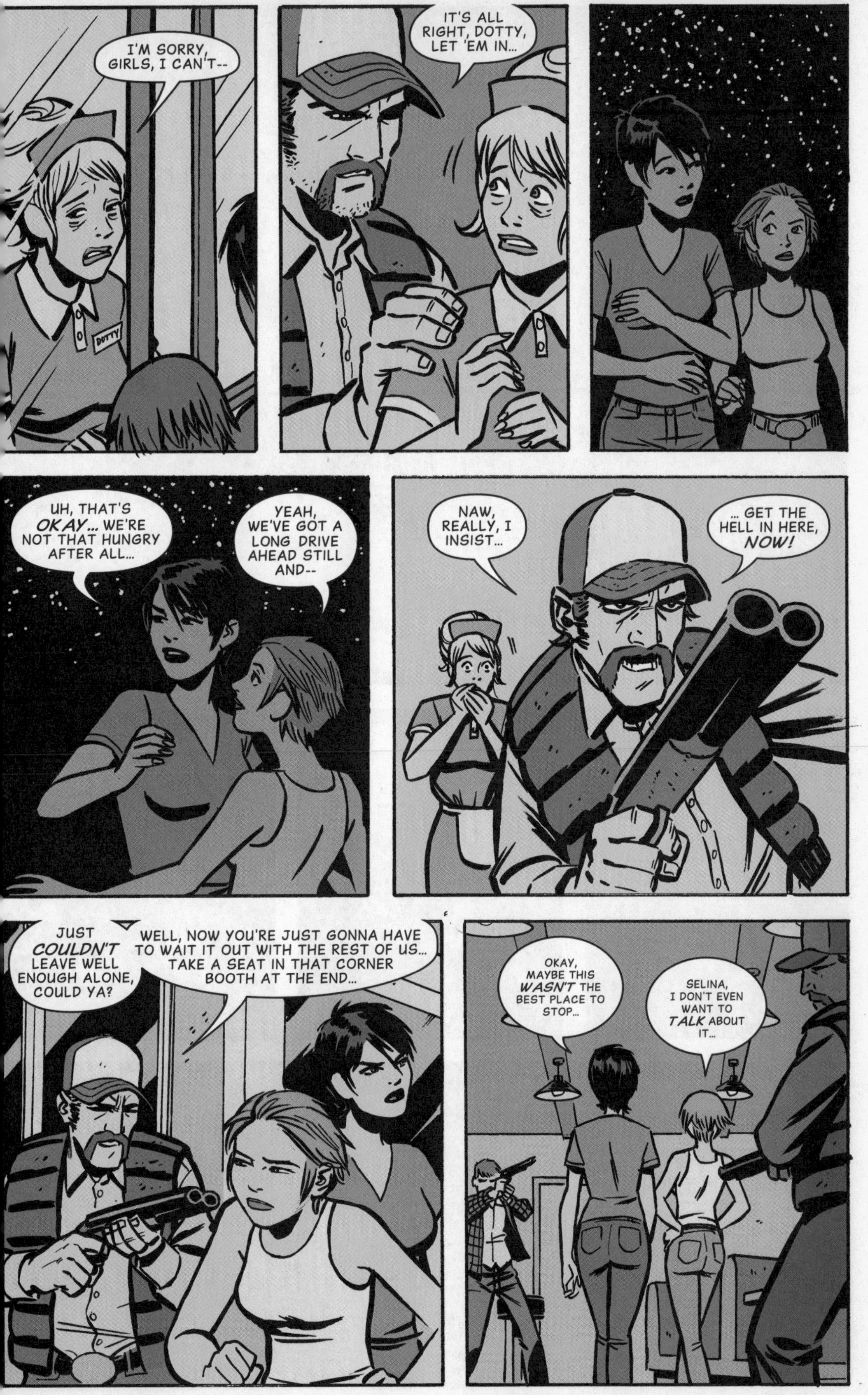
I'M SORRY, GIRLS, I CAN'T--
IT'S ALL RIGHT, DOTTY, LET 'EM IN...
DOTTY
UH, THAT'S OKAY... WE'RE NOT THAT HUNGRY AFTER ALL...
YEAH, WE'VE GOT A LONG DRIVE AHEAD STILL AND--
NAW, REALLY, I INSIST...
... GET THE HELL IN HERE, NOW!
JUST COULDN'T LEAVE WELL ENOUGH ALONE, COULD YA?
WELL, NOW YOU'RE JUST GONNA HAVE TO WAIT IT OUT WITH THE REST OF US... TAKE A SEAT IN THAT CORNER BOOTH AT THE END...
OKAY, MAYBE THIS WASN'T THE BEST PLACE TO STOP...
SELINA, I DON'T EVEN WANT TO TALK ABOUT IT...

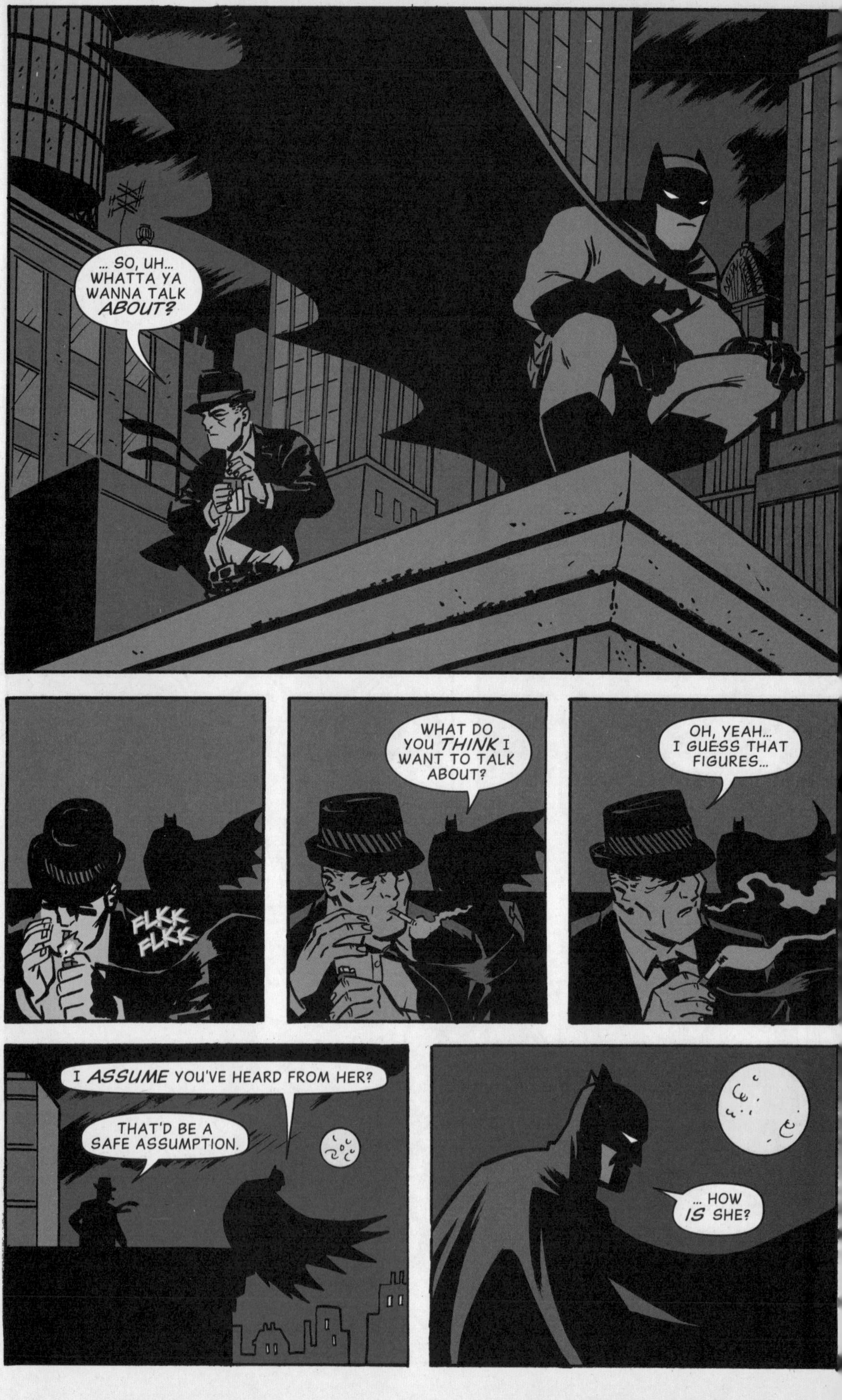
... SO, UH... WHATTA YA WANNA TALK ABOUT?
FLKK FLKK
WHAT DO YOU THINK I WANT TO TALK ABOUT?
OH, YEAH... I GUESS THAT FIGURES...
I ASSUME YOU'VE HEARD FROM HER?
THAT'D BE A SAFE ASSUMPTION.
... HOW IS SHE?

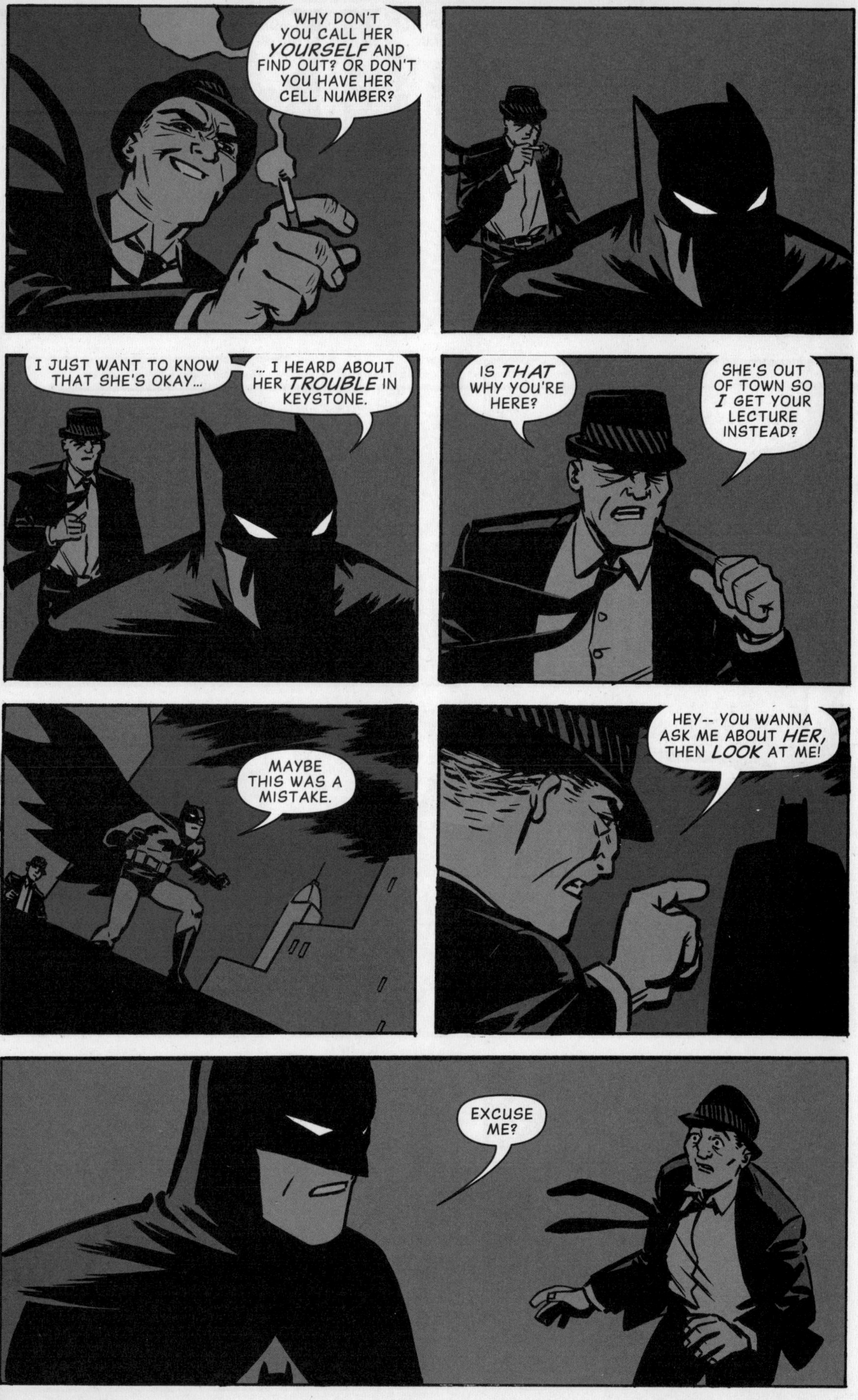
WHY DON'T YOU CALL HER YOURSELF AND FIND OUT? OR DON'T YOU HAVE HER CELL NUMBER?
I JUST WANT TO KNOW THAT SHE'S OKAY...
... I HEARD ABOUT HER TROUBLE IN KEYSTONE.
IS THAT WHY YOU'RE HERE?
SHE'S OUT OF TOWN SO I GET YOUR LECTURE INSTEAD?
MAYBE THIS WAS A MISTAKE.
HEY-- YOU WANNA ASK ME ABOUT HER, THEN LOOK AT ME!
EXCUSE ME?

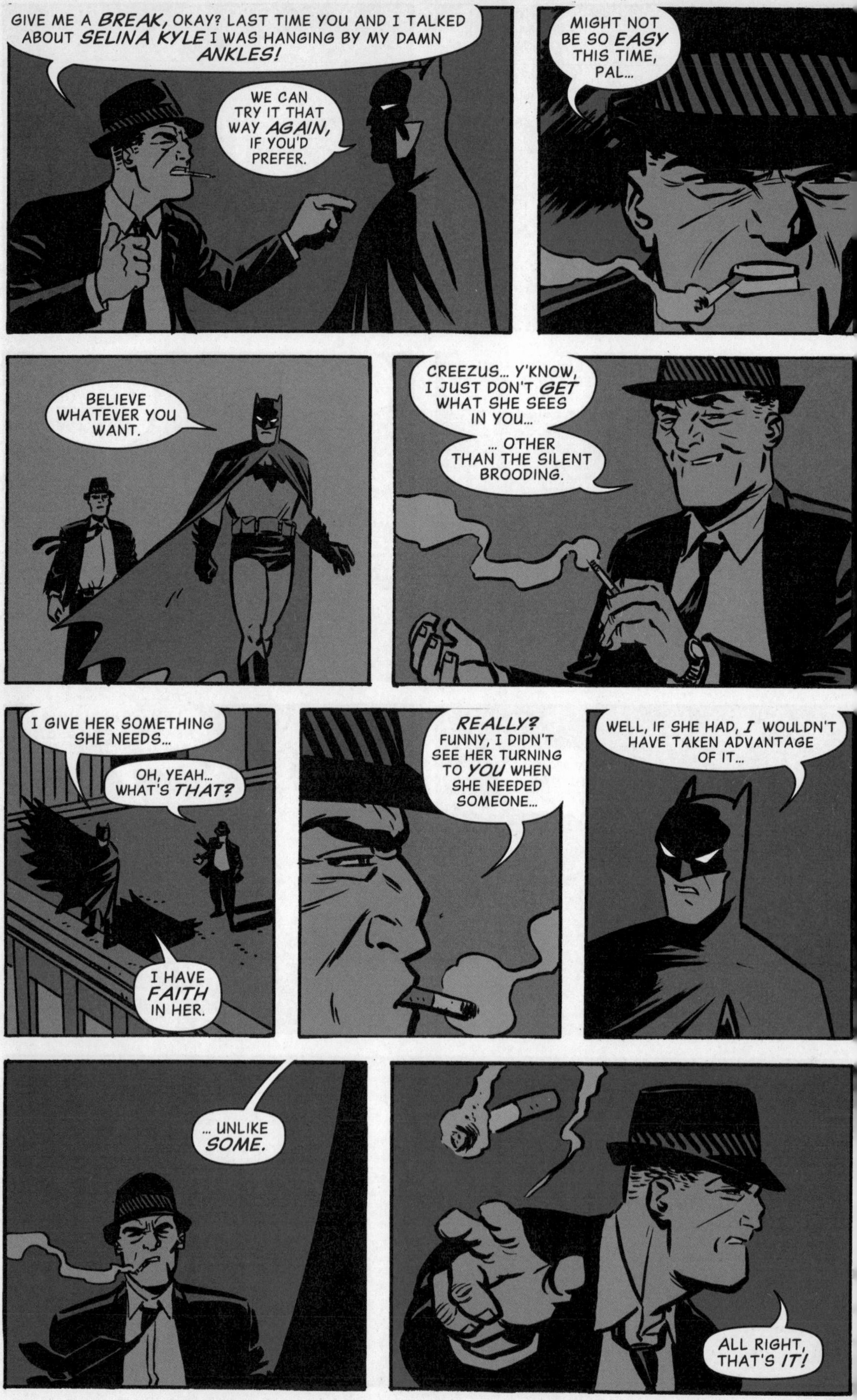
GIVE ME A BREAK, OKAY? LAST TIME YOU AND I TALKED ABOUT SELINA KYLE I WAS HANGING BY MY DAMN ANKLES!
WE CAN TRY IT THAT WAY AGAIN, IF YOU'D PREFER.
MIGHT NOT BE SO EASY THIS TIME, PAL...
BELIEVE WHATEVER YOU WANT.
CREEZUS... Y'KNOW, I JUST DON'T GET WHAT SHE SEES IN YOU...
... OTHER THAN THE SILENT BROODING.
I GIVE HER SOMETHING SHE NEEDS...
OH, YEAH... WHAT'S THAT?
I HAVE FAITH IN HER.
REALLY? FUNNY, I DIDN'T SEE HER TURNING TO YOU WHEN SHE NEEDED SOMEONE...
WELL, IF SHE HAD, I WOULDN'T HAVE TAKEN ADVANTAGE OF IT...
... UNLIKE SOME.
ALL RIGHT, THAT'S IT!

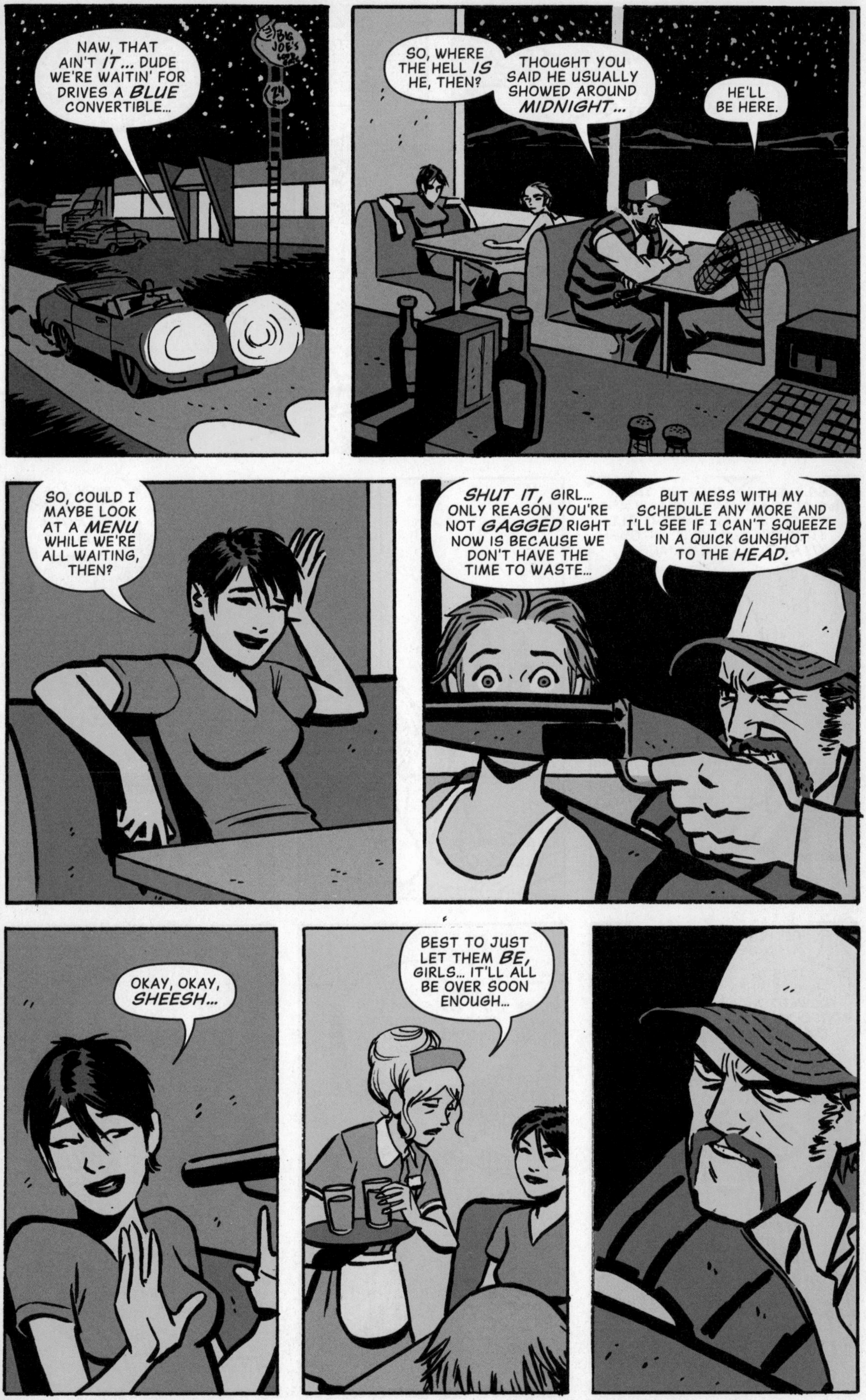
NAW, THAT AIN'T *IT*... DUDE WE'RE WAITIN' FOR DRIVES A *BLUE* CONVERTIBLE...
SO, WHERE THE HELL *IS* HE, THEN?
THOUGHT YOU SAID HE USUALLY SHOWED AROUND *MIDNIGHT*...
HE'LL BE HERE.
SO, COULD I MAYBE LOOK AT A *MENU* WHILE WE'RE ALL WAITING, THEN?
SHUT IT, GIRL... ONLY REASON YOU'RE NOT *GAGGED* RIGHT NOW IS BECAUSE WE DON'T HAVE THE TIME TO WASTE...
BUT MESS WITH MY SCHEDULE ANY MORE AND I'LL SEE IF I CAN'T SQUEEZE IN A QUICK GUNSHOT TO THE *HEAD.*
OKAY, OKAY, *SHEESH*...
BEST TO JUST LET THEM *BE,* GIRLS... IT'LL ALL BE OVER SOON ENOUGH...

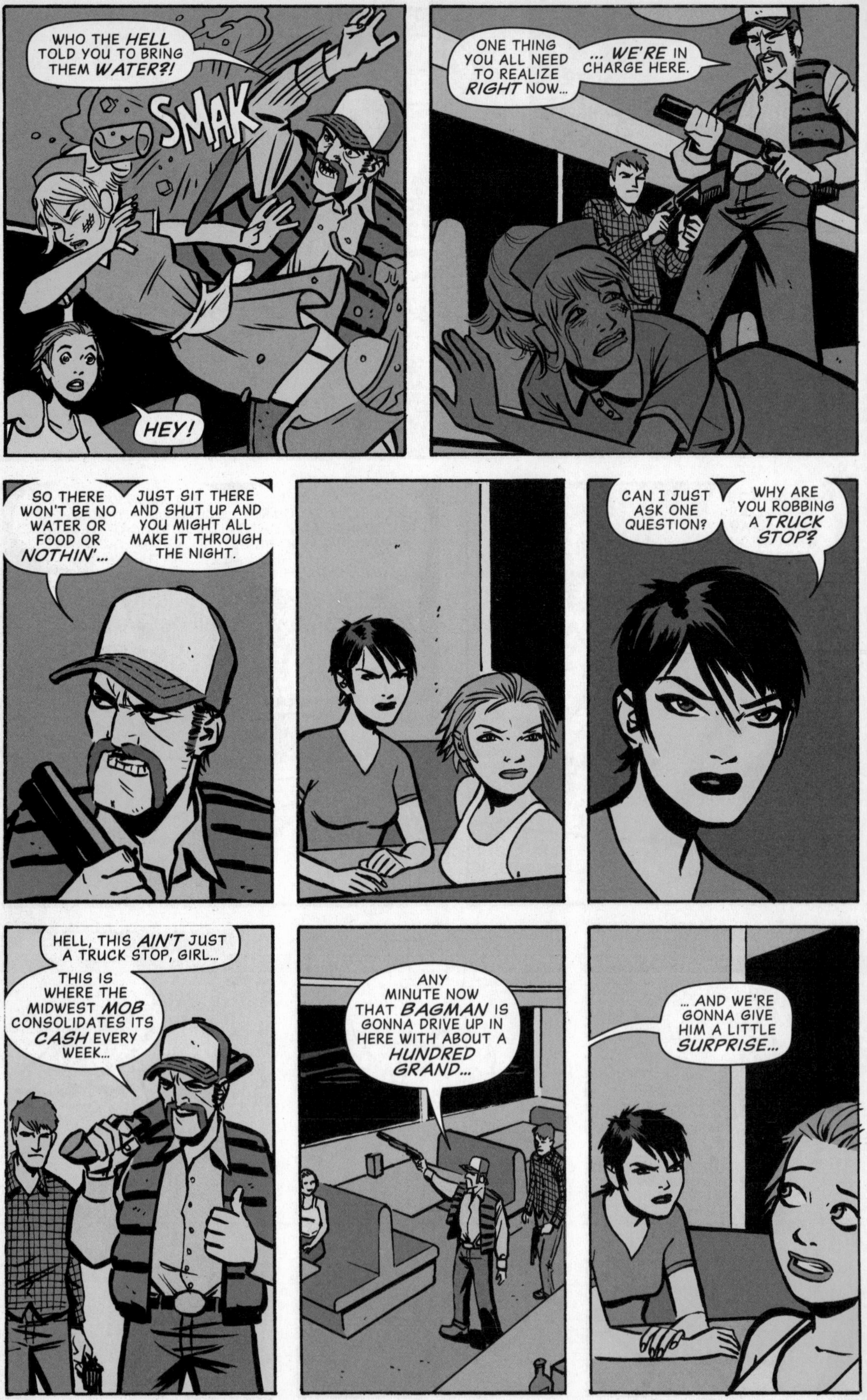
WHO THE HELL TOLD YOU TO BRING THEM WATER?!
SMAK
HEY!
ONE THING YOU ALL NEED TO REALIZE RIGHT NOW...
... WE'RE IN CHARGE HERE.
SO THERE WON'T BE NO WATER OR FOOD OR NOTHIN'...
JUST SIT THERE AND SHUT UP AND YOU MIGHT ALL MAKE IT THROUGH THE NIGHT.
CAN I JUST ASK ONE QUESTION?
WHY ARE YOU ROBBING A TRUCK STOP?
HELL, THIS AIN'T JUST A TRUCK STOP, GIRL...
THIS IS WHERE THE MIDWEST MOB CONSOLIDATES ITS CASH EVERY WEEK...
ANY MINUTE NOW THAT BAGMAN IS GONNA DRIVE UP IN HERE WITH ABOUT A HUNDRED GRAND...
... AND WE'RE GONNA GIVE HIM A LITTLE SURPRISE...

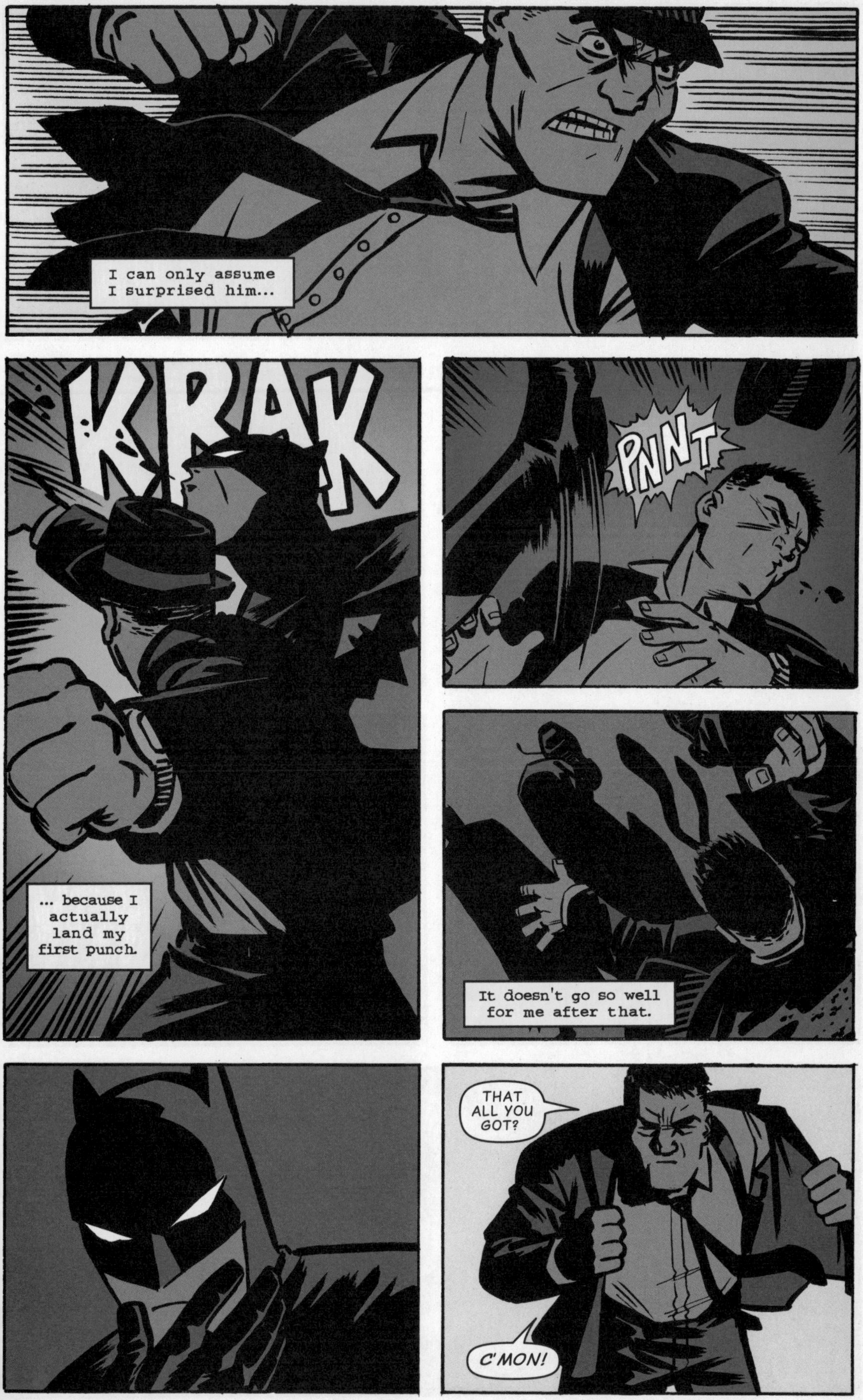
I can only assume I surprised him...
KRAK
... because I actually land my first punch.
PNNT
It doesn't go so well for me after that.
THAT ALL YOU GOT?
C'MON!

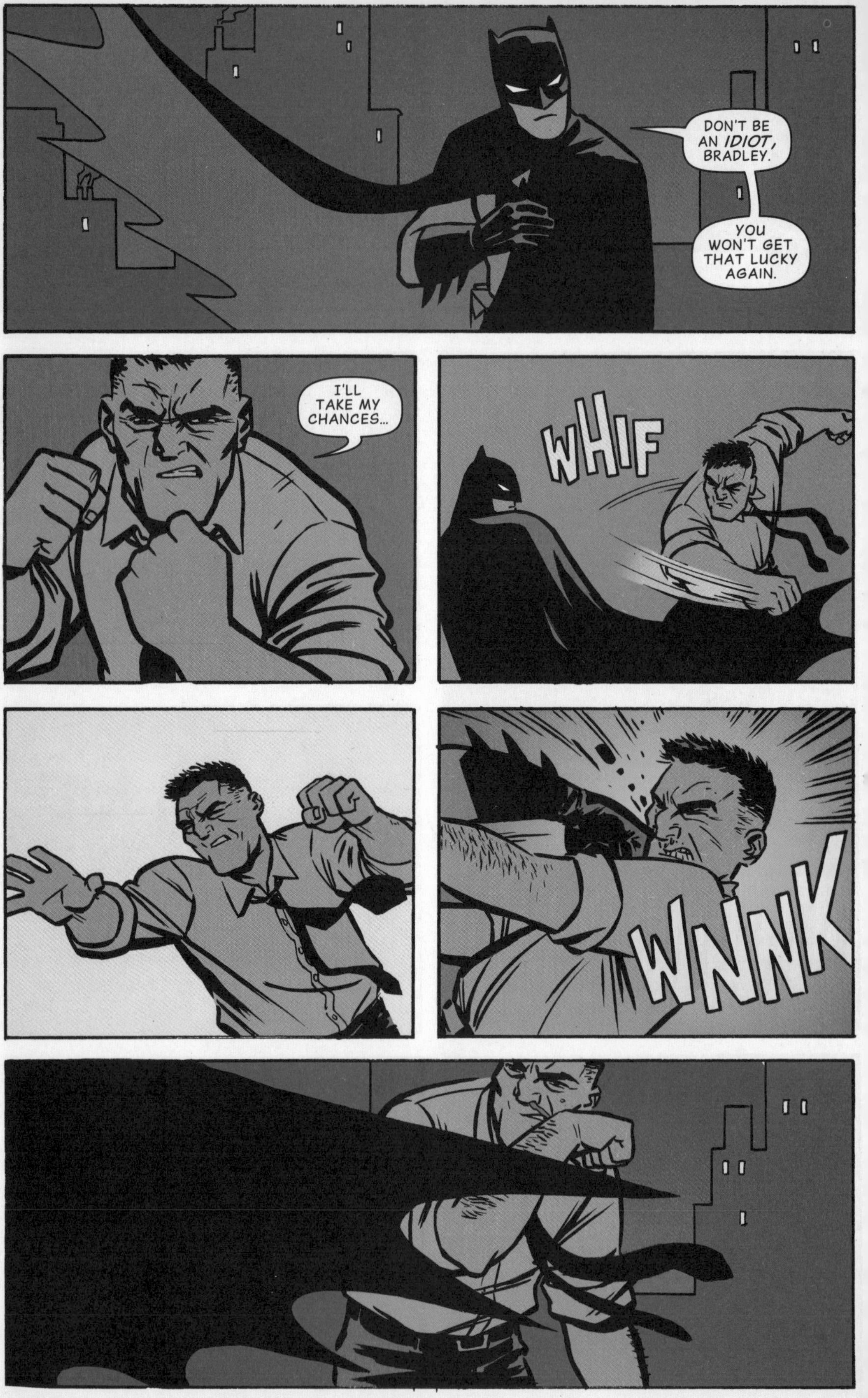
DON'T BE AN *IDIOT*, BRADLEY.
YOU WON'T GET THAT LUCKY AGAIN.
I'LL TAKE MY CHANCES...
WHIF
WNNK

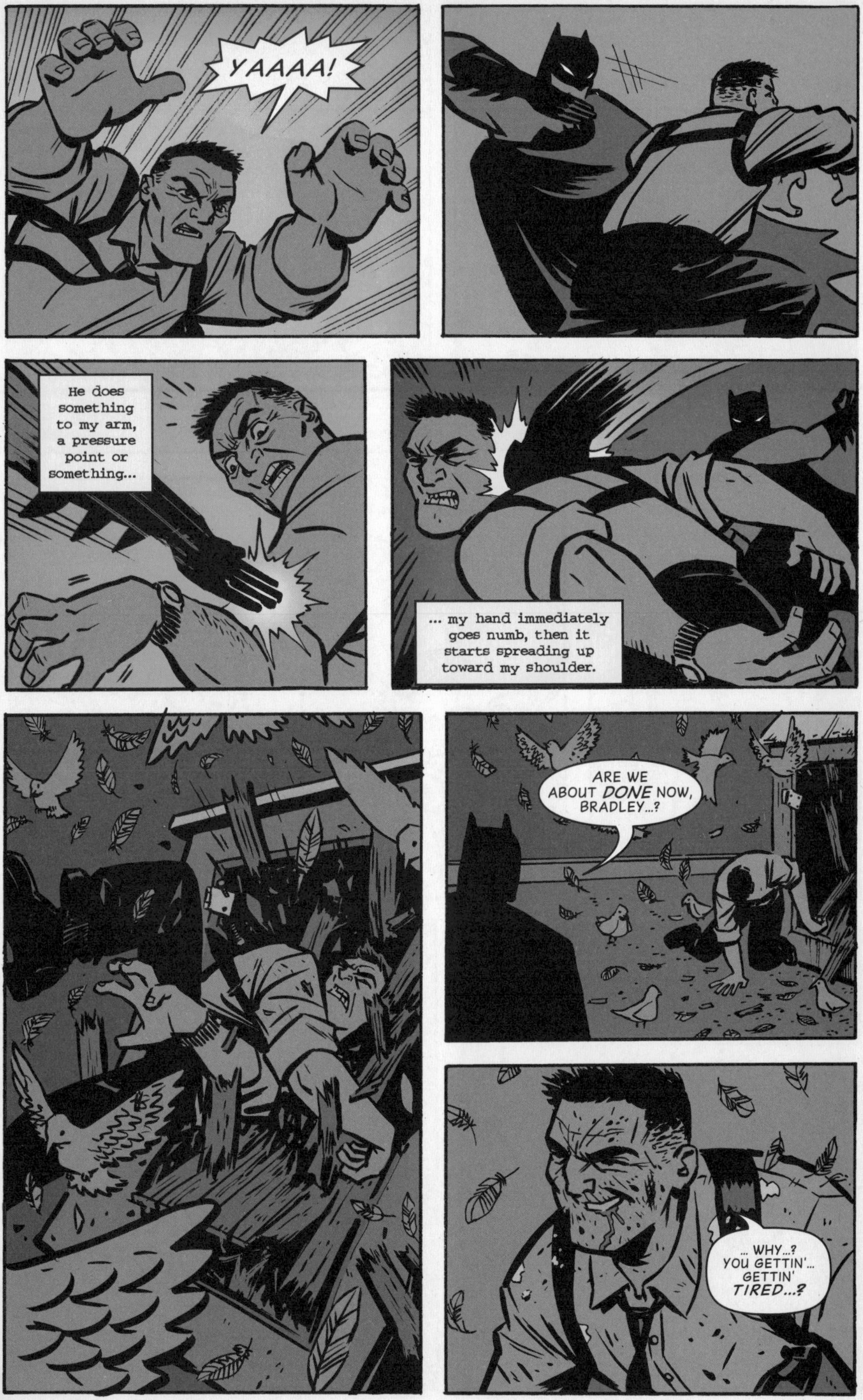
YAAAA!
He does something to my arm, a pressure point or something...
... my hand immediately goes numb, then it starts spreading up toward my shoulder.
ARE WE ABOUT DONE NOW, BRADLEY...?
... WHY...? YOU GETTIN'... GETTIN' TIRED...?

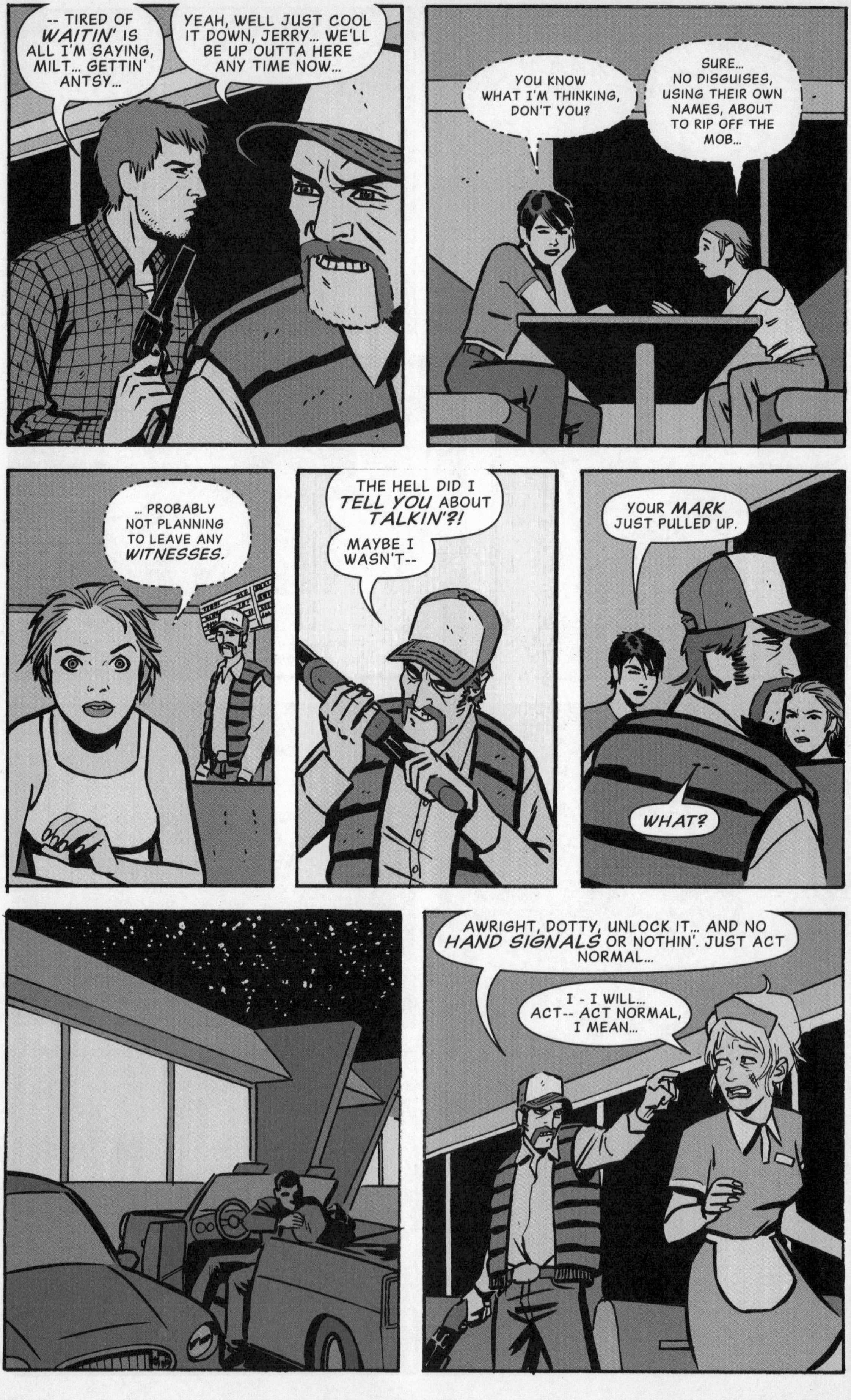
-- TIRED OF WAITIN' IS ALL I'M SAYING, MILT... GETTIN' ANTSY...
YEAH, WELL JUST COOL IT DOWN, JERRY... WE'LL BE UP OUTTA HERE ANY TIME NOW...
YOU KNOW WHAT I'M THINKING, DON'T YOU?
SURE... NO DISGUISES, USING THEIR OWN NAMES, ABOUT TO RIP OFF THE MOB...
... PROBABLY NOT PLANNING TO LEAVE ANY WITNESSES.
THE HELL DID I TELL YOU ABOUT TALKIN'?!
MAYBE I WASN'T--
YOUR MARK JUST PULLED UP.
WHAT?
AWRIGHT, DOTTY, UNLOCK IT... AND NO HAND SIGNALS OR NOTHIN'. JUST ACT NORMAL...
I - I WILL... ACT-- ACT NORMAL, I MEAN...

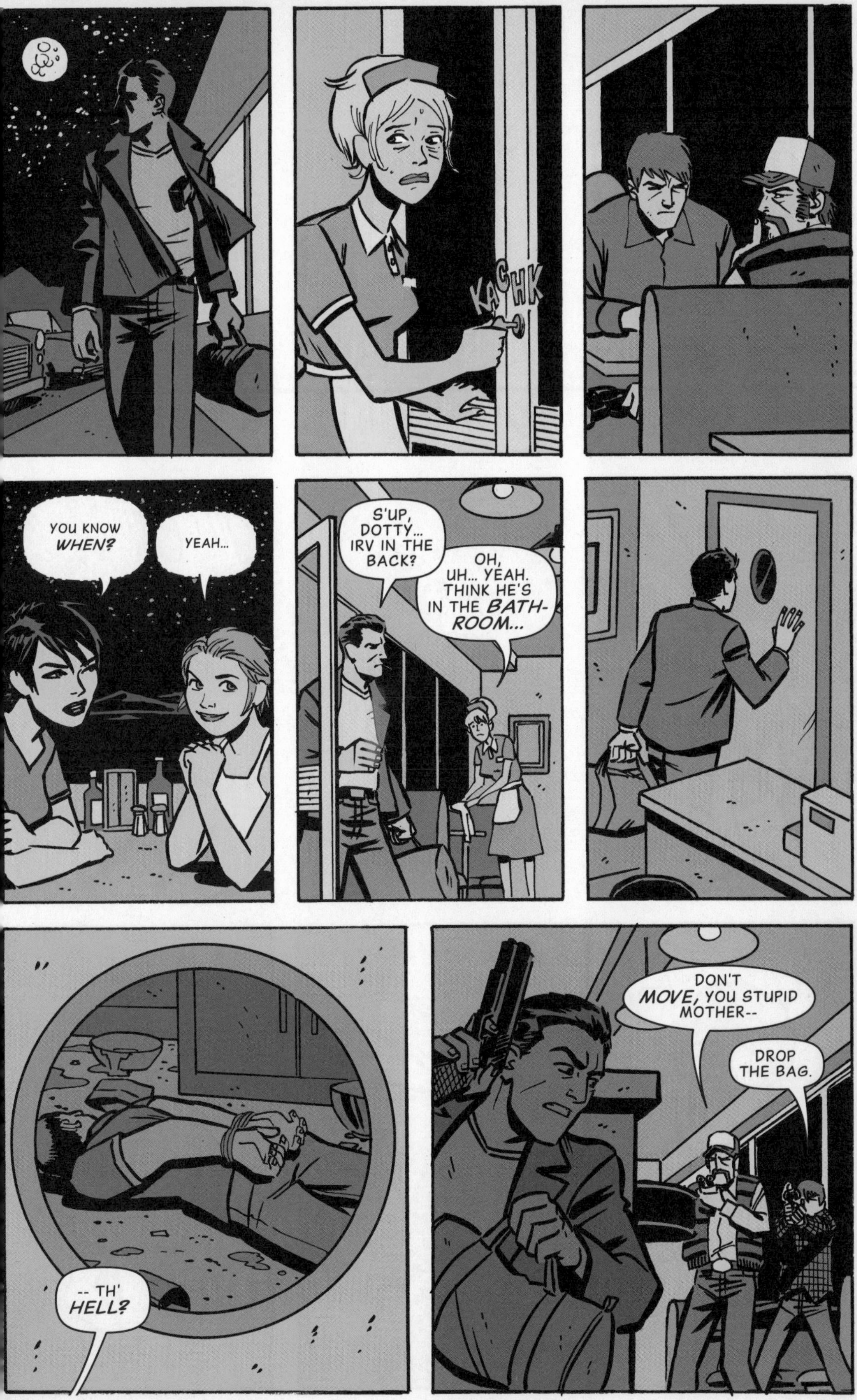
KACHK
YOU KNOW *WHEN?*
YEAH...
S'UP, DOTTY... IRV IN THE BACK?
OH, UH... YEAH. THINK HE'S IN THE *BATH-ROOM...*
-- TH' *HELL?*
DON'T *MOVE,* YOU STUPID MOTHER--
DROP THE BAG.

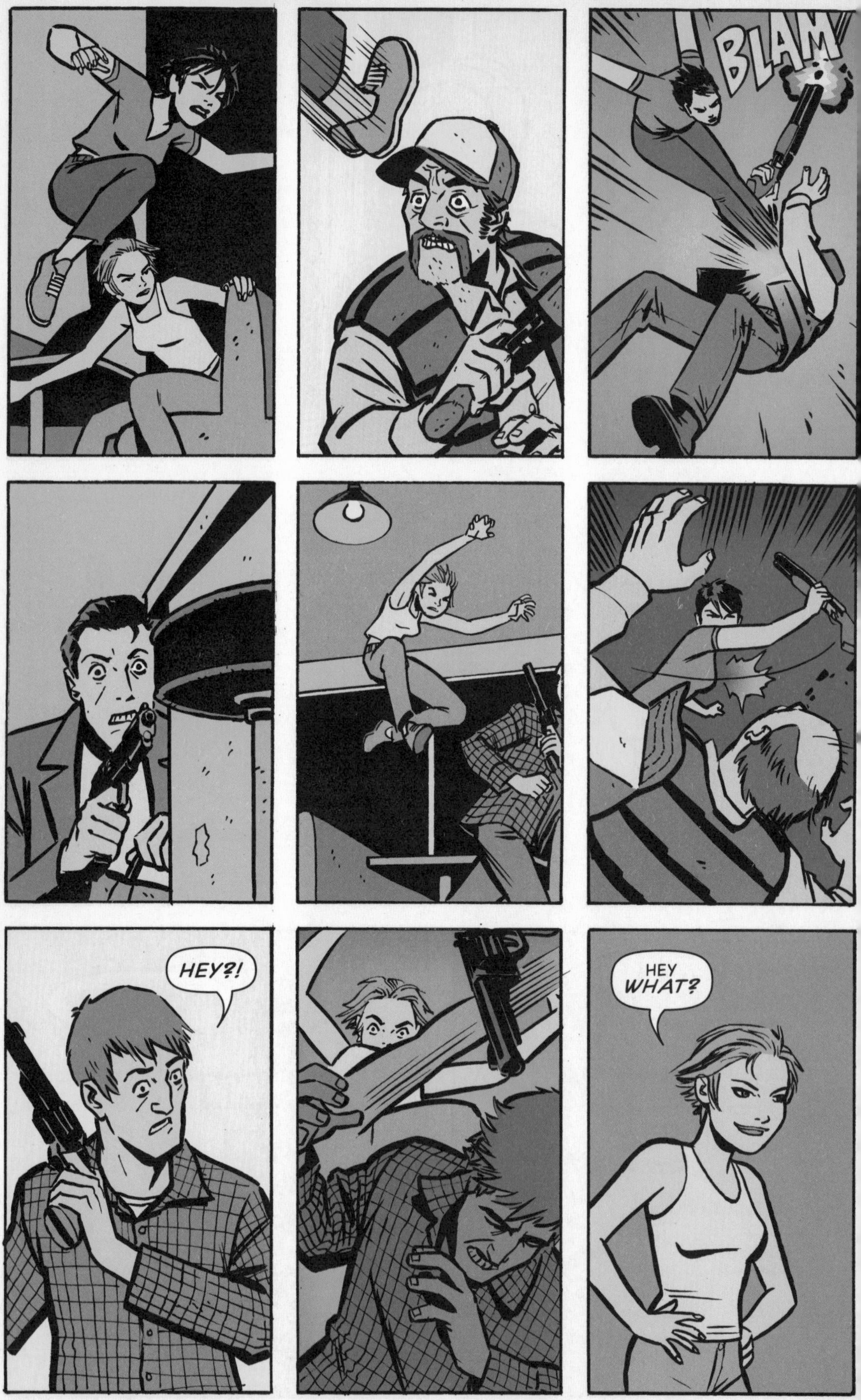
BLAM
HEY?!
HEY WHAT?

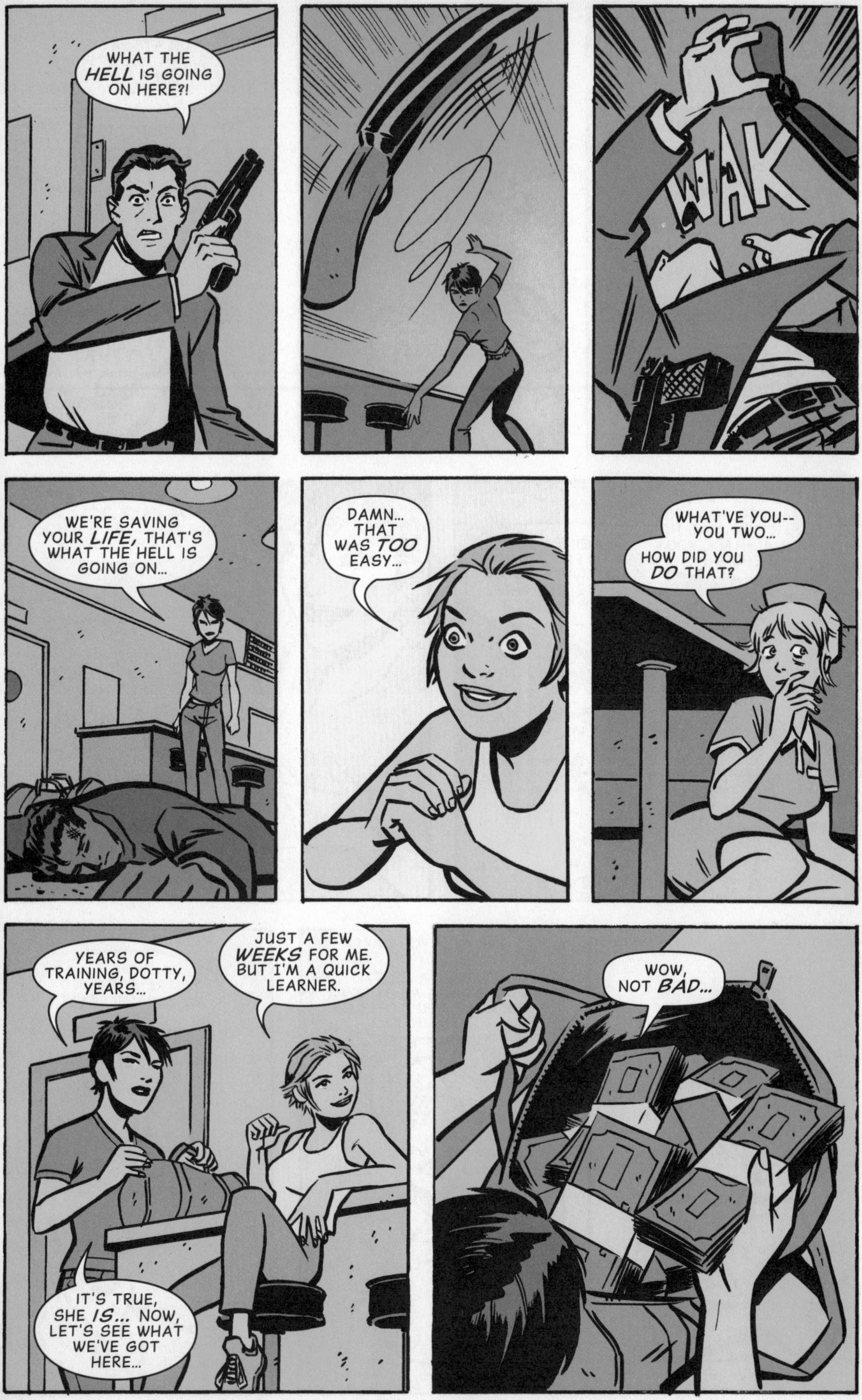
WHAT THE HELL IS GOING ON HERE?!
WAK
WE'RE SAVING YOUR LIFE, THAT'S WHAT THE HELL IS GOING ON...
DAMN... THAT WAS TOO EASY...
WHAT'VE YOU-- YOU TWO...
HOW DID YOU DO THAT?
YEARS OF TRAINING, DOTTY, YEARS...
JUST A FEW WEEKS FOR ME. BUT I'M A QUICK LEARNER.
IT'S TRUE, SHE IS... NOW, LET'S SEE WHAT WE'VE GOT HERE...
WOW, NOT BAD...

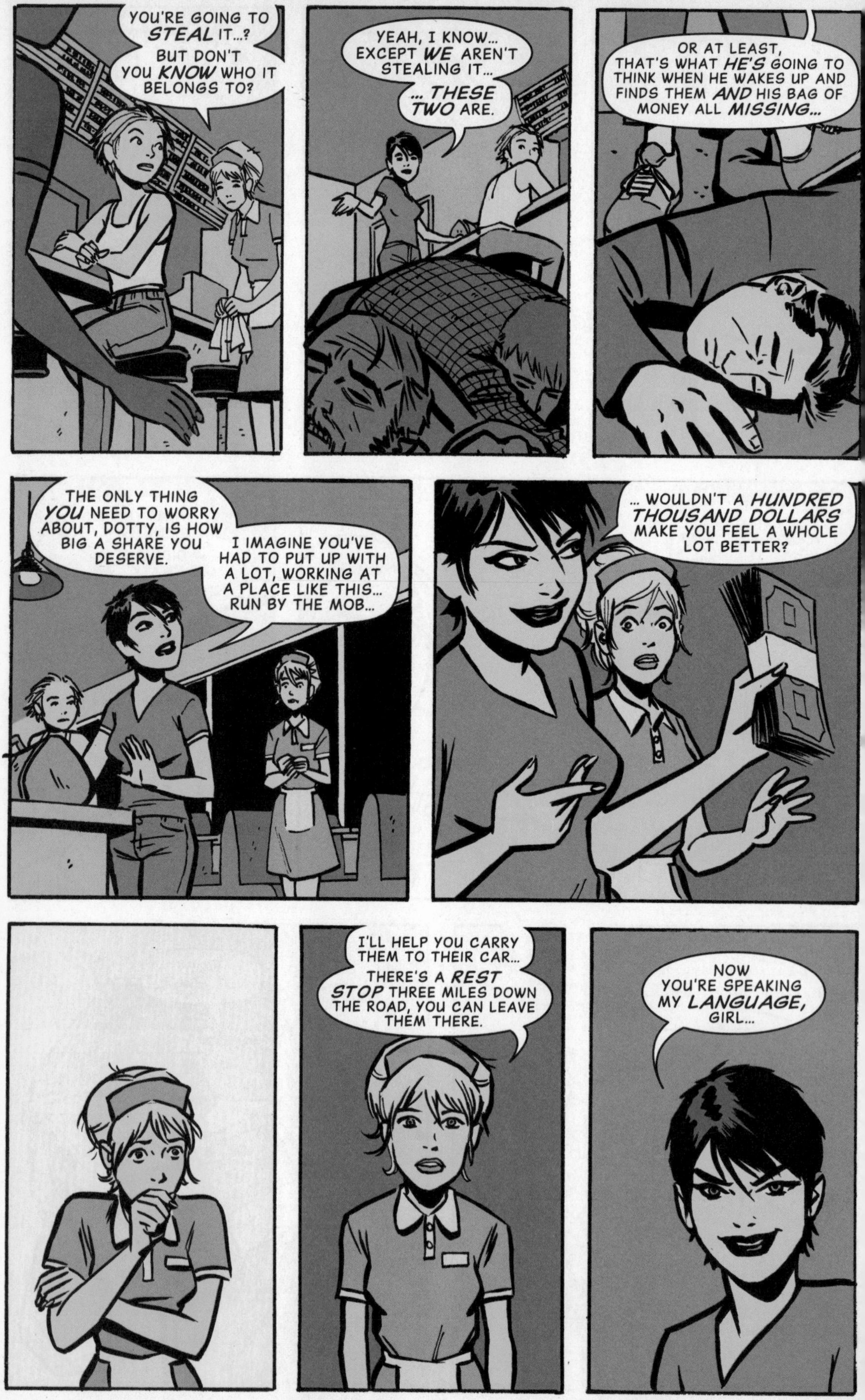
YOU'RE GOING TO STEAL IT...?
BUT DON'T YOU KNOW WHO IT BELONGS TO?
YEAH, I KNOW... EXCEPT WE AREN'T STEALING IT...
... THESE TWO ARE.
OR AT LEAST, THAT'S WHAT HE'S GOING TO THINK WHEN HE WAKES UP AND FINDS THEM AND HIS BAG OF MONEY ALL MISSING...
THE ONLY THING YOU NEED TO WORRY ABOUT, DOTTY, IS HOW BIG A SHARE YOU DESERVE.
I IMAGINE YOU'VE HAD TO PUT UP WITH A LOT, WORKING AT A PLACE LIKE THIS... RUN BY THE MOB...
... WOULDN'T A HUNDRED THOUSAND DOLLARS MAKE YOU FEEL A WHOLE LOT BETTER?
I'LL HELP YOU CARRY THEM TO THEIR CAR...
THERE'S A REST STOP THREE MILES DOWN THE ROAD, YOU CAN LEAVE THEM THERE.
NOW YOU'RE SPEAKING MY LANGUAGE, GIRL...

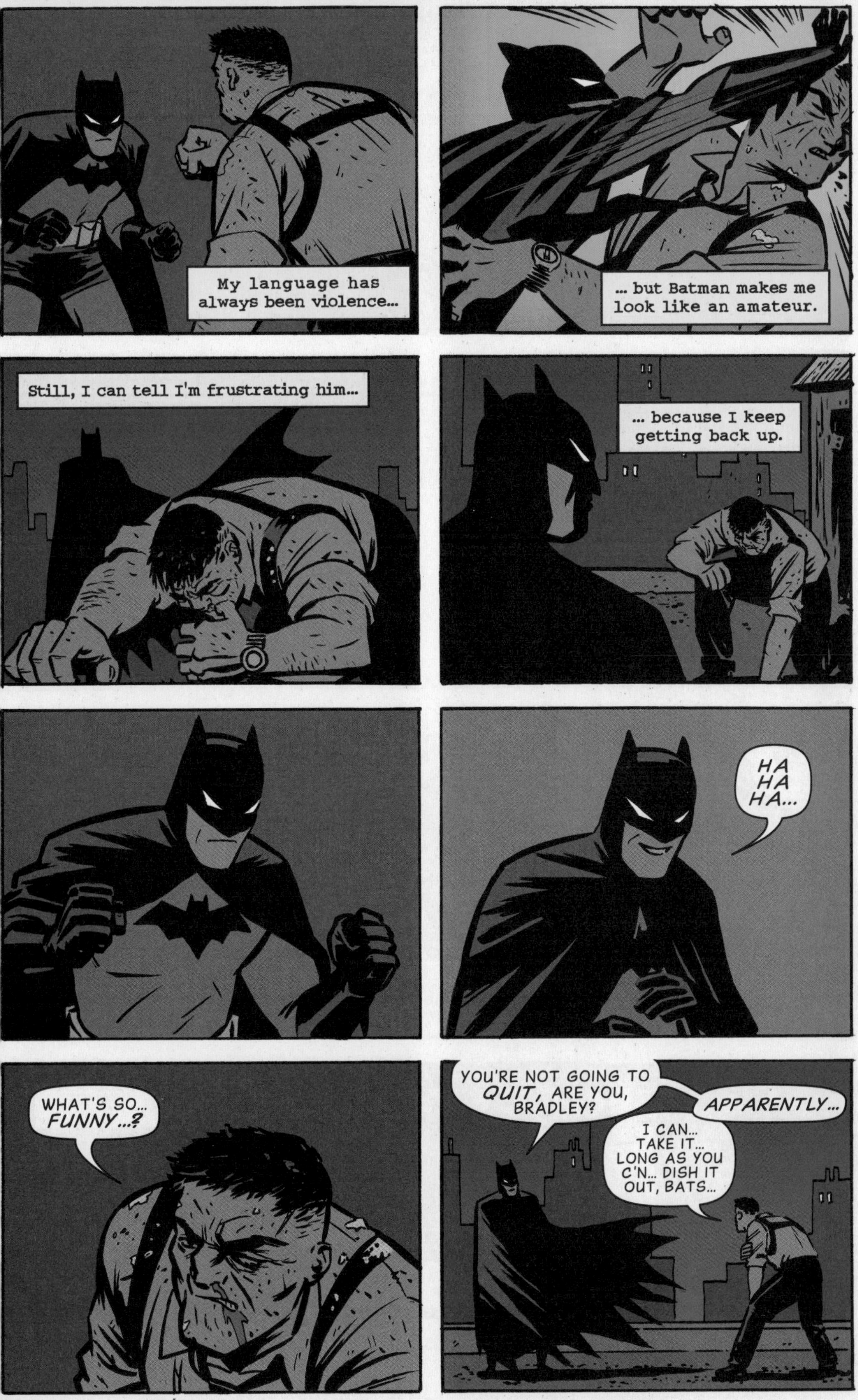
My language has always been violence...
... but Batman makes me look like an amateur.
Still, I can tell I'm frustrating him...
... because I keep getting back up.
HA HA HA...
WHAT'S SO... FUNNY...?
YOU'RE NOT GOING TO QUIT, ARE YOU, BRADLEY?
APPARENTLY...
I CAN... TAKE IT... LONG AS YOU C'N... DISH IT OUT, BATS...

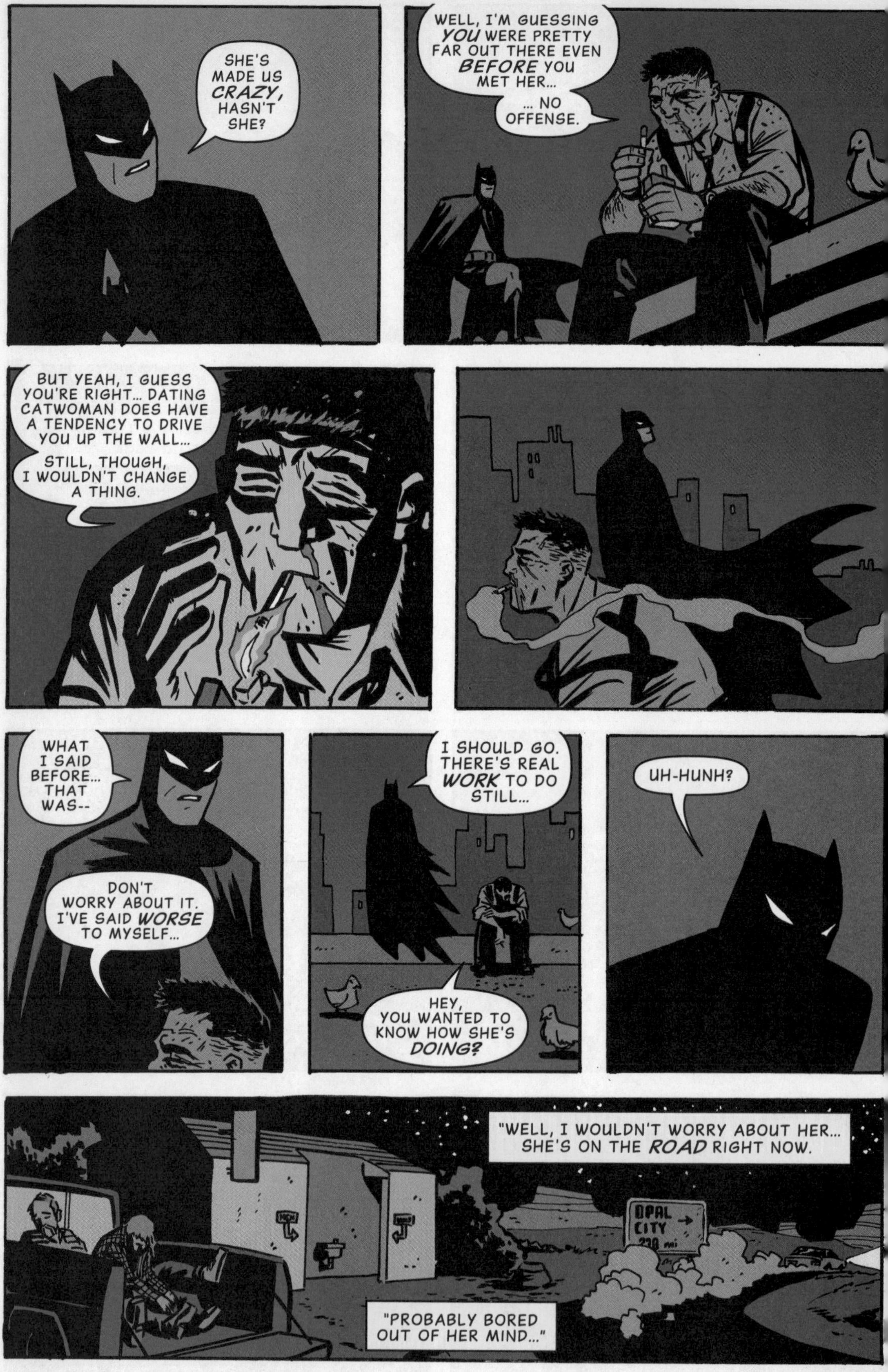

SHE'S MADE US CRAZY, HASN'T SHE?
WELL, I'M GUESSING YOU WERE PRETTY FAR OUT THERE EVEN BEFORE YOU MET HER...
... NO OFFENSE.
BUT YEAH, I GUESS YOU'RE RIGHT... DATING CATWOMAN DOES HAVE A TENDENCY TO DRIVE YOU UP THE WALL...
STILL, THOUGH, I WOULDN'T CHANGE A THING.
WHAT I SAID BEFORE... THAT WAS--
DON'T WORRY ABOUT IT. I'VE SAID WORSE TO MYSELF...
I SHOULD GO. THERE'S REAL WORK TO DO STILL...
HEY, YOU WANTED TO KNOW HOW SHE'S DOING?
UH-HUNH?
"WELL, I WOULDN'T WORRY ABOUT HER... SHE'S ON THE ROAD RIGHT NOW.
OPAL CITY →
"PROBABLY BORED OUT OF HER MIND..."

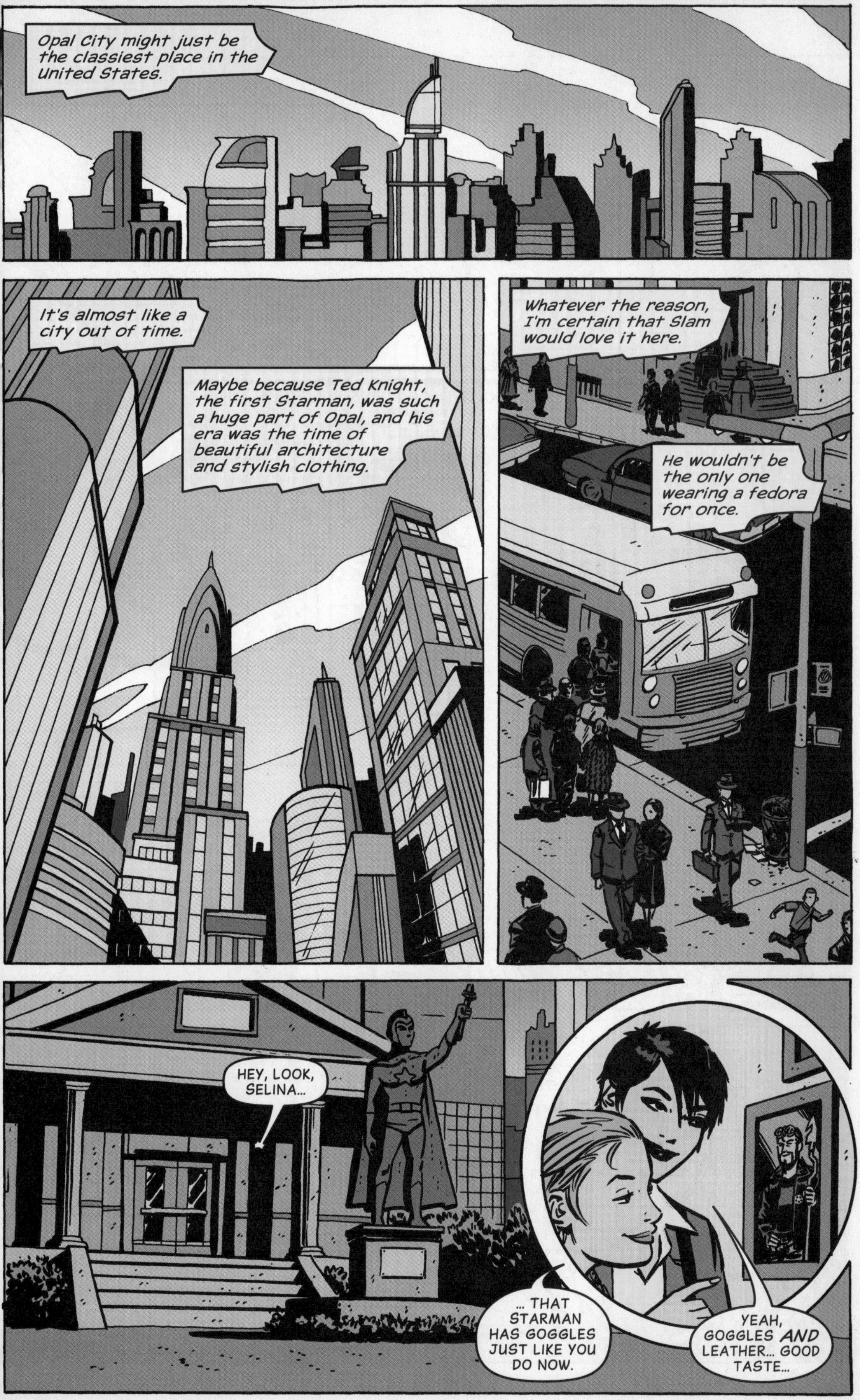
Opal City might just be the classiest place in the United States.
It's almost like a city out of time.
Maybe because Ted Knight, the first Starman, was such a huge part of Opal, and his era was the time of beautiful architecture and stylish clothing.
Whatever the reason, I'm certain that Slam would love it here.
He wouldn't be the only one wearing a fedora for once.
HEY, LOOK, SELINA...
... THAT STARMAN HAS GOGGLES JUST LIKE YOU DO NOW.
YEAH, GOGGLES *AND* LEATHER... GOOD TASTE...

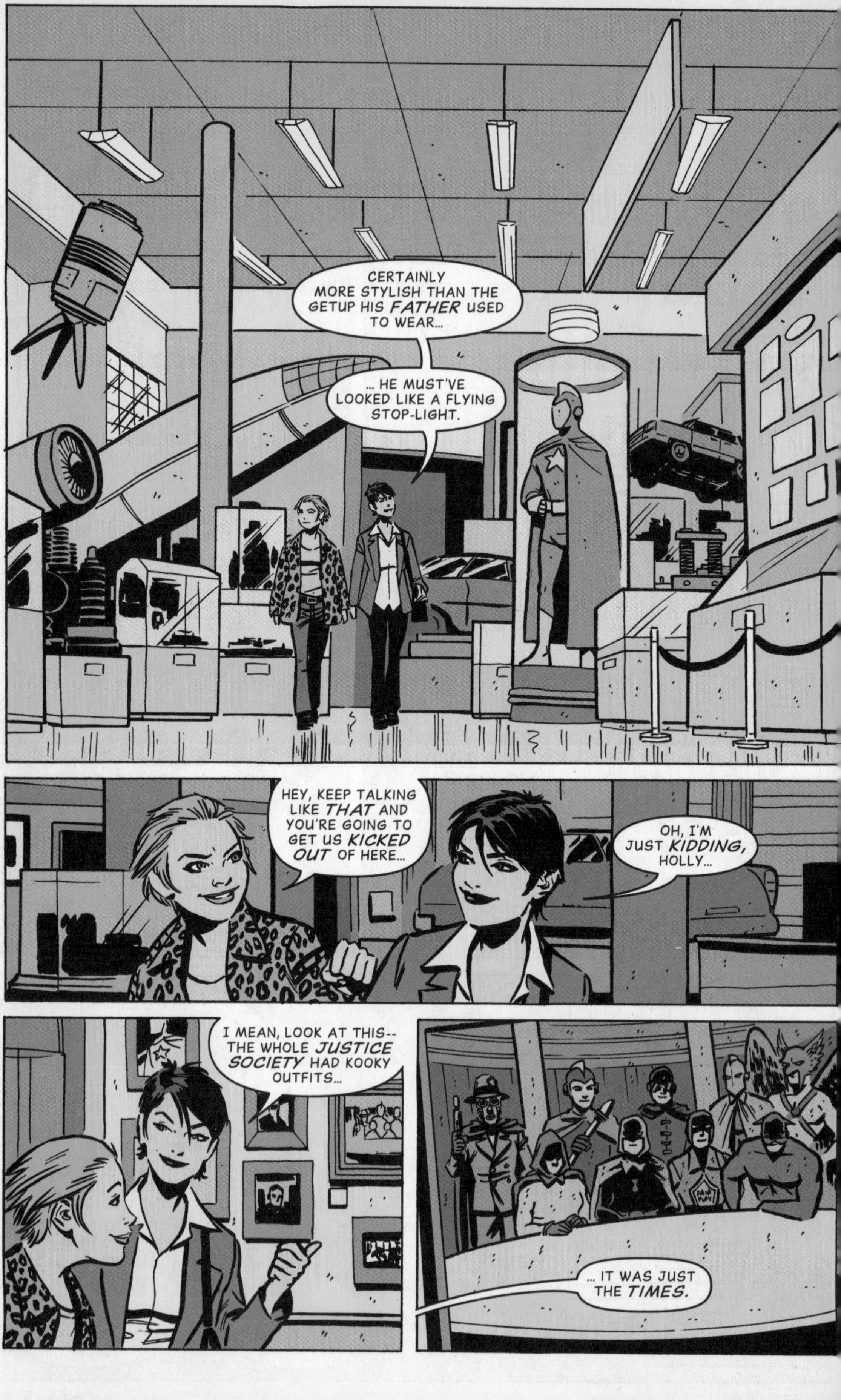
CERTAINLY MORE STYLISH THAN THE GETUP HIS FATHER USED TO WEAR...
... HE MUST'VE LOOKED LIKE A FLYING STOP-LIGHT.
HEY, KEEP TALKING LIKE THAT AND YOU'RE GOING TO GET US KICKED OUT OF HERE...
OH, I'M JUST KIDDING, HOLLY...
I MEAN, LOOK AT THIS-- THE WHOLE JUSTICE SOCIETY HAD KOOKY OUTFITS...
... IT WAS JUST THE TIMES.

HA... YOU KNOW WHAT, MAYBE *YOU* SHOULD TRY TO JOIN THE *JSA.* SINCE YOU'RE TRYING TO POLISH UP YOUR IMAGE..

WILDCAT'D PUT IN A GOOD WORD FOR YOU, PROBABLY.

AH, YEAH... I DON'T *THINK* SO...

BESIDES, JUST BECAUSE I'M NOT STAKING THIS MUSEUM OUT FOR A *SCORE* DOESN'T MEAN I'M EXACTLY *MISS LAW-AND-ORDER* FOR THE NEW MILLENNIUM.

YOU SHOULD KNOW BY NOW, *GIRL,* THAT *WHATEVER* SIDE I'M ON...

... I PLAY BY MY *OWN* RULES.

I KNOW... I KNOW...

I JUST THOUGHT IT'D BE FUNNY, SEEING *YOU* SITTING AROUND A TABLE WITH HAWKMAN AND CAPTAIN MARVEL...

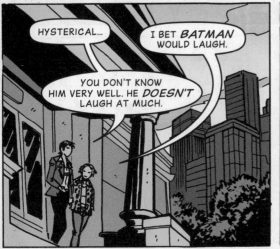

HYSTERICAL...

I BET *BATMAN* WOULD LAUGH.

YOU DON'T KNOW HIM VERY WELL. HE *DOESN'T* LAUGH AT MUCH.

NOW, C'MON, I THOUGHT WE WERE GOING *SHOPPING* BEFORE DINNER TONIGHT?

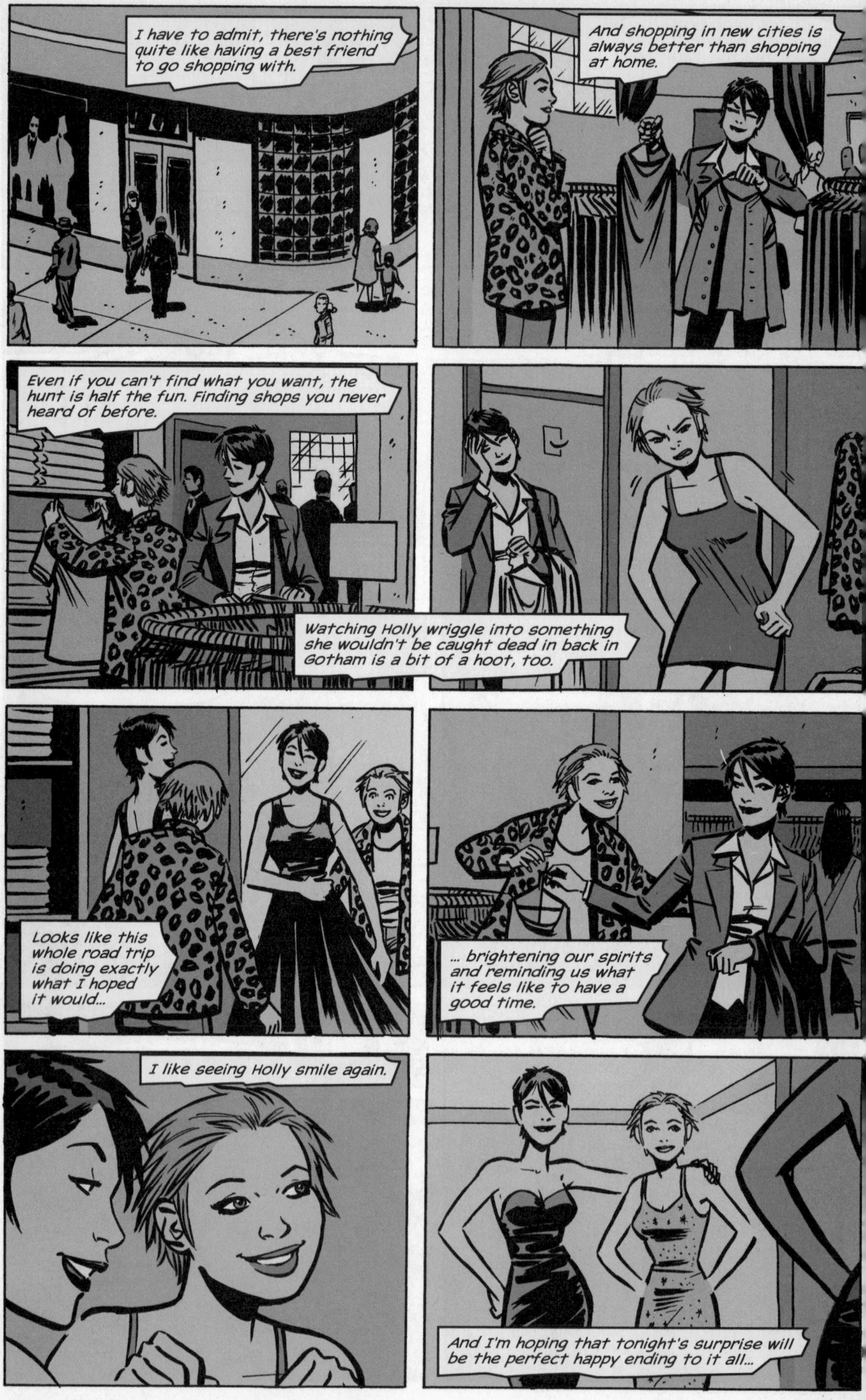
I have to admit, there's nothing quite like having a best friend to go shopping with.
And shopping in new cities is always better than shopping at home.
Even if you can't find what you want, the hunt is half the fun. Finding shops you never heard of before.
Watching Holly wriggle into something she wouldn't be caught dead in back in Gotham is a bit of a hoot, too.
Looks like this whole road trip is doing exactly what I hoped it would...
... brightening our spirits and reminding us what it feels like to have a good time.
I like seeing Holly smile again.
And I'm hoping that tonight's surprise will be the perfect happy ending to it all...

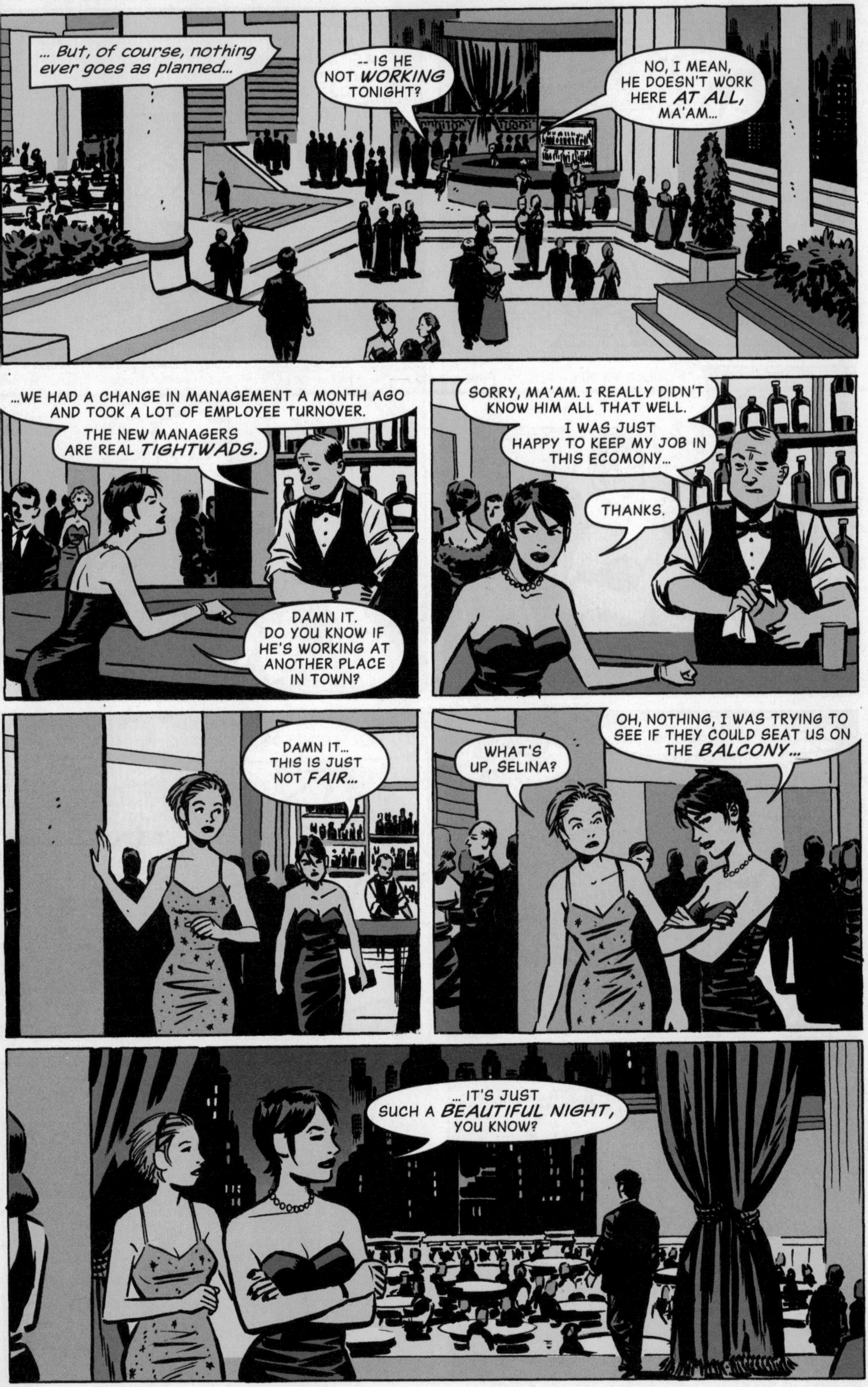
... But, of course, nothing ever goes as planned...
-- IS HE NOT WORKING TONIGHT?
NO, I MEAN, HE DOESN'T WORK HERE AT ALL, MA'AM...
...WE HAD A CHANGE IN MANAGEMENT A MONTH AGO AND TOOK A LOT OF EMPLOYEE TURNOVER.
THE NEW MANAGERS ARE REAL TIGHTWADS.
DAMN IT. DO YOU KNOW IF HE'S WORKING AT ANOTHER PLACE IN TOWN?
SORRY, MA'AM. I REALLY DIDN'T KNOW HIM ALL THAT WELL.
I WAS JUST HAPPY TO KEEP MY JOB IN THIS ECOMONY...
THANKS.
DAMN IT... THIS IS JUST NOT FAIR...
WHAT'S UP, SELINA?
OH, NOTHING, I WAS TRYING TO SEE IF THEY COULD SEAT US ON THE BALCONY...
... IT'S JUST SUCH A BEAUTIFUL NIGHT, YOU KNOW?

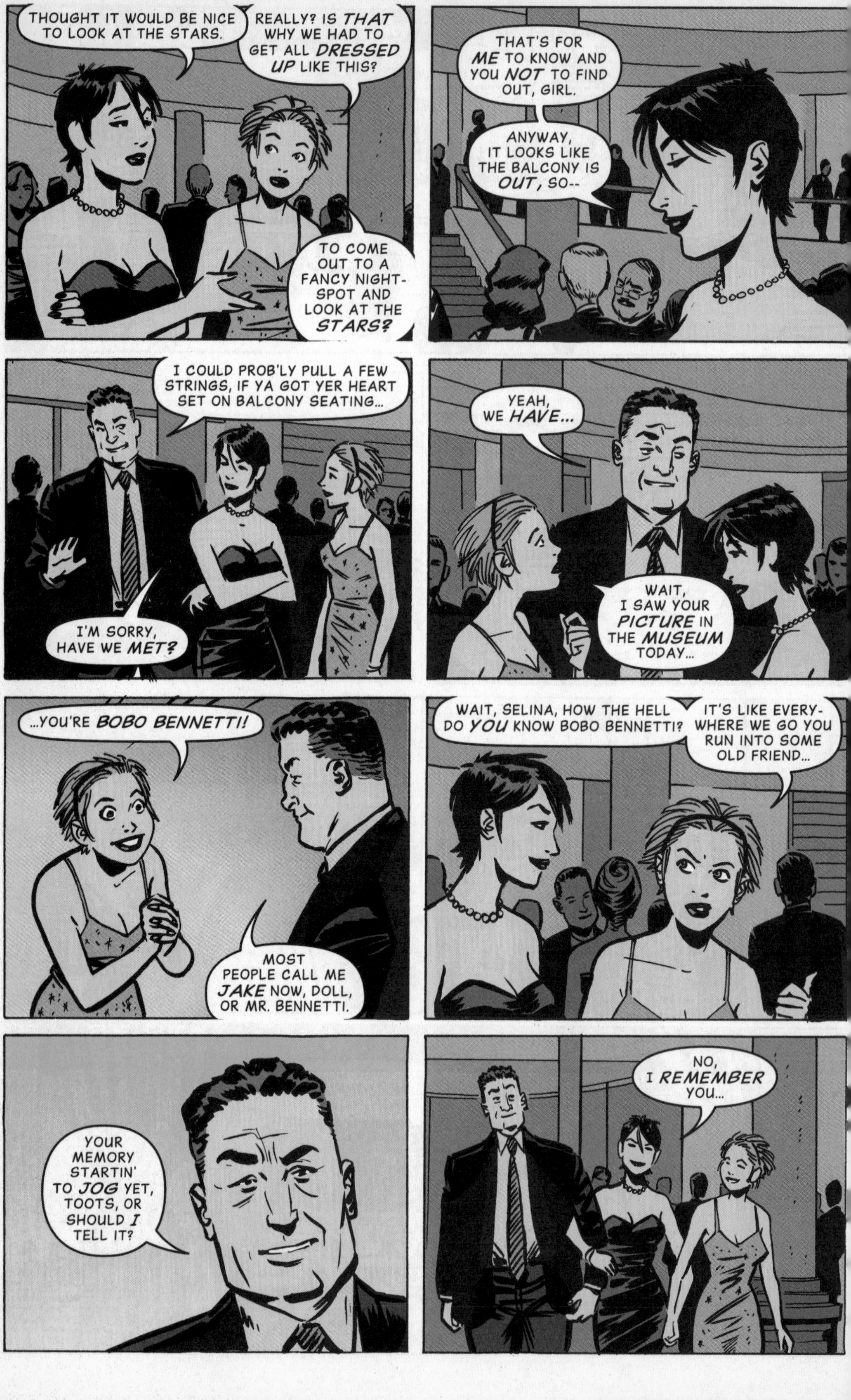
THOUGHT IT WOULD BE NICE TO LOOK AT THE STARS.
REALLY? IS THAT WHY WE HAD TO GET ALL DRESSED UP LIKE THIS?
TO COME OUT TO A FANCY NIGHT-SPOT AND LOOK AT THE STARS?
THAT'S FOR ME TO KNOW AND YOU NOT TO FIND OUT, GIRL.
ANYWAY, IT LOOKS LIKE THE BALCONY IS OUT, SO--
I COULD PROB'LY PULL A FEW STRINGS, IF YA GOT YER HEART SET ON BALCONY SEATING...
I'M SORRY, HAVE WE MET?
YEAH, WE HAVE...
WAIT, I SAW YOUR PICTURE IN THE MUSEUM TODAY...
...YOU'RE BOBO BENNETTI!
MOST PEOPLE CALL ME JAKE NOW, DOLL, OR MR. BENNETTI.
WAIT, SELINA, HOW THE HELL DO YOU KNOW BOBO BENNETTI?
IT'S LIKE EVERY-WHERE WE GO YOU RUN INTO SOME OLD FRIEND...
YOUR MEMORY STARTIN' TO JOG YET, TOOTS, OR SHOULD I TELL IT?
NO, I REMEMBER YOU...

FIVE YEARS AGO...

LOCK KEEP PRISON

-- NO, THAT'S *NOT* WHAT I'M GETTING AT, GEORGE...

I'M JUST SAYING IN MY DAY, YOU'D NEVER OF SEEN ALL THESE TATTOOS AND PIERCED EARS AND NOSES AND JUNK ON A *PRO* BALL-PLAYER, Y'KNOW?

I MEAN, PEOPLE JUST HAD MORE RESPECT FOR--

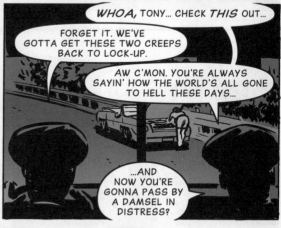

WHOA, TONY... CHECK *THIS* OUT...

FORGET IT. WE'VE GOTTA GET THESE TWO CREEPS BACK TO LOCK-UP.

AW C'MON. YOU'RE ALWAYS SAYIN' HOW THE WORLD'S ALL GONE TO HELL THESE DAYS...

...AND NOW YOU'RE GONNA PASS BY A DAMSEL IN DISTRESS?

ALL RIGHT, BUT LET ME DO THE TALKING...

OH YEAH, YOU GOT A REAL *WAY* WITH THE LADIES, I'M SURE...

MAYBE YOU CAN LECTURE HER ABOUT THAT SHORT SKIRT...

'SCUSE US, MA'AM. MIGHT WE BE OF SOME *ASSISTANCE?*

OH, THANKS *SO MUCH* FOR STOPPING. I DON'T KNOW WHAT'S *WRONG.* IT JUST STALLED OUT RIGHT HERE IN THE MIDDLE OF THE STREET...

WELL, DON'T YOU FRET, LITTLE LADY... LET'S JUST GIVE 'ER A *LOOK-SEE...*

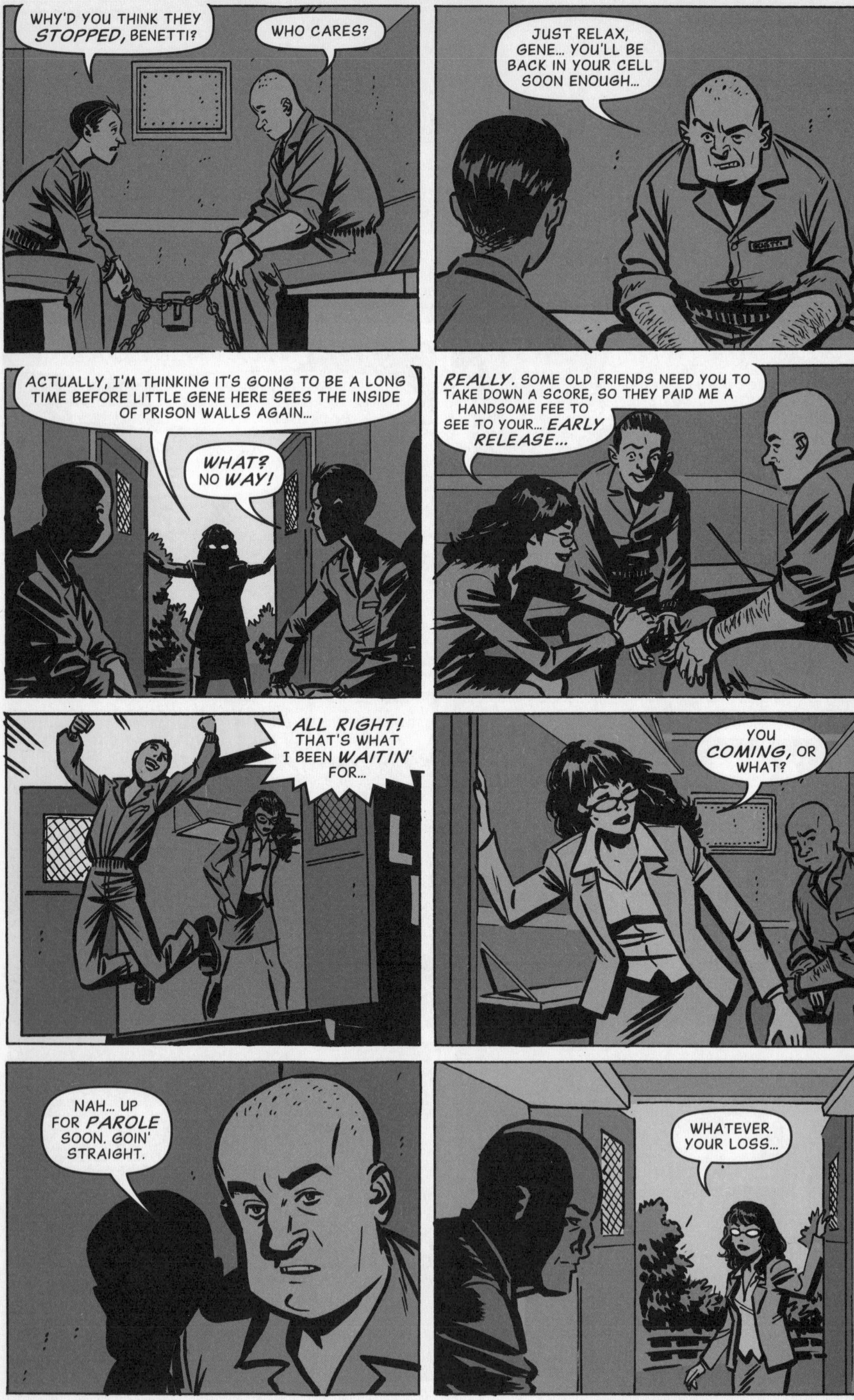
WHY'D YOU THINK THEY STOPPED, BENETTI?
WHO CARES?
JUST RELAX, GENE... YOU'LL BE BACK IN YOUR CELL SOON ENOUGH...
ACTUALLY, I'M THINKING IT'S GOING TO BE A LONG TIME BEFORE LITTLE GENE HERE SEES THE INSIDE OF PRISON WALLS AGAIN...
WHAT? NO WAY!
REALLY. SOME OLD FRIENDS NEED YOU TO TAKE DOWN A SCORE, SO THEY PAID ME A HANDSOME FEE TO SEE TO YOUR... EARLY RELEASE...
ALL RIGHT! THAT'S WHAT I BEEN WAITIN' FOR...
YOU COMING, OR WHAT?
NAH... UP FOR PAROLE SOON. GOIN' STRAIGHT.
WHATEVER. YOUR LOSS...

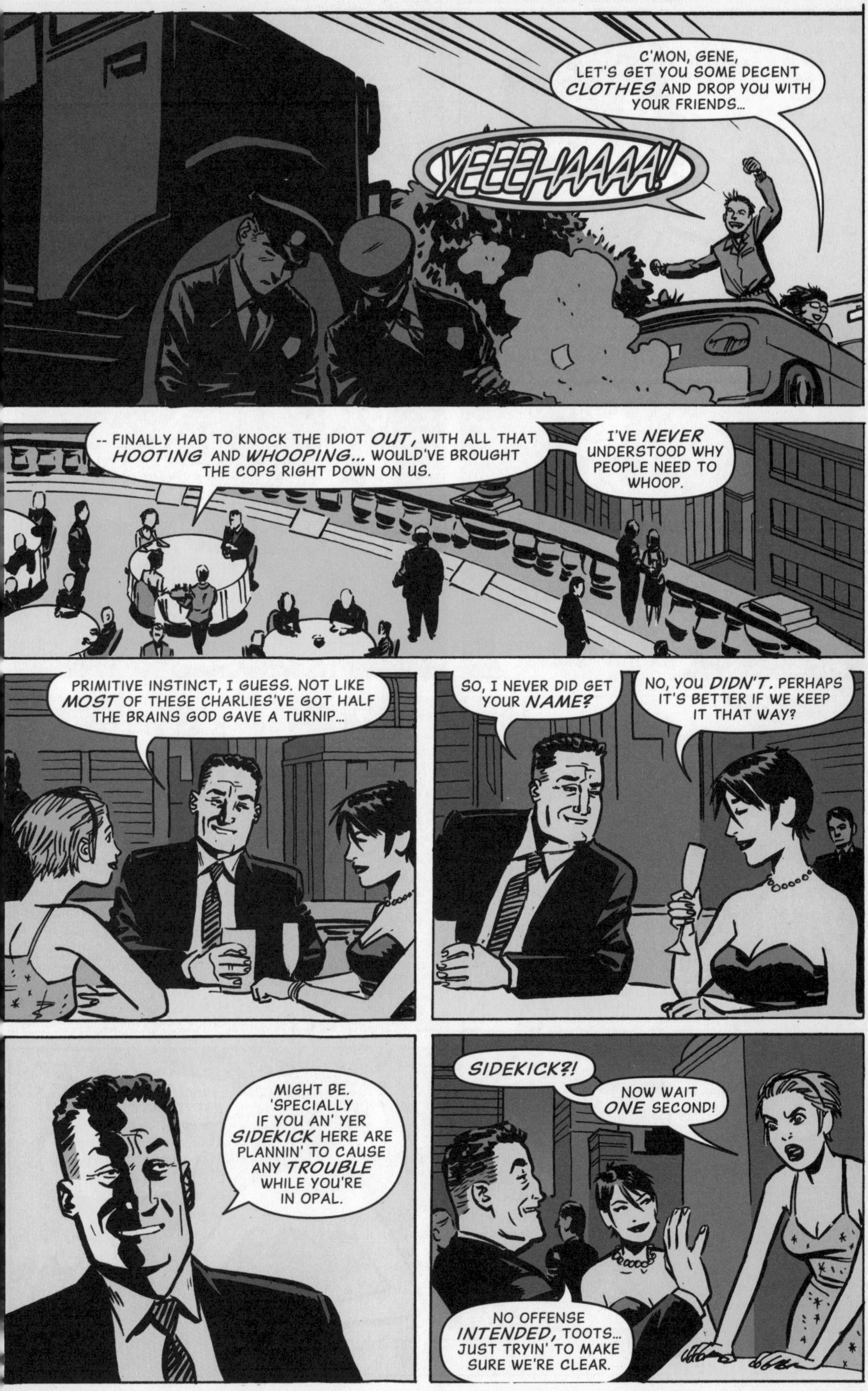
C'MON, GENE, LET'S GET YOU SOME DECENT CLOTHES AND DROP YOU WITH YOUR FRIENDS...
YEEEHAAAA!
-- FINALLY HAD TO KNOCK THE IDIOT OUT, WITH ALL THAT HOOTING AND WHOOPING... WOULD'VE BROUGHT THE COPS RIGHT DOWN ON US.
I'VE NEVER UNDERSTOOD WHY PEOPLE NEED TO WHOOP.
PRIMITIVE INSTINCT, I GUESS. NOT LIKE MOST OF THESE CHARLIES'VE GOT HALF THE BRAINS GOD GAVE A TURNIP...
SO, I NEVER DID GET YOUR NAME?
NO, YOU DIDN'T. PERHAPS IT'S BETTER IF WE KEEP IT THAT WAY?
MIGHT BE. 'SPECIALLY IF YOU AN' YER SIDEKICK HERE ARE PLANNIN' TO CAUSE ANY TROUBLE WHILE YOU'RE IN OPAL.
SIDEKICK?!
NOW WAIT ONE SECOND!
NO OFFENSE INTENDED, TOOTS... JUST TRYIN' TO MAKE SURE WE'RE CLEAR.

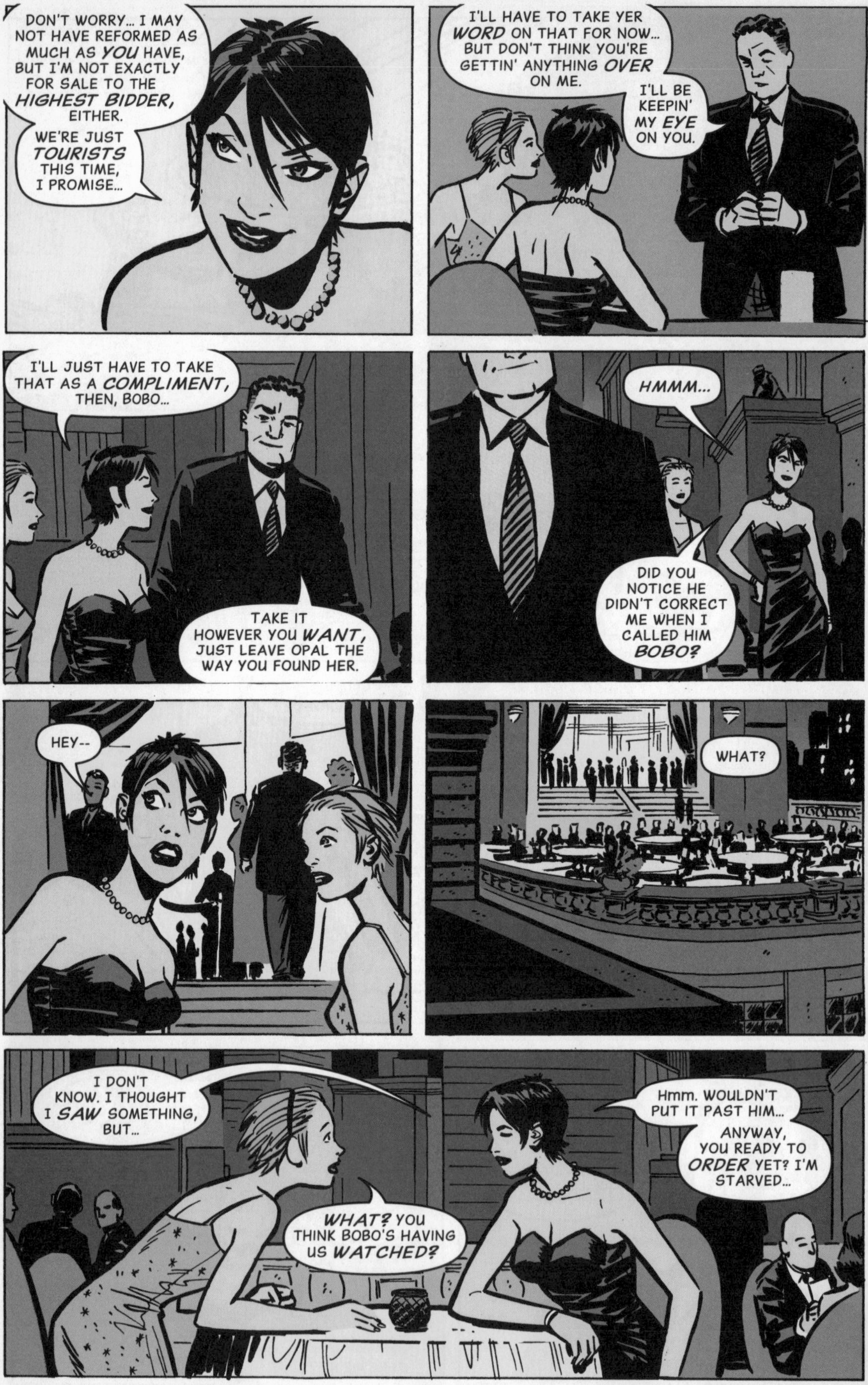
DON'T WORRY... I MAY NOT HAVE REFORMED AS MUCH AS YOU HAVE, BUT I'M NOT EXACTLY FOR SALE TO THE HIGHEST BIDDER, EITHER.
WE'RE JUST TOURISTS THIS TIME, I PROMISE...
I'LL HAVE TO TAKE YER WORD ON THAT FOR NOW... BUT DON'T THINK YOU'RE GETTIN' ANYTHING OVER ON ME.
I'LL BE KEEPIN' MY EYE ON YOU.
I'LL JUST HAVE TO TAKE THAT AS A COMPLIMENT, THEN, BOBO...
TAKE IT HOWEVER YOU WANT, JUST LEAVE OPAL THE WAY YOU FOUND HER.
HMMM...
DID YOU NOTICE HE DIDN'T CORRECT ME WHEN I CALLED HIM BOBO?
HEY--
WHAT?
I DON'T KNOW. I THOUGHT I SAW SOMETHING, BUT...
WHAT? YOU THINK BOBO'S HAVING US WATCHED?
Hmm. WOULDN'T PUT IT PAST HIM...
ANYWAY, YOU READY TO ORDER YET? I'M STARVED...

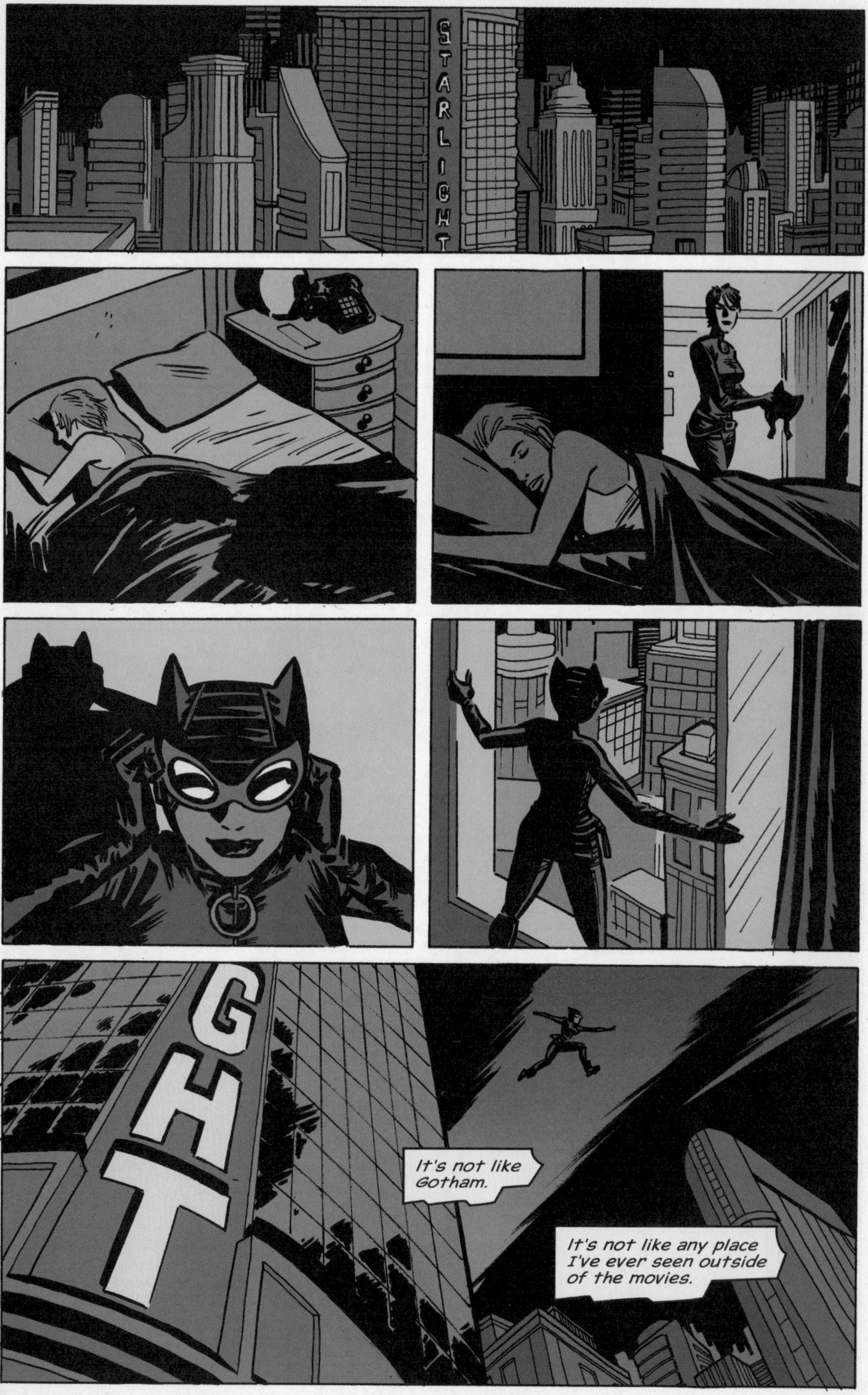
STARLIGHT
GHT
It's not like Gotham.
It's not like any place I've ever seen outside of the movies.

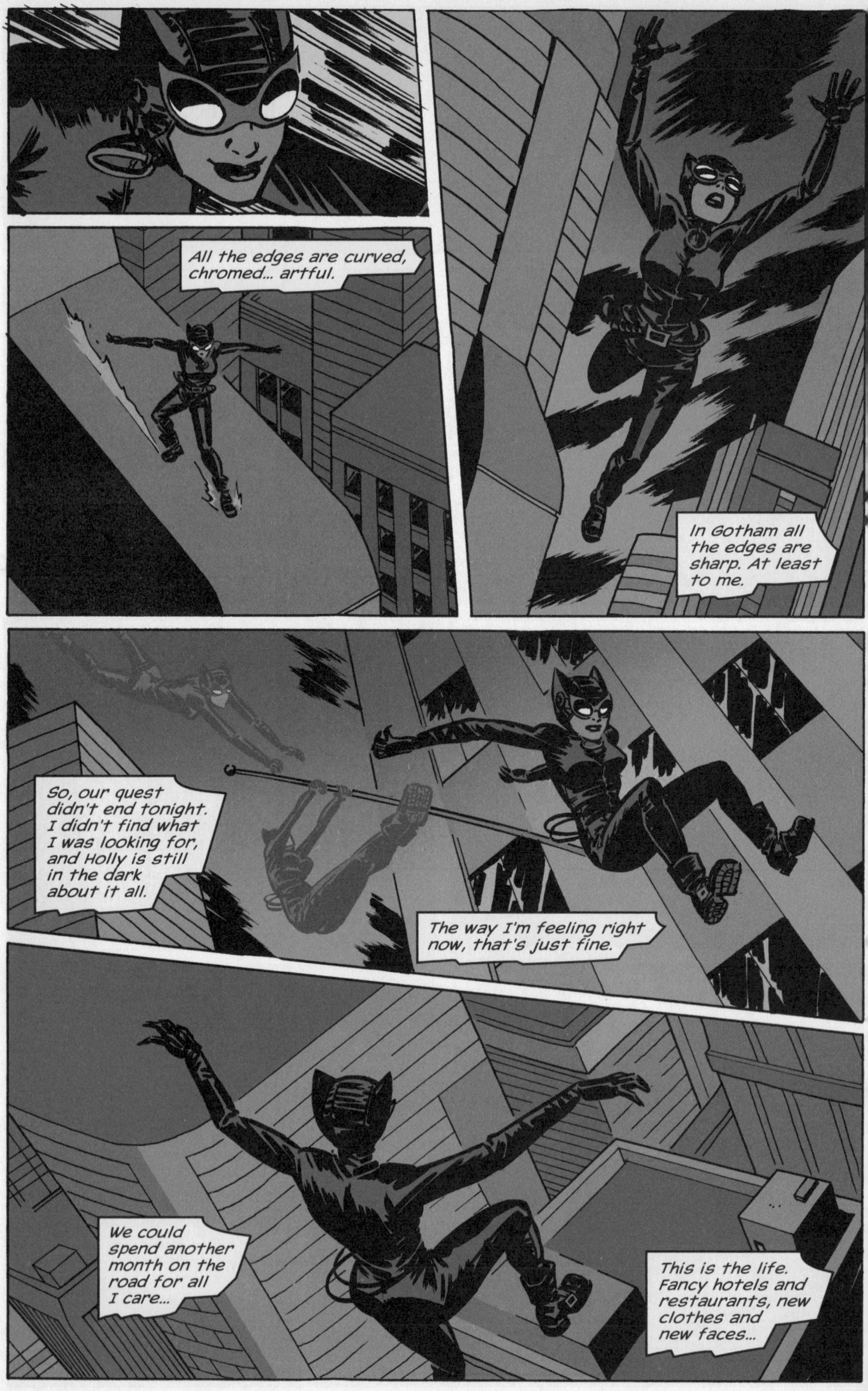
All the edges are curved, chromed... artful.
In Gotham all the edges are sharp. At least to me.
So, our quest didn't end tonight. I didn't find what I was looking for, and Holly is still in the dark about it all.
The way I'm feeling right now, that's just fine.
We could spend another month on the road for all I care...
This is the life. Fancy hotels and restaurants, new clothes and new faces...

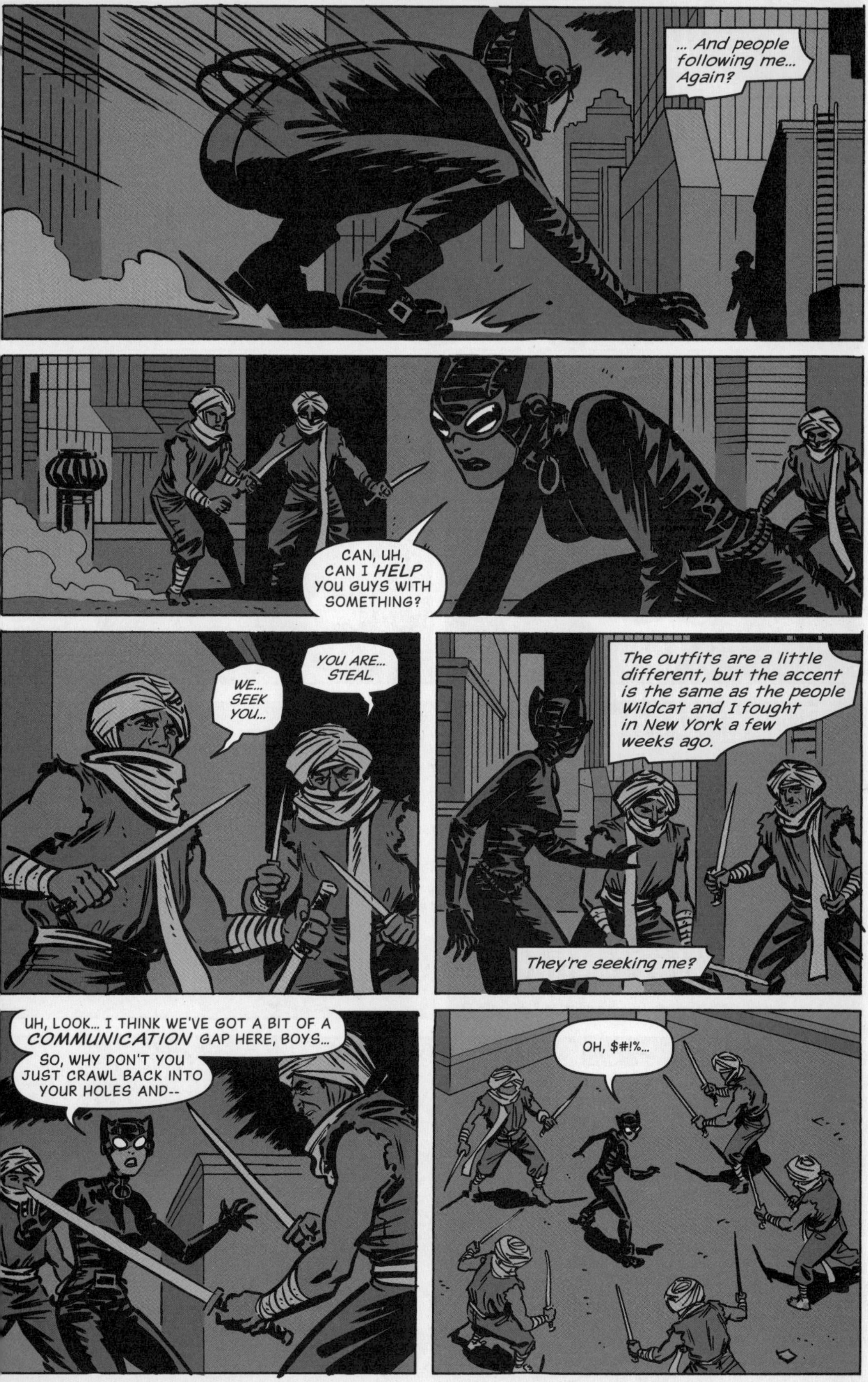

... And people following me... Again?
CAN, UH, CAN I HELP YOU GUYS WITH SOMETHING?
WE... SEEK YOU...
YOU ARE... STEAL.
The outfits are a little different, but the accent is the same as the people Wildcat and I fought in New York a few weeks ago.
They're seeking me?
UH, LOOK... I THINK WE'VE GOT A BIT OF A COMMUNICATION GAP HERE, BOYS...
SO, WHY DON'T YOU JUST CRAWL BACK INTO YOUR HOLES AND--
OH, $#!%...

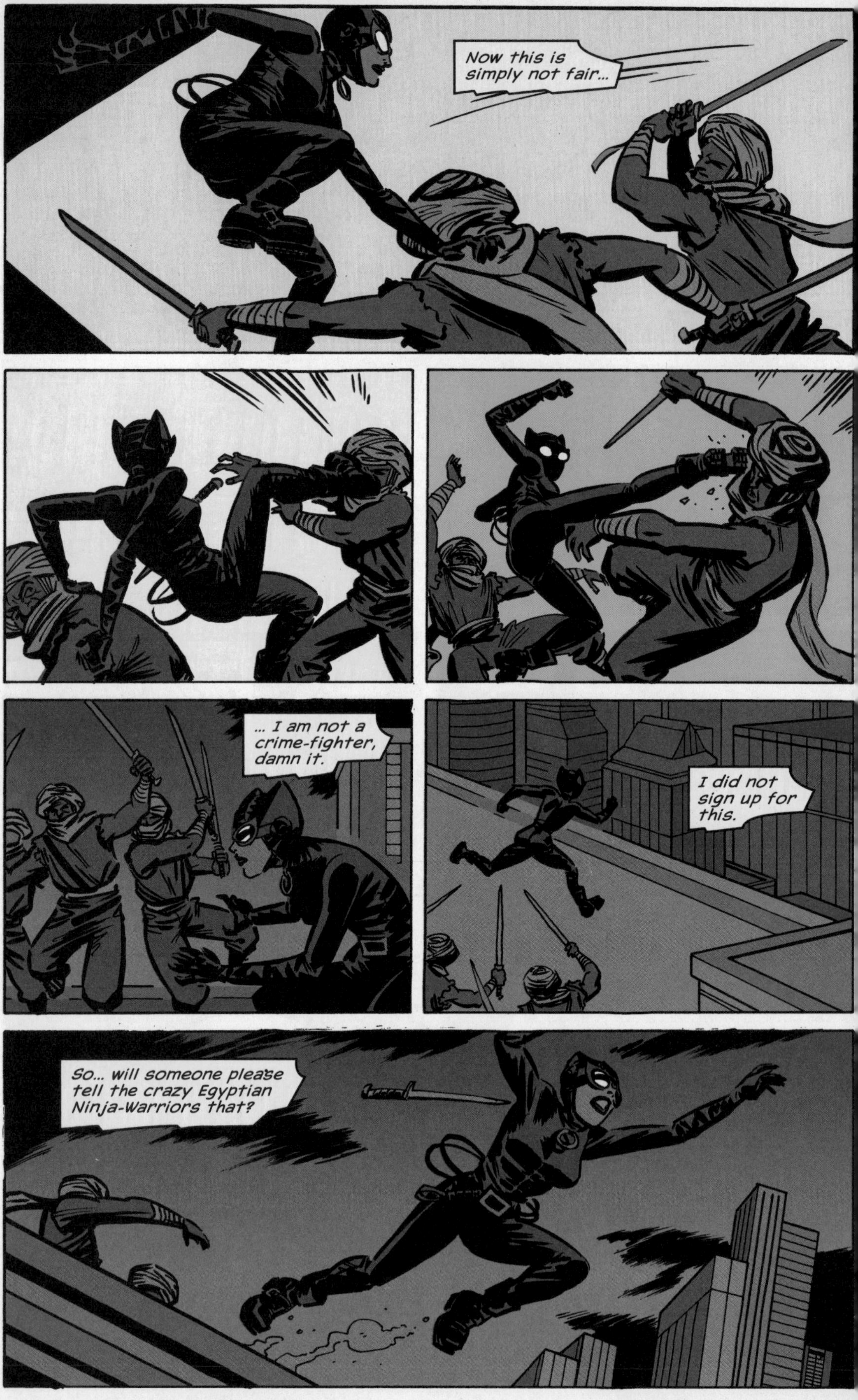
Now this is simply not fair...
... I am not a crime-fighter, damn it.
I did not sign up for this.
So... will someone please tell the crazy Egyptian Ninja-Warriors that?

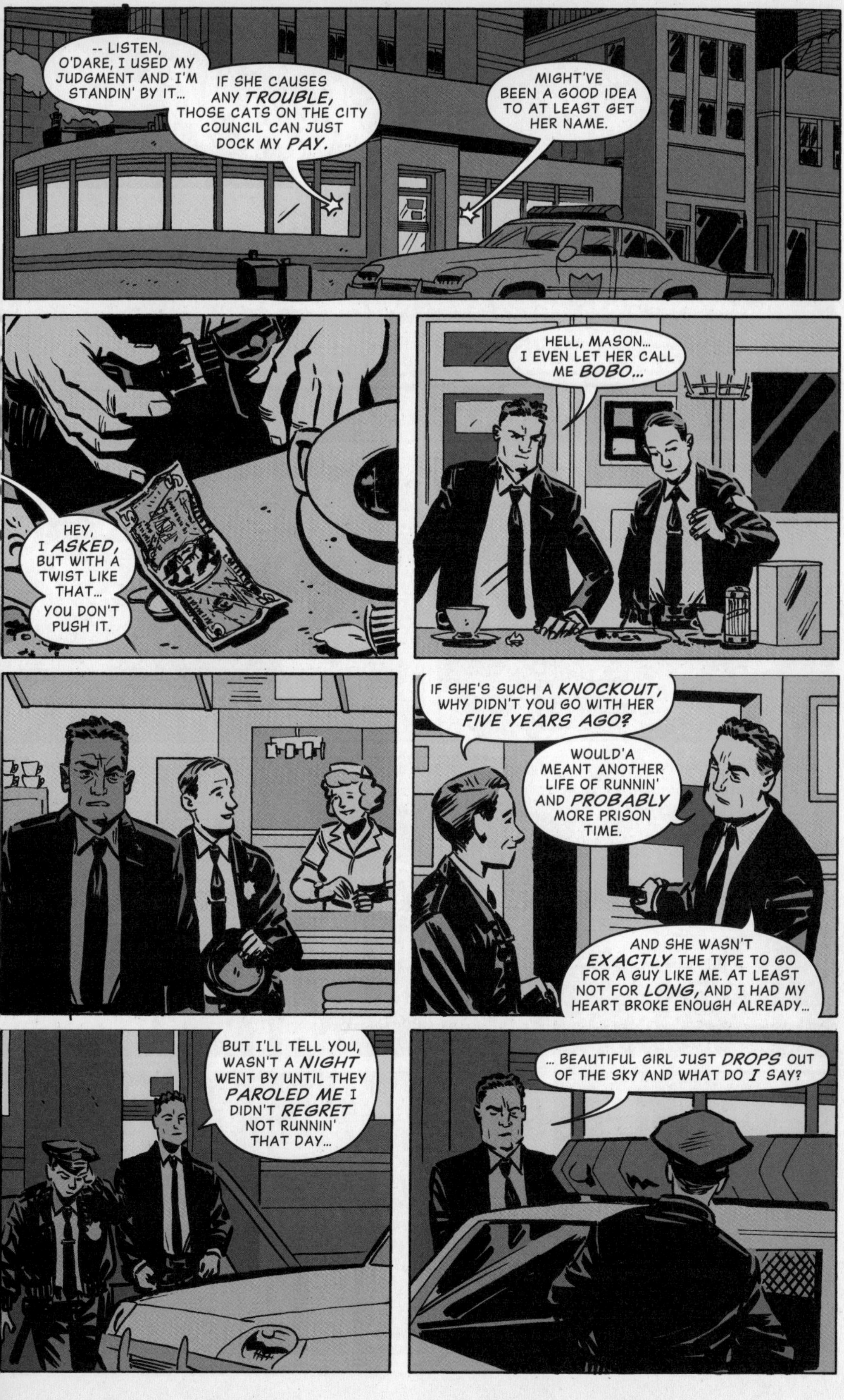
-- LISTEN, O'DARE, I USED MY JUDGMENT AND I'M STANDIN' BY IT...
IF SHE CAUSES ANY TROUBLE, THOSE CATS ON THE CITY COUNCIL CAN JUST DOCK MY PAY.
MIGHT'VE BEEN A GOOD IDEA TO AT LEAST GET HER NAME.
HEY, I ASKED, BUT WITH A TWIST LIKE THAT...
YOU DON'T PUSH IT.
HELL, MASON... I EVEN LET HER CALL ME BOBO...
IF SHE'S SUCH A KNOCKOUT, WHY DIDN'T YOU GO WITH HER FIVE YEARS AGO?
WOULD'A MEANT ANOTHER LIFE OF RUNNIN' AND PROBABLY MORE PRISON TIME.
AND SHE WASN'T EXACTLY THE TYPE TO GO FOR A GUY LIKE ME. AT LEAST NOT FOR LONG, AND I HAD MY HEART BROKE ENOUGH ALREADY...
BUT I'LL TELL YOU, WASN'T A NIGHT WENT BY UNTIL THEY PAROLED ME I DIDN'T REGRET NOT RUNNIN' THAT DAY...
... BEAUTIFUL GIRL JUST DROPS OUT OF THE SKY AND WHAT DO I SAY?

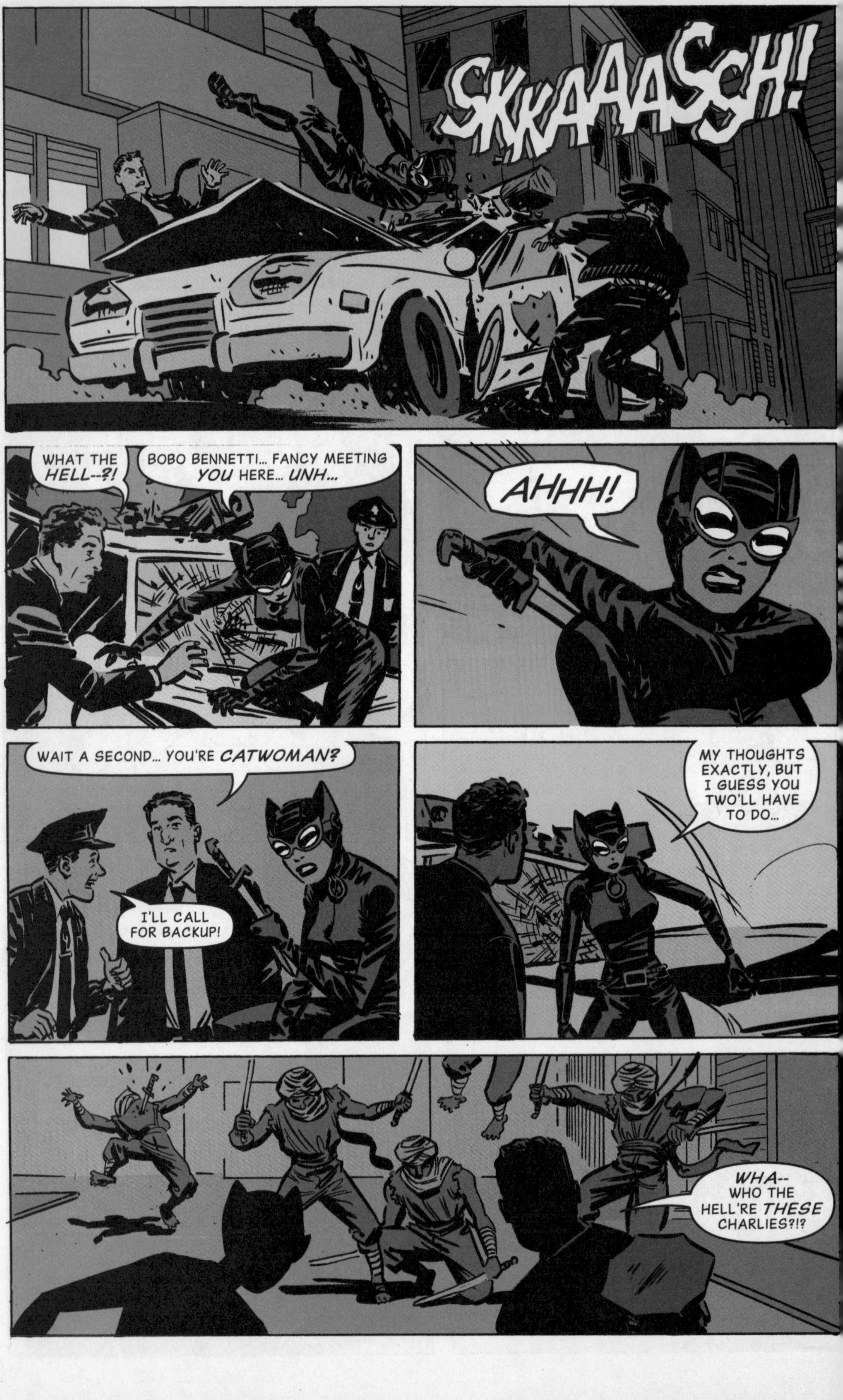
SKKAAASSGH!
WHAT THE HELL--?!
BOBO BENNETTI... FANCY MEETING YOU HERE... UNH...
AHHH!
WAIT A SECOND... YOU'RE CATWOMAN?
I'LL CALL FOR BACKUP!
MY THOUGHTS EXACTLY, BUT I GUESS YOU TWO'LL HAVE TO DO...
WHA-- WHO THE HELL'RE THESE CHARLIES?!?

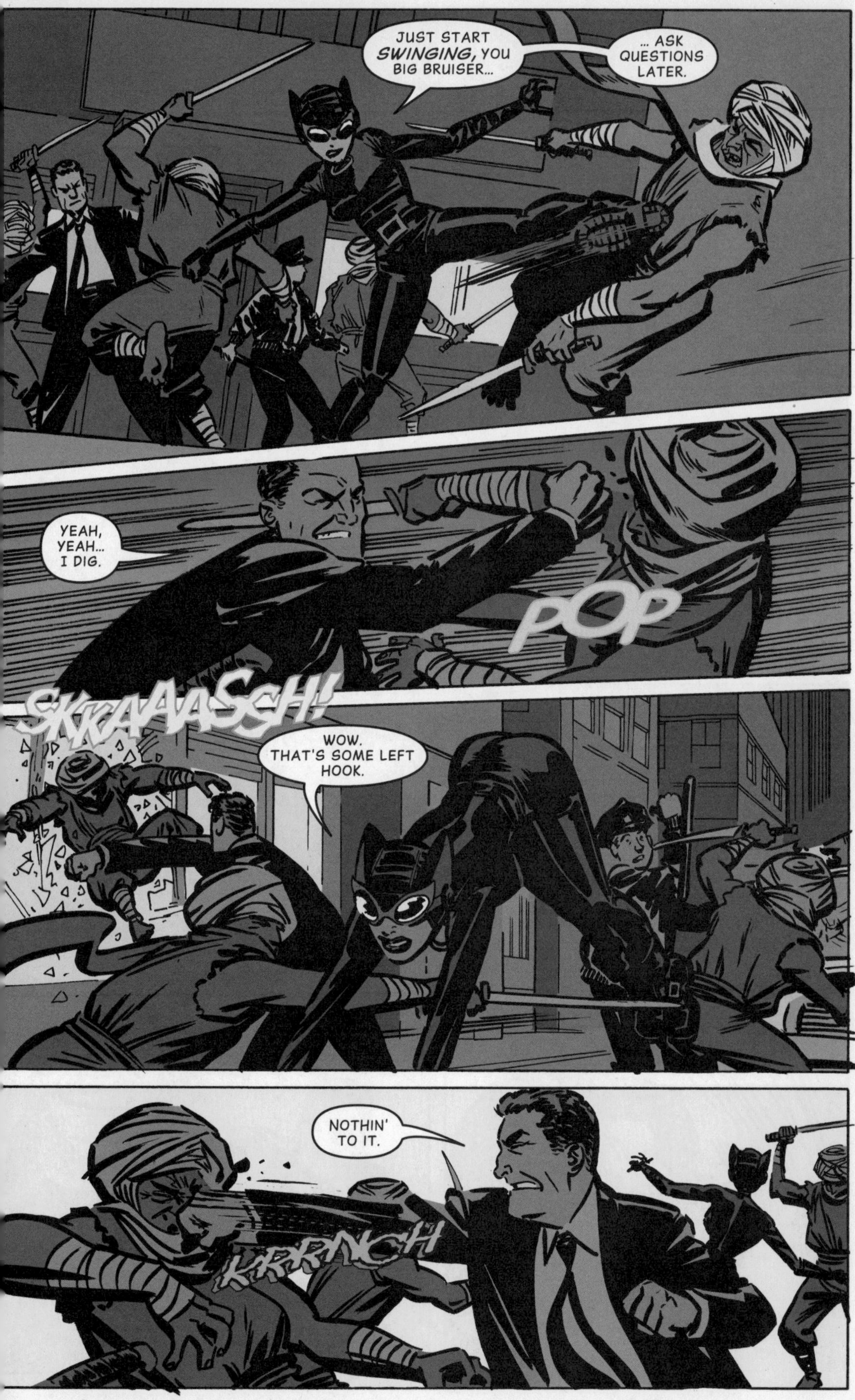

JUST START SWINGING, YOU BIG BRUISER...
... ASK QUESTIONS LATER.
YEAH, YEAH... I DIG.
POP
SKKAAAASSGH!
WOW. THAT'S SOME LEFT HOOK.
NOTHIN' TO IT.
KRRRNCH

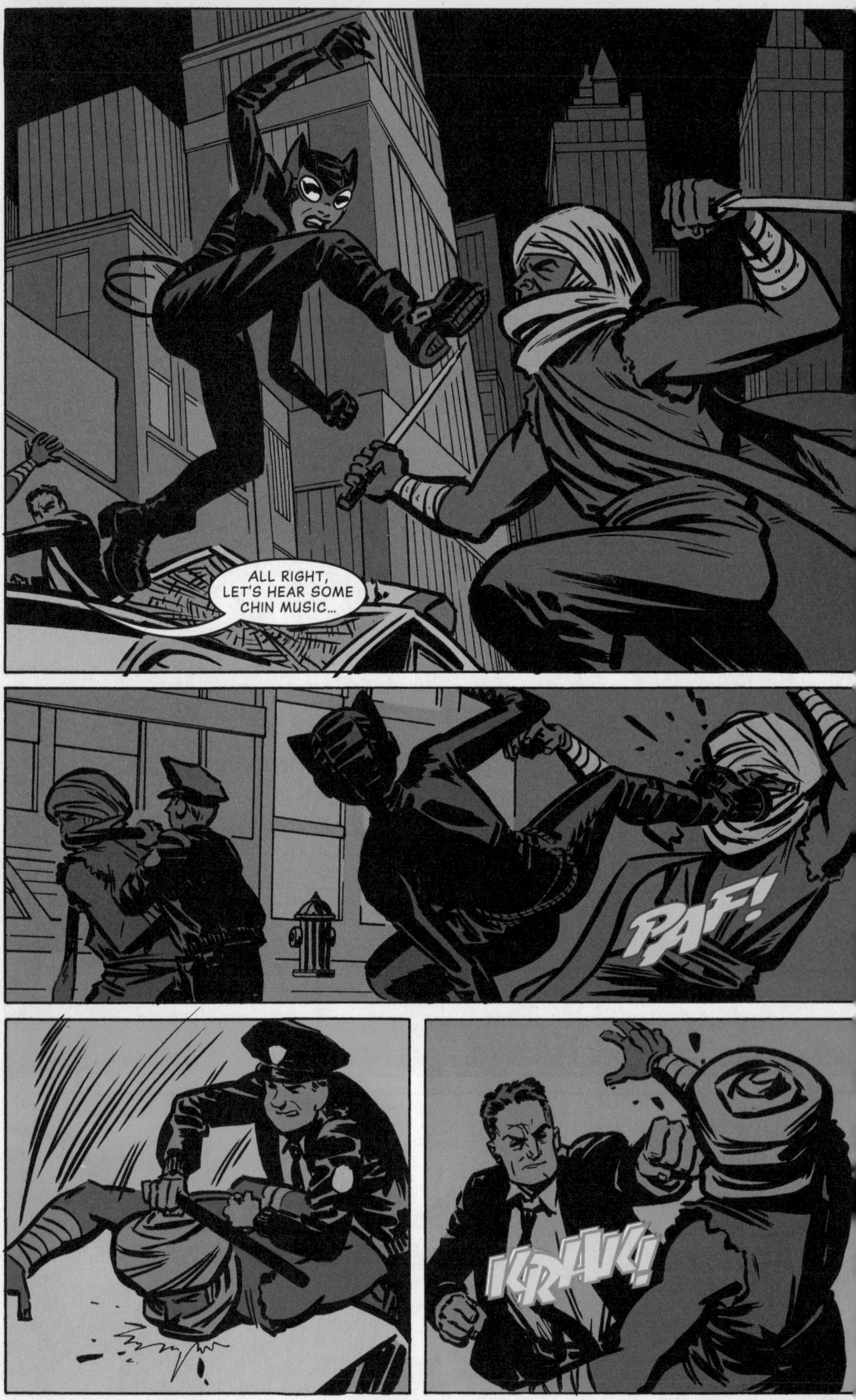
ALL RIGHT, LET'S HEAR SOME CHIN MUSIC...
PAF!
KRAK!

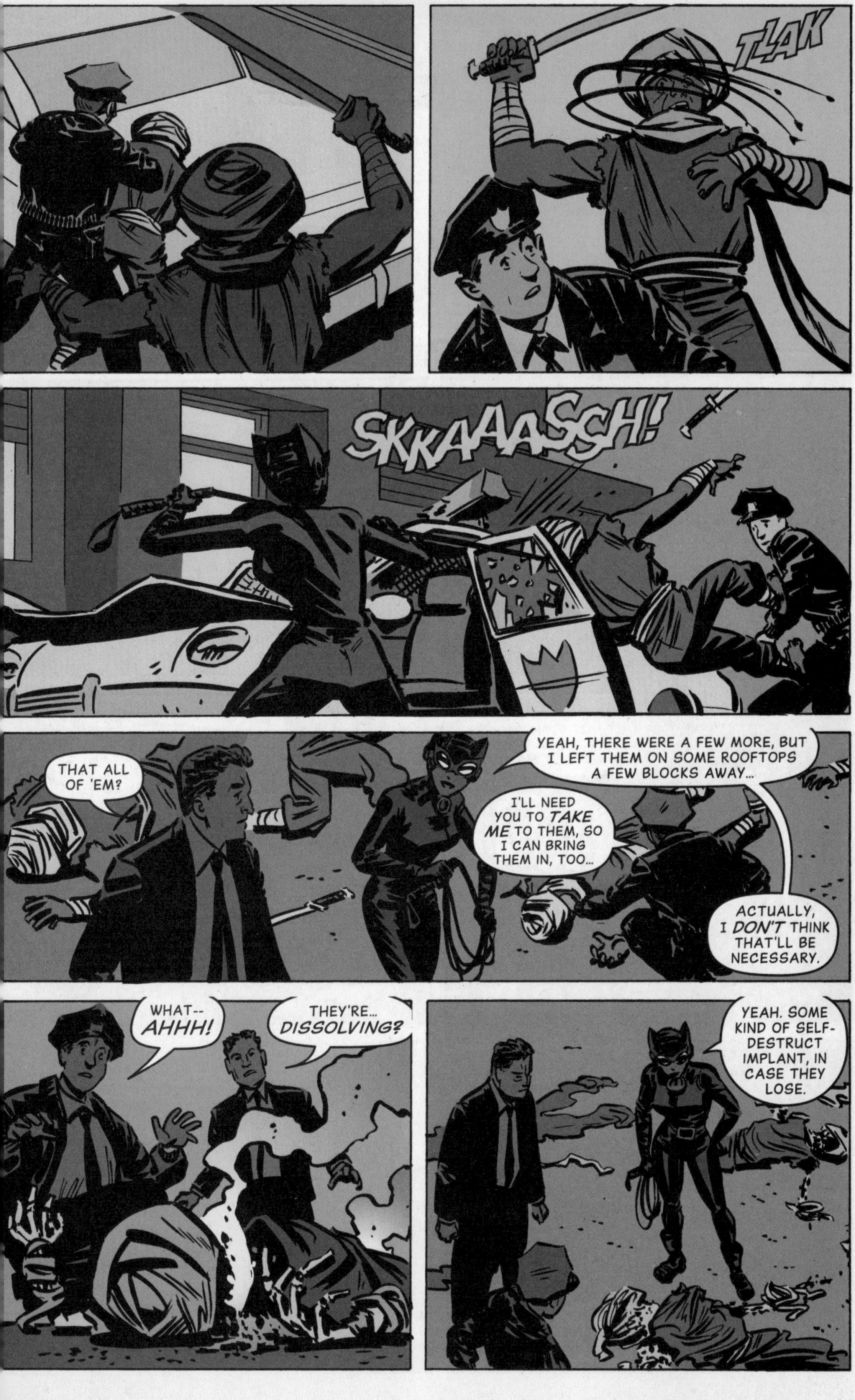
TLAK
SKKAAASSCH!
THAT ALL OF 'EM?
YEAH, THERE WERE A FEW MORE, BUT I LEFT THEM ON SOME ROOFTOPS A FEW BLOCKS AWAY...
I'LL NEED YOU TO *TAKE ME* TO THEM, SO I CAN BRING THEM IN, TOO...
ACTUALLY, I *DON'T* THINK THAT'LL BE NECESSARY.
WHAT-- *AHHH!*
THEY'RE... *DISSOLVING?*
YEAH. SOME KIND OF SELF-DESTRUCT IMPLANT, IN CASE THEY LOSE.

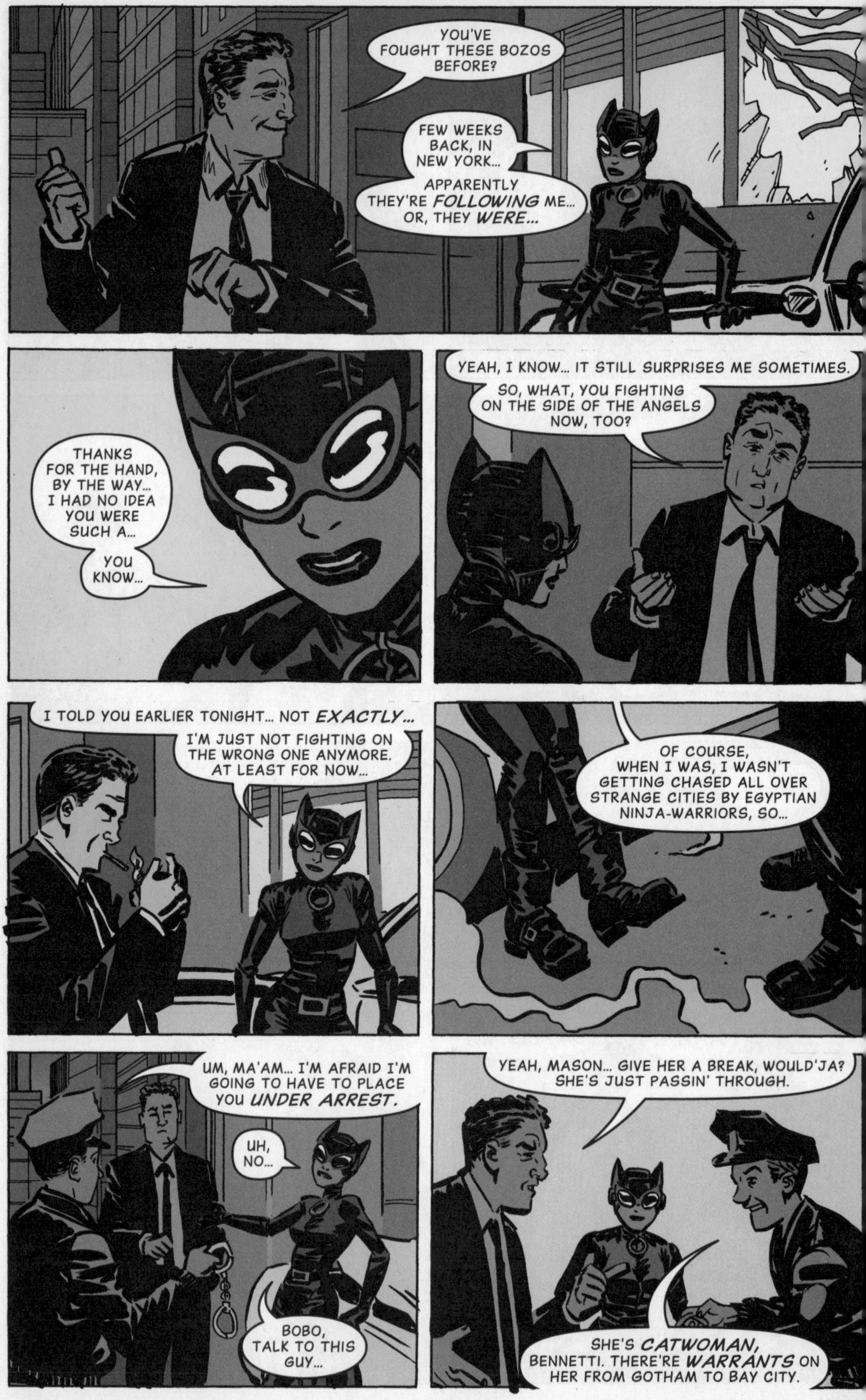
YOU'VE FOUGHT THESE BOZOS BEFORE?
FEW WEEKS BACK, IN NEW YORK...
APPARENTLY THEY'RE *FOLLOWING* ME... OR, THEY *WERE...*
THANKS FOR THE HAND, BY THE WAY... I HAD NO IDEA YOU WERE SUCH A...
YOU KNOW...
YEAH, I KNOW... IT STILL SURPRISES ME SOMETIMES.
SO, WHAT, YOU FIGHTING ON THE SIDE OF THE ANGELS NOW, TOO?
I TOLD YOU EARLIER TONIGHT... NOT *EXACTLY...*
I'M JUST NOT FIGHTING ON THE WRONG ONE ANYMORE. AT LEAST FOR NOW...
OF COURSE, WHEN I WAS, I WASN'T GETTING CHASED ALL OVER STRANGE CITIES BY EGYPTIAN NINJA-WARRIORS, SO...
UM, MA'AM... I'M AFRAID I'M GOING TO HAVE TO PLACE YOU *UNDER ARREST.*
UH, NO...
BOBO, TALK TO THIS GUY...
YEAH, MASON... GIVE HER A BREAK, WOULD'JA? SHE'S JUST PASSIN' THROUGH.
SHE'S *CATWOMAN,* BENNETTI. THERE'RE *WARRANTS* ON HER FROM GOTHAM TO BAY CITY.

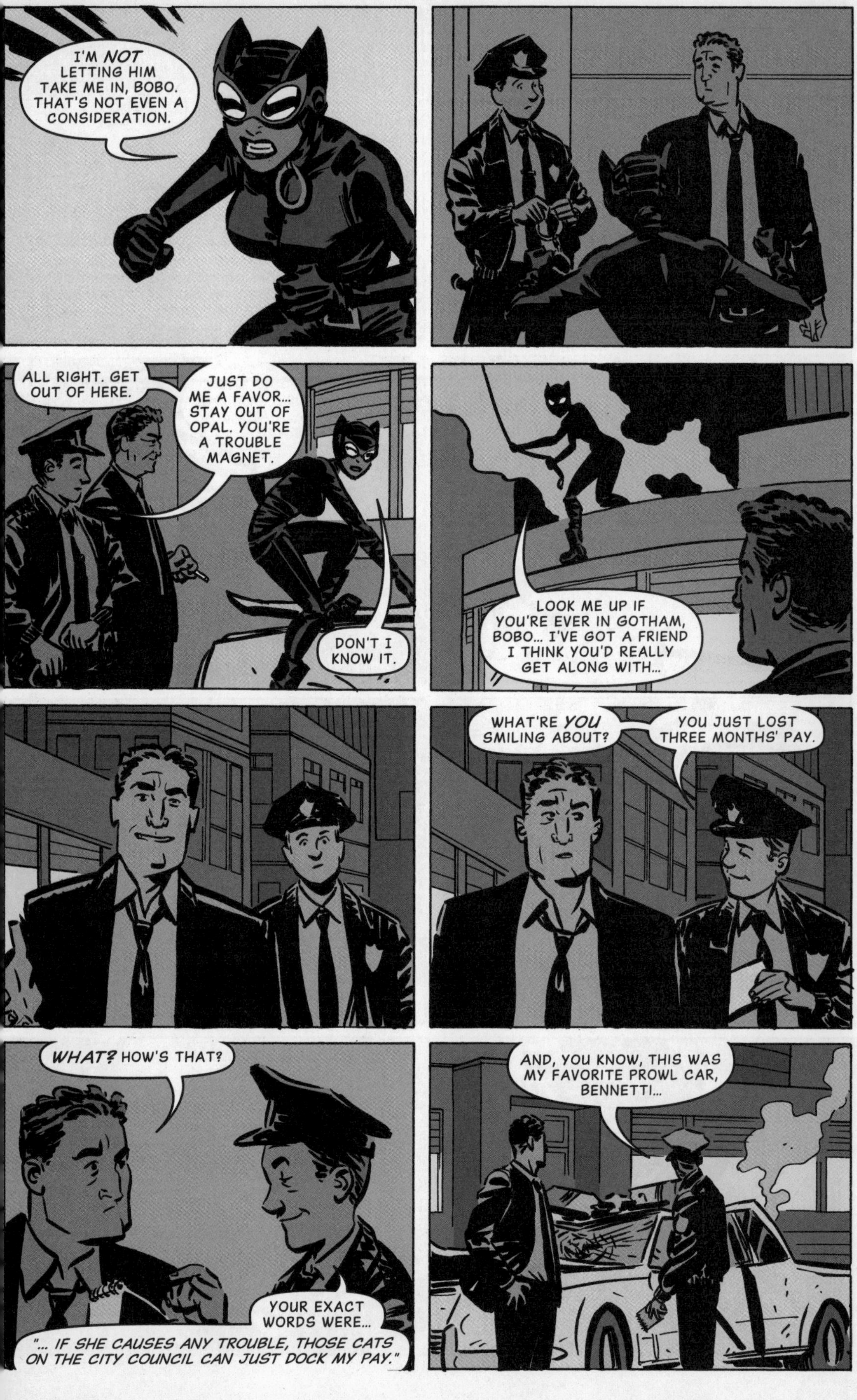
I'M NOT LETTING HIM TAKE ME IN, BOBO. THAT'S NOT EVEN A CONSIDERATION.
ALL RIGHT. GET OUT OF HERE.
JUST DO ME A FAVOR... STAY OUT OF OPAL. YOU'RE A TROUBLE MAGNET.
DON'T I KNOW IT.
LOOK ME UP IF YOU'RE EVER IN GOTHAM, BOBO... I'VE GOT A FRIEND I THINK YOU'D REALLY GET ALONG WITH...
WHAT'RE YOU SMILING ABOUT?
YOU JUST LOST THREE MONTHS' PAY.
WHAT? HOW'S THAT?
YOUR EXACT WORDS WERE...
"... IF SHE CAUSES ANY TROUBLE, THOSE CATS ON THE CITY COUNCIL CAN JUST DOCK MY PAY."
AND, YOU KNOW, THIS WAS MY FAVORITE PROWL CAR, BENNETTI...

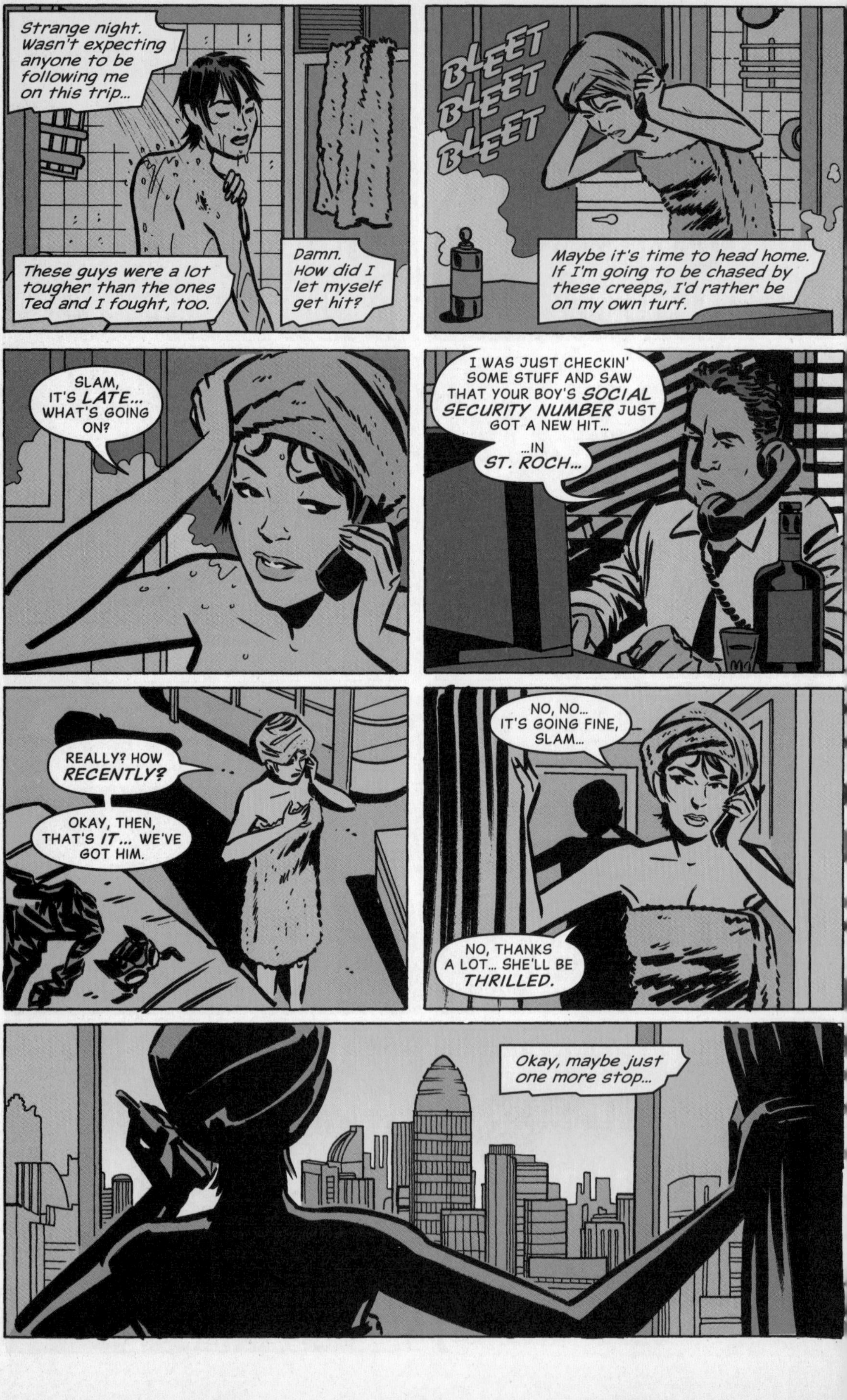
Strange night. Wasn't expecting anyone to be following me on this trip...
These guys were a lot tougher than the ones Ted and I fought, too.
Damn. How did I let myself get hit?
BLEET BLEET BLEET
Maybe it's time to head home. If I'm going to be chased by these creeps, I'd rather be on my own turf.
SLAM, IT'S LATE... WHAT'S GOING ON?
I WAS JUST CHECKIN' SOME STUFF AND SAW THAT YOUR BOY'S SOCIAL SECURITY NUMBER JUST GOT A NEW HIT...
...IN ST. ROCH...
REALLY? HOW RECENTLY?
OKAY, THEN, THAT'S IT... WE'VE GOT HIM.
NO, NO... IT'S GOING FINE, SLAM...
NO, THANKS A LOT... SHE'LL BE THRILLED.
Okay, maybe just one more stop...

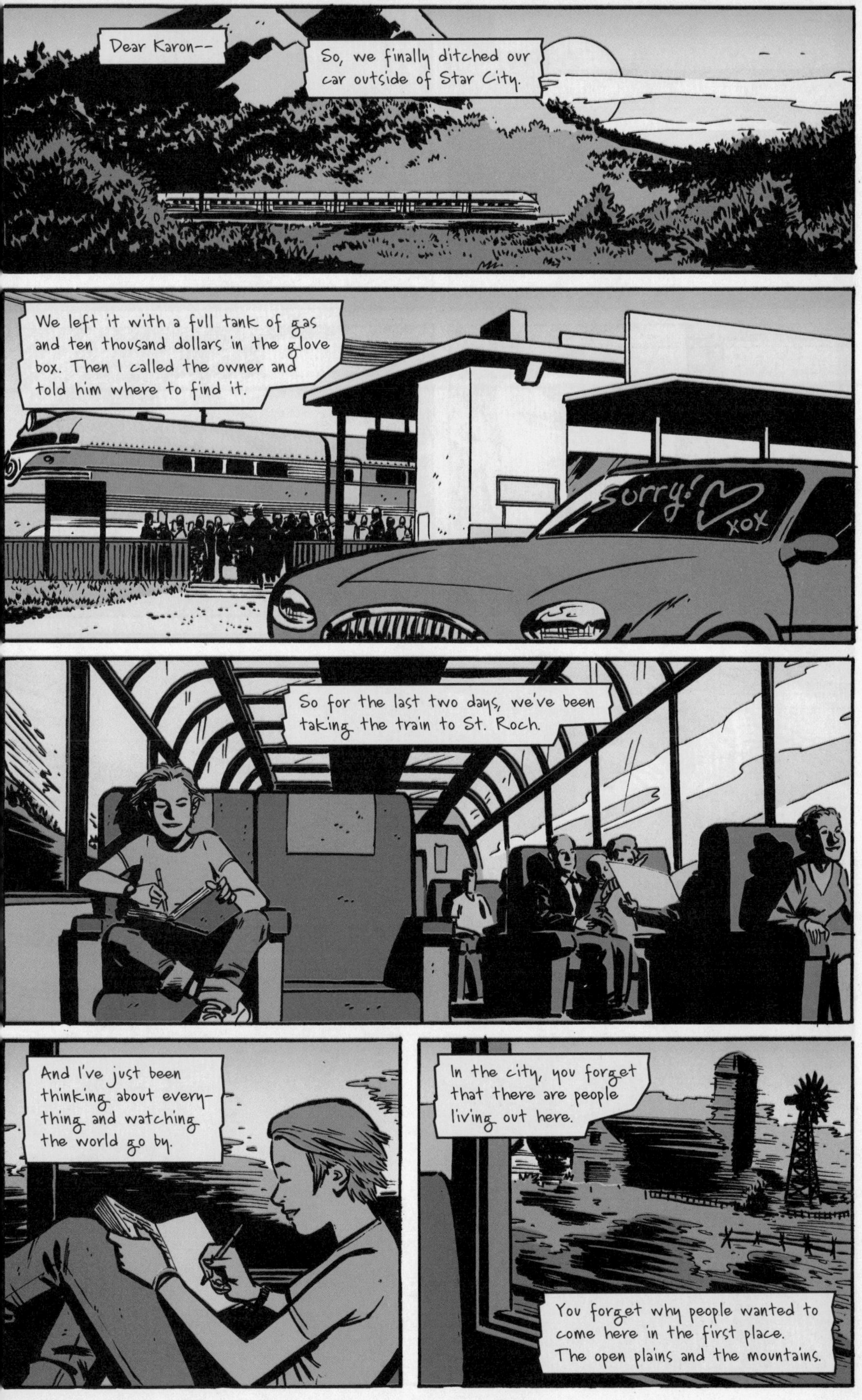
Dear Karon--
So, we finally ditched our car outside of Star City.
We left it with a full tank of gas and ten thousand dollars in the glove box. Then I called the owner and told him where to find it.
sorry! xox
So for the last two days, we've been taking the train to St. Roch.
And I've just been thinking about every-thing and watching the world go by.
In the city, you forget that there are people living out here.
You forget why people wanted to come here in the first place. The open plains and the mountains.

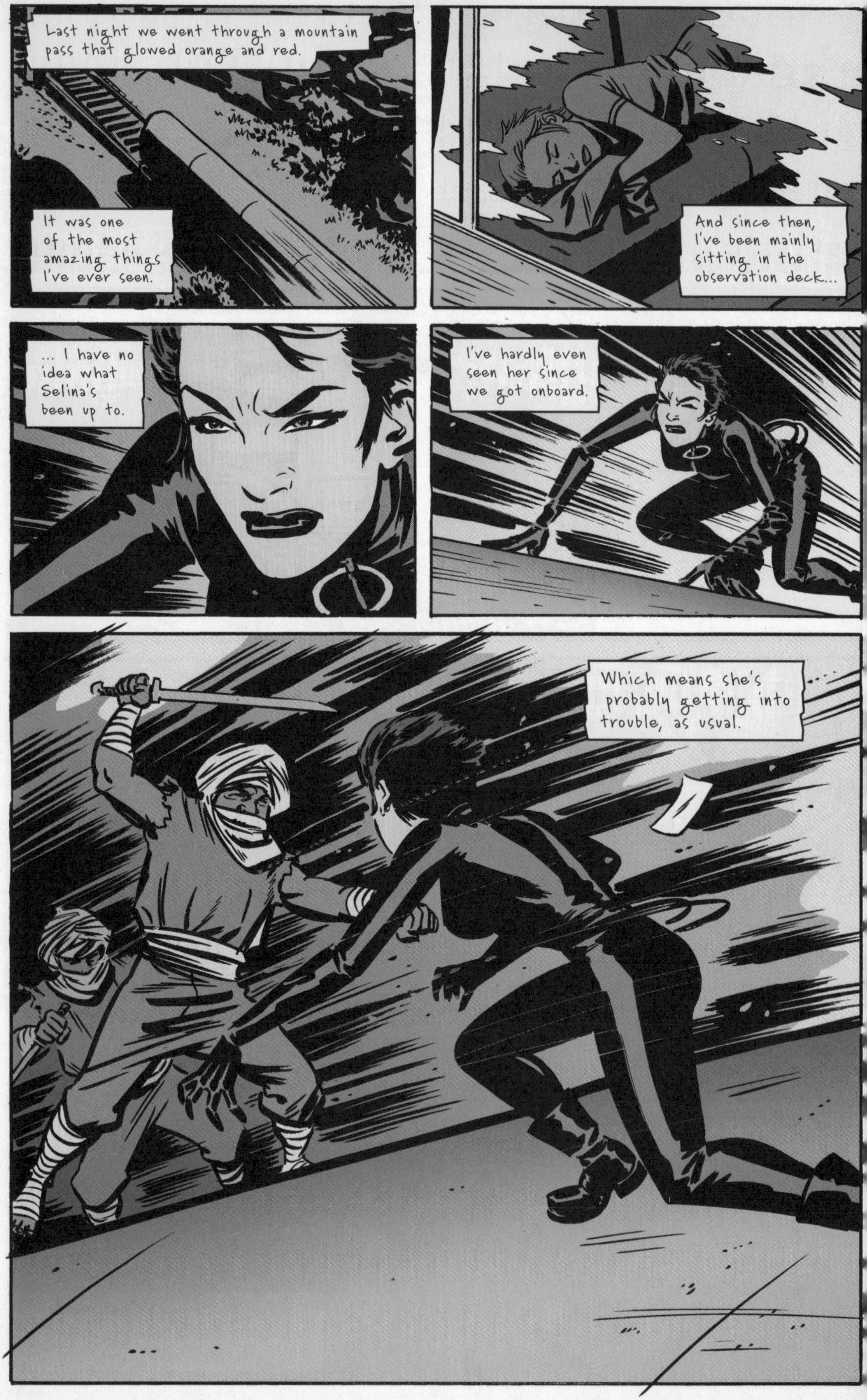
Last night we went through a mountain pass that glowed orange and red.
It was one of the most amazing things I've ever seen.
And since then, I've been mainly sitting in the observation deck...
... I have no idea what Selina's been up to.
I've hardly even seen her since we got onboard.
Which means she's probably getting into trouble, as usual.

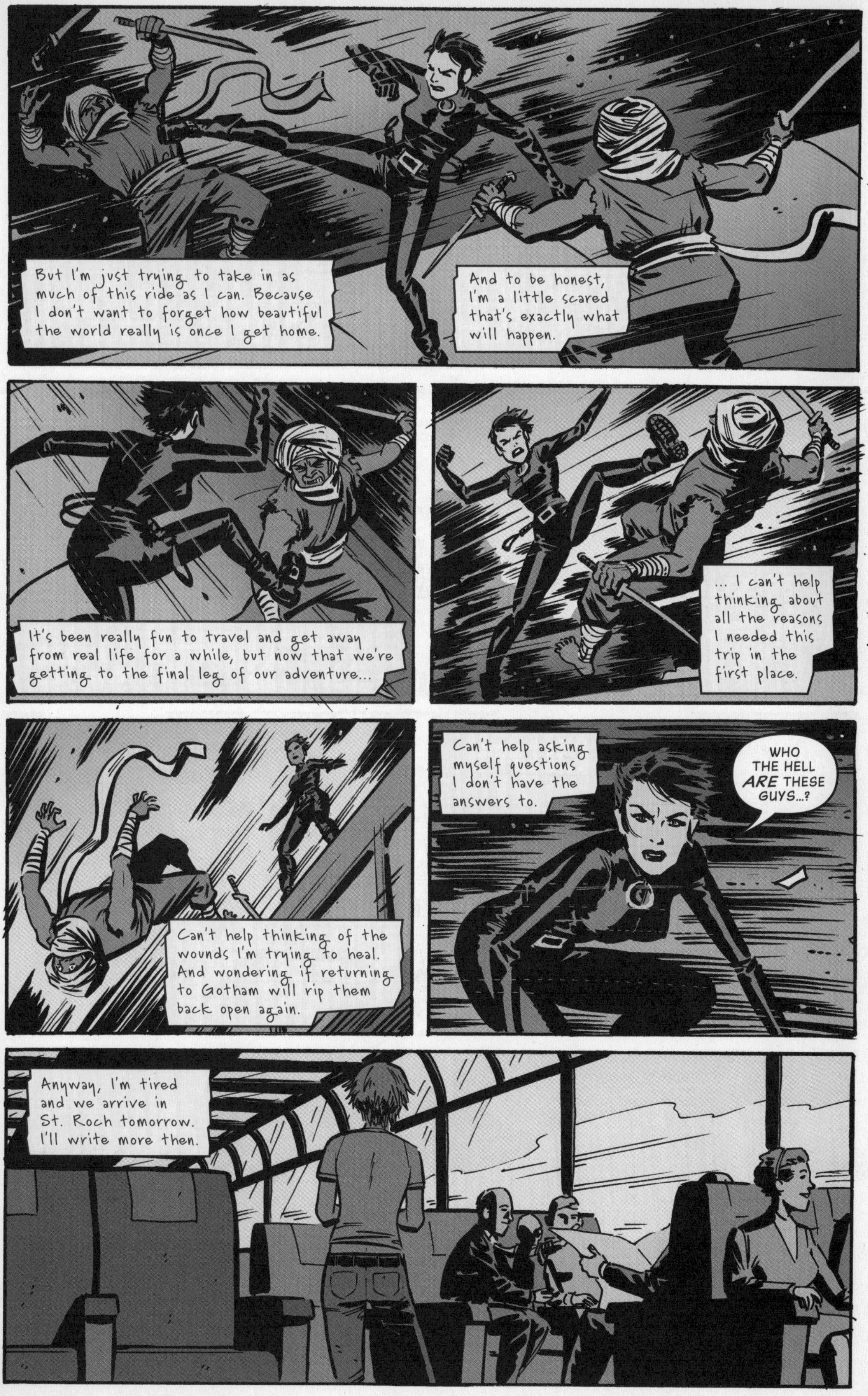

But I'm just trying to take in as much of this ride as I can. Because I don't want to forget how beautiful the world really is once I get home.
And to be honest, I'm a little scared that's exactly what will happen.
It's been really fun to travel and get away from real life for a while, but now that we're getting to the final leg of our adventure...
... I can't help thinking about all the reasons I needed this trip in the first place.
Can't help thinking of the wounds I'm trying to heal. And wondering if returning to Gotham will rip them back open again.
Can't help asking myself questions I don't have the answers to.
WHO THE HELL *ARE* THESE GUYS...?
Anyway, I'm tired and we arrive in St. Roch tomorrow. I'll write more then.

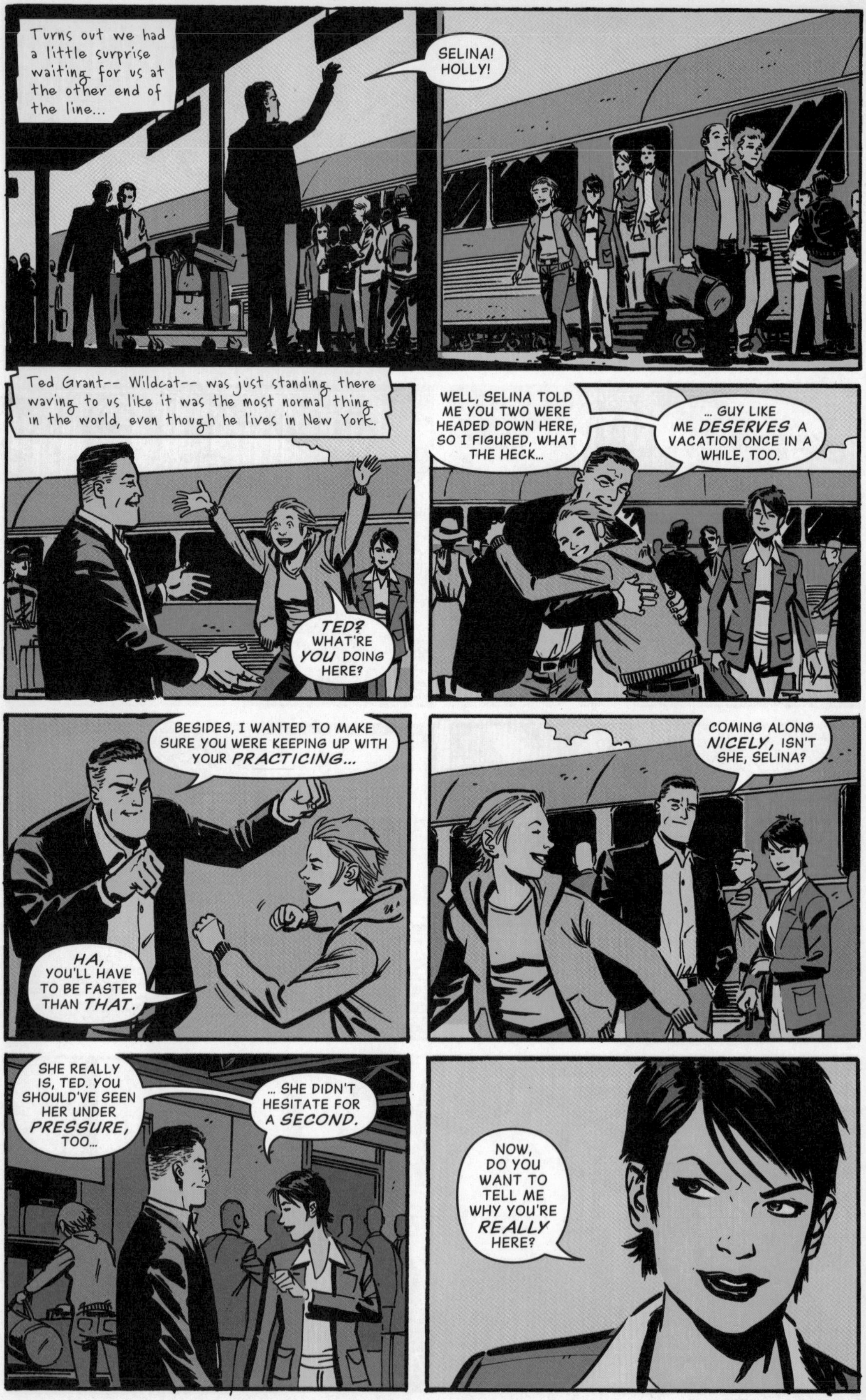
Turns out we had a little surprise waiting for us at the other end of the line...
SELINA! HOLLY!
Ted Grant-- Wildcat-- was just standing there waving to us like it was the most normal thing in the world, even though he lives in New York.
TED? WHAT'RE YOU DOING HERE?
WELL, SELINA TOLD ME YOU TWO WERE HEADED DOWN HERE, SO I FIGURED, WHAT THE HECK...
... GUY LIKE ME DESERVES A VACATION ONCE IN A WHILE, TOO.
BESIDES, I WANTED TO MAKE SURE YOU WERE KEEPING UP WITH YOUR PRACTICING...
HA, YOU'LL HAVE TO BE FASTER THAN THAT.
COMING ALONG NICELY, ISN'T SHE, SELINA?
SHE REALLY IS, TED. YOU SHOULD'VE SEEN HER UNDER PRESSURE, TOO...
... SHE DIDN'T HESITATE FOR A SECOND.
NOW, DO YOU WANT TO TELL ME WHY YOU'RE REALLY HERE?

Of course, once we get checked into our hotel, Ted and Selina disappear on some private errand.

I'm beginning to wonder if they'd let me in on all their secrets if I really was a sidekick. But I just can't see myself in a mask.

Oh well, whatever, let them have their secrets...

NO, YOU'RE NOT *LISTENING* TO ME. IT'S NOT THAT I GOT *LOST*, IT'S THAT THE WHOLE DANG BUILDING JUST *DISAPPEARED.*

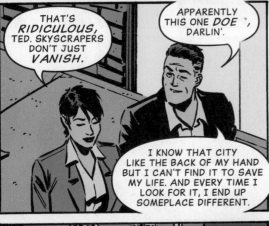

THAT'S *RIDICULOUS,* TED. SKYSCRAPERS DON'T JUST *VANISH.*

APPARENTLY THIS ONE *DOE*, DARLIN'.

I KNOW THAT CITY LIKE THE BACK OF MY HAND BUT I CAN'T FIND IT TO SAVE MY LIFE. AND EVERY TIME I LOOK FOR IT, I END UP SOMEPLACE DIFFERENT.

SO, CONSIDERING IT HAD SOME KIND OF ANCIENT TEMPLE INSIDE IT, AND THAT THOSE CRAZY NINJAS WE FOUGHT THERE HAVE BEEN ALL OVER YOU SINCE THAT NIGHT...

... I'M REALLY STARTING TO WONDER WHAT THE HELL IS GOING ON.

SO YOU CAME ALL THIS WAY JUST TO TELL ME THAT?

NO, I CAME DOWN HERE BECAUSE A FRIEND OF MINE LIVES HERE WHO I THINK MIGHT HAVE SOME ANSWERS ABOUT ALL THIS...

SAINT ROCK'S
BAR AND GRILL

OKAY, JUST WAIT HERE ONE MINUTE AND WE'LL GO SEE YOUR FRIEND, THEN...

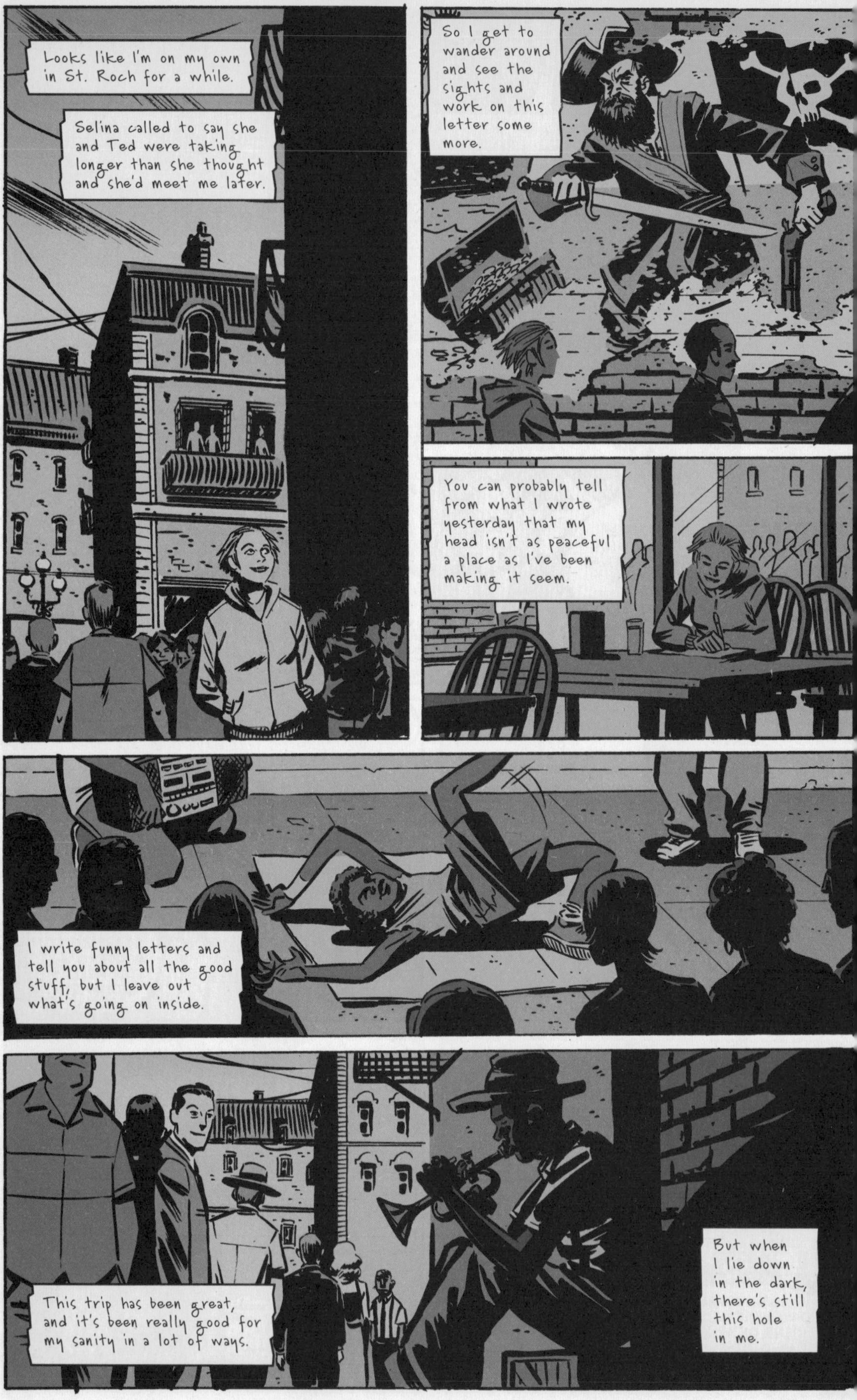

Looks like I'm on my own in St. Roch for a while.
Selina called to say she and Ted were taking longer than she thought and she'd meet me later.
So I get to wander around and see the sights and work on this letter some more.
You can probably tell from what I wrote yesterday that my head isn't as peaceful a place as I've been making it seem.
I write funny letters and tell you about all the good stuff, but I leave out what's going on inside.
This trip has been great, and it's been really good for my sanity in a lot of ways.
But when I lie down in the dark, there's still this hole in me.

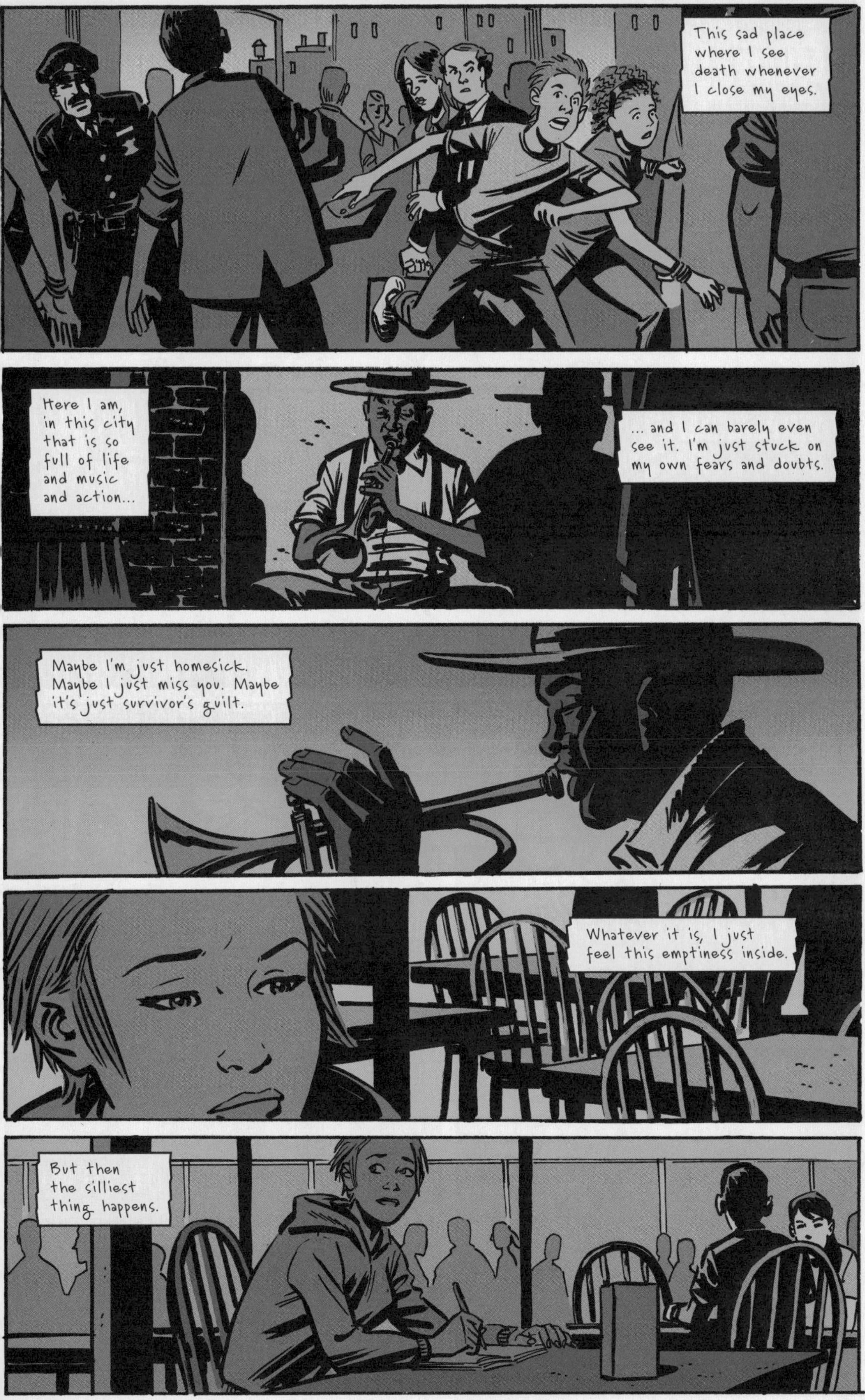
This sad place where I see death whenever I close my eyes.
Here I am, in this city that is so full of life and music and action...
... and I can barely even see it. I'm just stuck on my own fears and doubts.
Maybe I'm just homesick. Maybe I just miss you. Maybe it's just survivor's guilt.
Whatever it is, I just feel this emptiness inside.
But then the silliest thing happens.

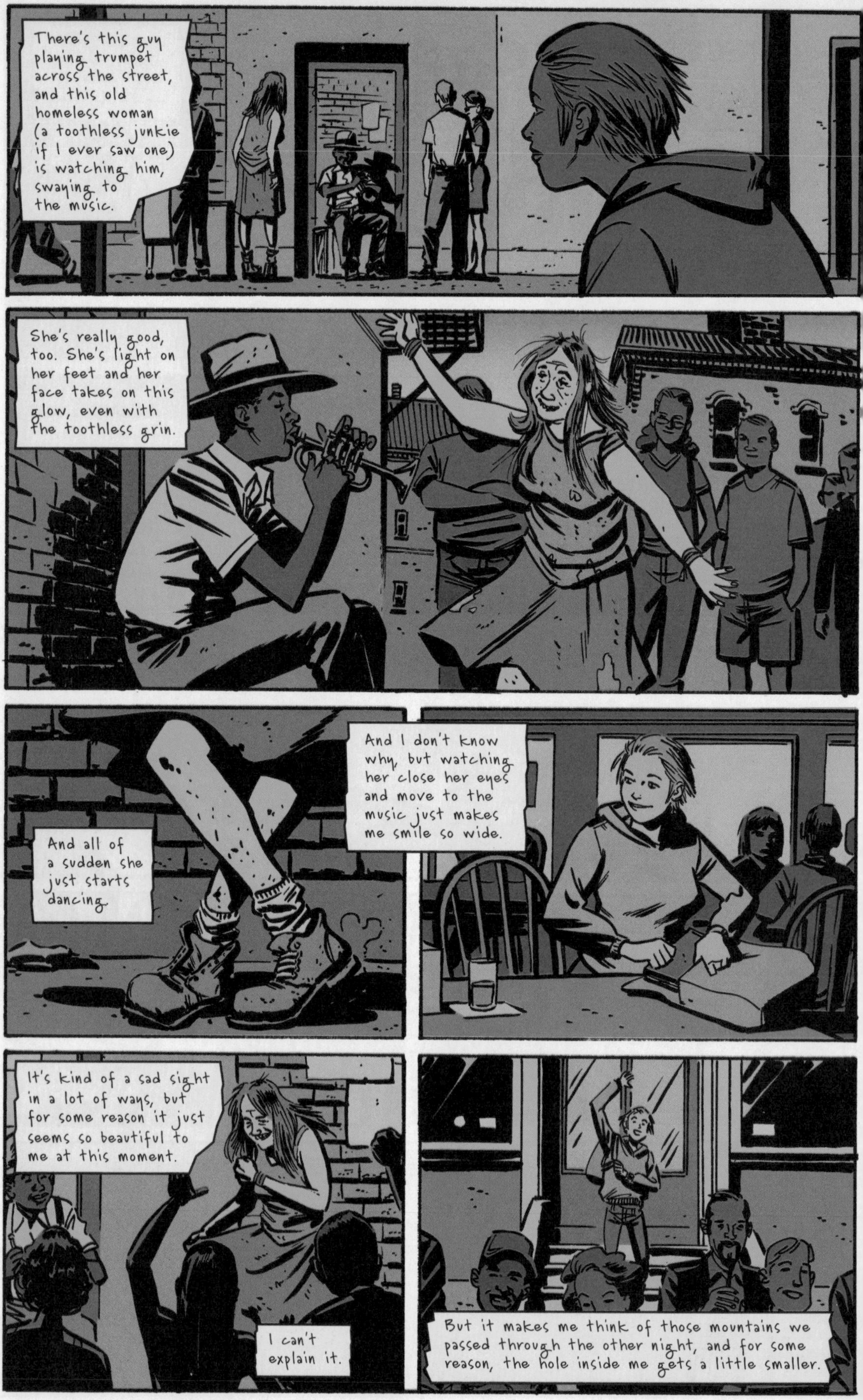
There's this guy playing trumpet across the street, and this old homeless woman (a toothless junkie if I ever saw one) is watching him, swaying to the music.
She's really good, too. She's light on her feet and her face takes on this glow, even with the toothless grin.
And all of a sudden she just starts dancing.
And I don't know why, but watching her close her eyes and move to the music just makes me smile so wide.
It's kind of a sad sight in a lot of ways, but for some reason it just seems so beautiful to me at this moment.
I can't explain it.
But it makes me think of those mountains we passed through the other night, and for some reason, the hole inside me gets a little smaller.

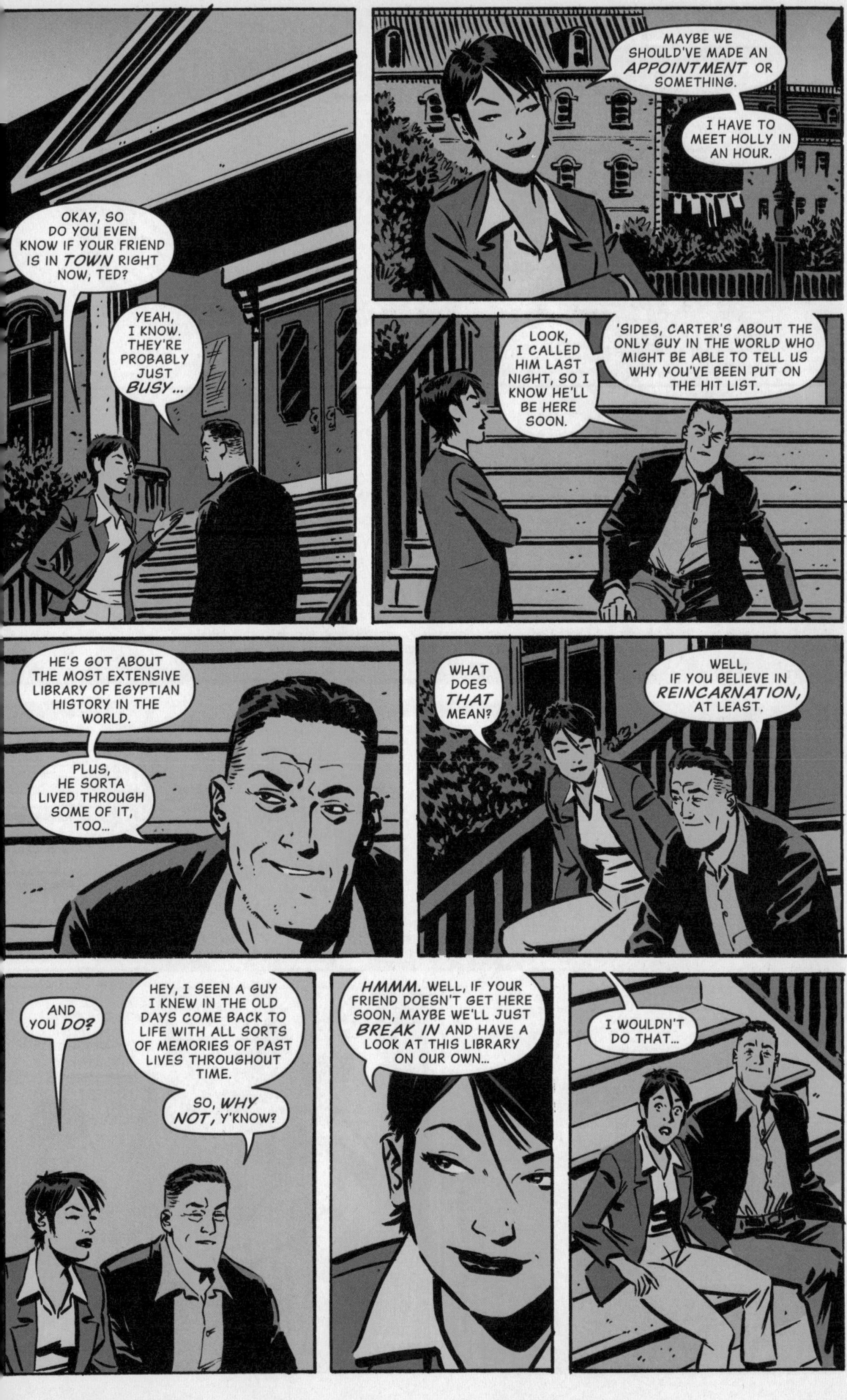
OKAY, SO DO YOU EVEN KNOW IF YOUR FRIEND IS IN TOWN RIGHT NOW, TED?
YEAH, I KNOW. THEY'RE PROBABLY JUST BUSY...
MAYBE WE SHOULD'VE MADE AN APPOINTMENT OR SOMETHING.
I HAVE TO MEET HOLLY IN AN HOUR.
LOOK, I CALLED HIM LAST NIGHT, SO I KNOW HE'LL BE HERE SOON.
'SIDES, CARTER'S ABOUT THE ONLY GUY IN THE WORLD WHO MIGHT BE ABLE TO TELL US WHY YOU'VE BEEN PUT ON THE HIT LIST.
HE'S GOT ABOUT THE MOST EXTENSIVE LIBRARY OF EGYPTIAN HISTORY IN THE WORLD.
PLUS, HE SORTA LIVED THROUGH SOME OF IT, TOO...
WHAT DOES THAT MEAN?
WELL, IF YOU BELIEVE IN REINCARNATION, AT LEAST.
AND YOU DO?
HEY, I SEEN A GUY I KNEW IN THE OLD DAYS COME BACK TO LIFE WITH ALL SORTS OF MEMORIES OF PAST LIVES THROUGHOUT TIME.
SO, WHY NOT, Y'KNOW?
HMMM. WELL, IF YOUR FRIEND DOESN'T GET HERE SOON, MAYBE WE'LL JUST BREAK IN AND HAVE A LOOK AT THIS LIBRARY ON OUR OWN...
I WOULDN'T DO THAT...

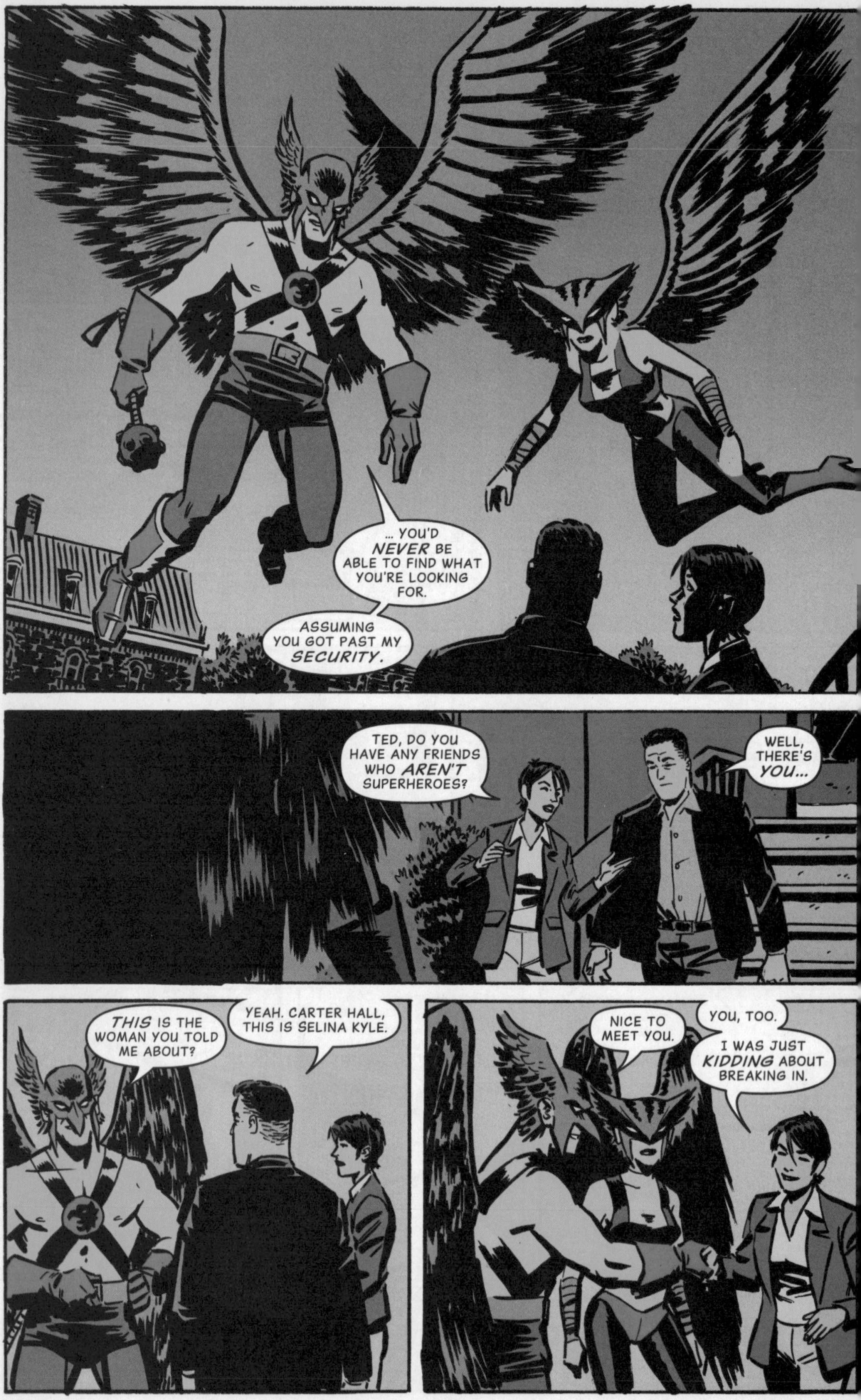

... YOU'D NEVER BE ABLE TO FIND WHAT YOU'RE LOOKING FOR.
ASSUMING YOU GOT PAST MY SECURITY.
TED, DO YOU HAVE ANY FRIENDS WHO AREN'T SUPERHEROES?
WELL, THERE'S YOU...
THIS IS THE WOMAN YOU TOLD ME ABOUT?
YEAH. CARTER HALL, THIS IS SELINA KYLE.
NICE TO MEET YOU.
YOU, TOO.
I WAS JUST KIDDING ABOUT BREAKING IN.

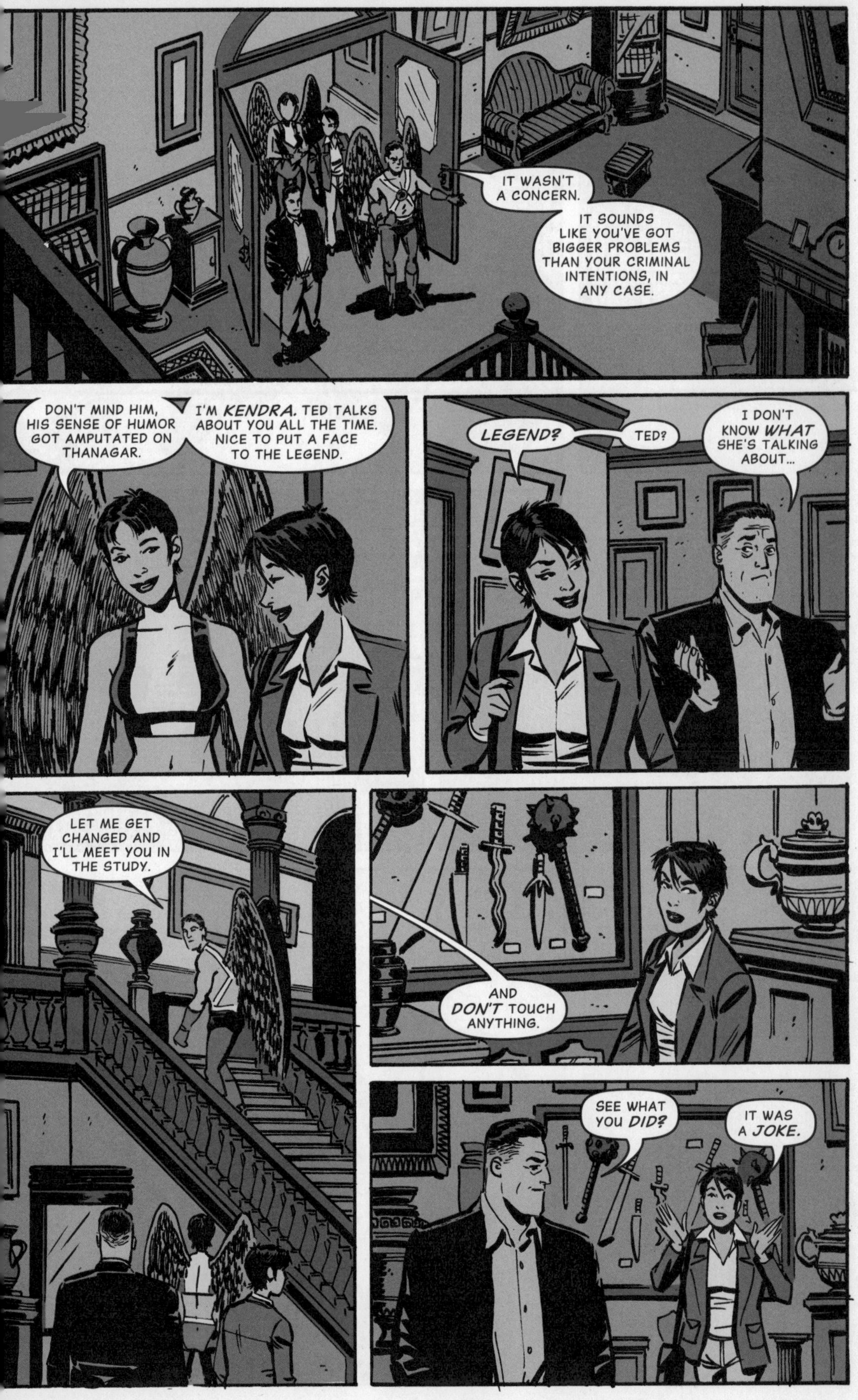
IT WASN'T A CONCERN.
IT SOUNDS LIKE YOU'VE GOT BIGGER PROBLEMS THAN YOUR CRIMINAL INTENTIONS, IN ANY CASE.
DON'T MIND HIM, HIS SENSE OF HUMOR GOT AMPUTATED ON THANAGAR.
I'M *KENDRA.* TED TALKS ABOUT YOU ALL THE TIME. NICE TO PUT A FACE TO THE LEGEND.
LEGEND?
TED?
I DON'T KNOW *WHAT* SHE'S TALKING ABOUT...
LET ME GET CHANGED AND I'LL MEET YOU IN THE STUDY.
AND *DON'T* TOUCH ANYTHING.
SEE WHAT YOU *DID?*
IT WAS A *JOKE.*

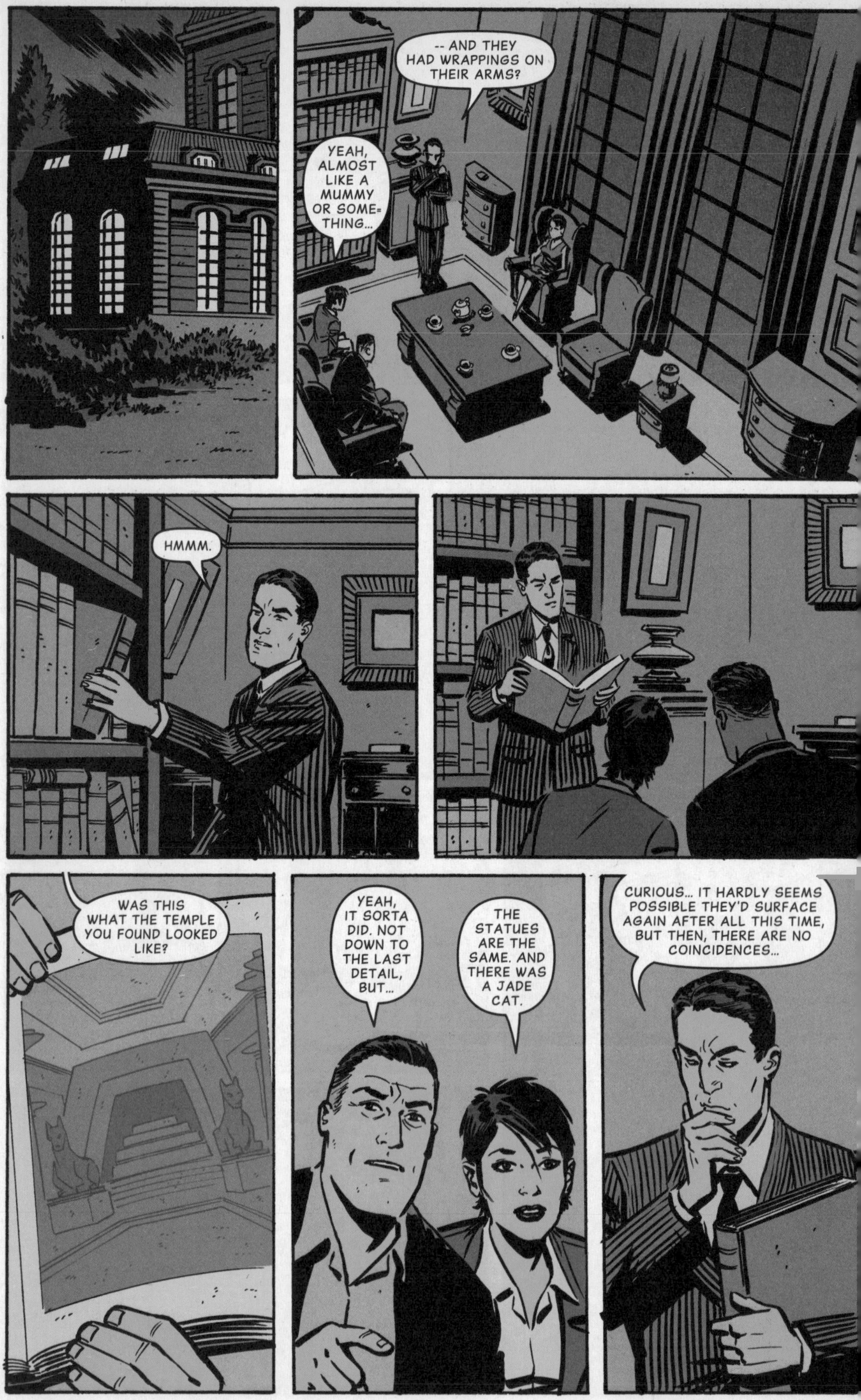
-- AND THEY HAD WRAPPINGS ON THEIR ARMS?
YEAH, ALMOST LIKE A MUMMY OR SOME-THING...
HMMM.
WAS THIS WHAT THE TEMPLE YOU FOUND LOOKED LIKE?
YEAH, IT SORTA DID. NOT DOWN TO THE LAST DETAIL, BUT...
THE STATUES ARE THE SAME. AND THERE WAS A JADE CAT.
CURIOUS... IT HARDLY SEEMS POSSIBLE THEY'D SURFACE AGAIN AFTER ALL THIS TIME, BUT THEN, THERE ARE NO COINCIDENCES...

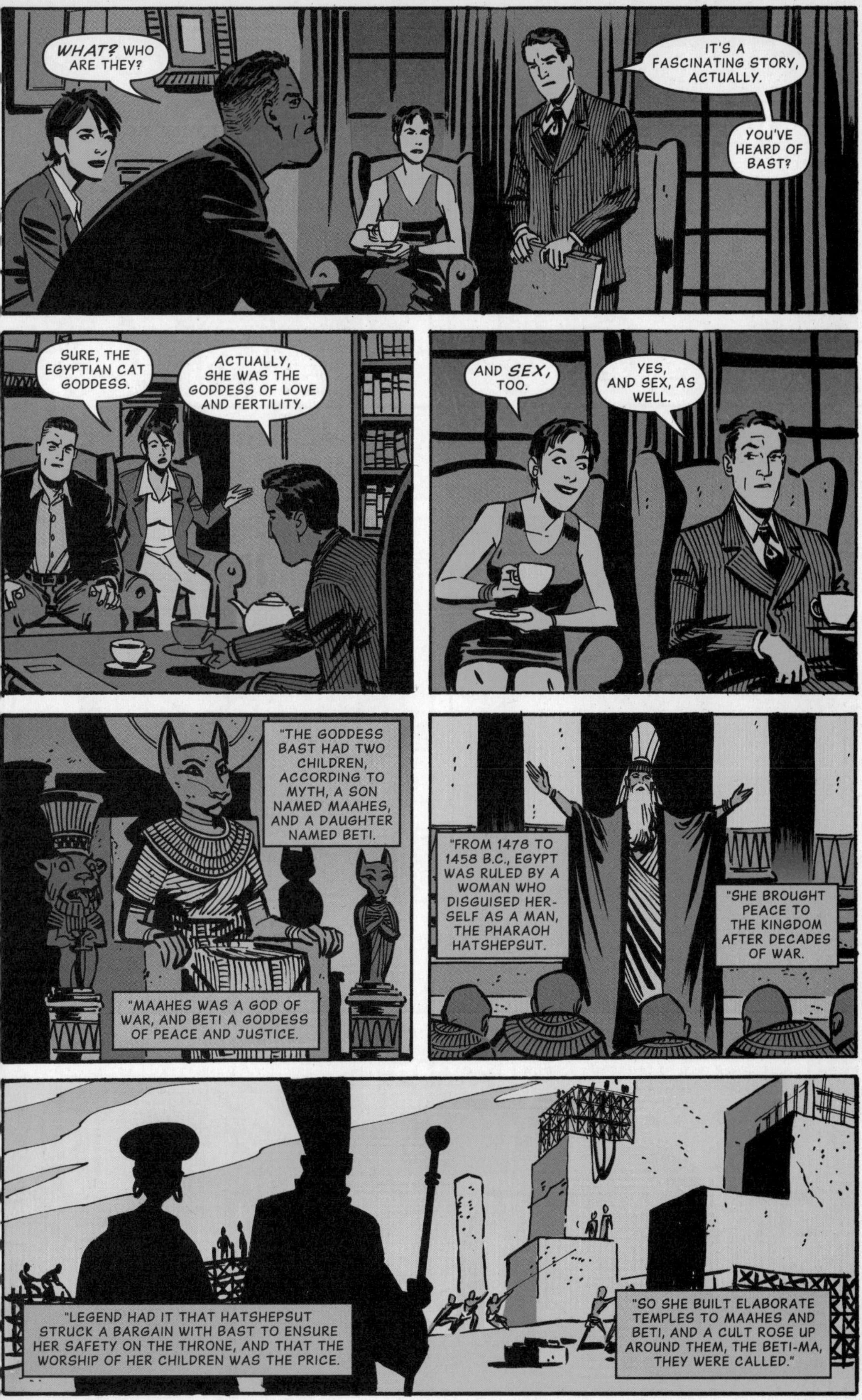

WHAT? WHO ARE THEY?
IT'S A FASCINATING STORY, ACTUALLY.
YOU'VE HEARD OF BAST?
SURE, THE EGYPTIAN CAT GODDESS.
ACTUALLY, SHE WAS THE GODDESS OF LOVE AND FERTILITY.
AND SEX, TOO.
YES, AND SEX, AS WELL.
"THE GODDESS BAST HAD TWO CHILDREN, ACCORDING TO MYTH, A SON NAMED MAAHES, AND A DAUGHTER NAMED BETI.
"MAAHES WAS A GOD OF WAR, AND BETI A GODDESS OF PEACE AND JUSTICE.
"FROM 1478 TO 1458 B.C., EGYPT WAS RULED BY A WOMAN WHO DISGUISED HER-SELF AS A MAN, THE PHARAOH HATSHEPSUT.
"SHE BROUGHT PEACE TO THE KINGDOM AFTER DECADES OF WAR.
"LEGEND HAD IT THAT HATSHEPSUT STRUCK A BARGAIN WITH BAST TO ENSURE HER SAFETY ON THE THRONE, AND THAT THE WORSHIP OF HER CHILDREN WAS THE PRICE.
"SO SHE BUILT ELABORATE TEMPLES TO MAAHES AND BETI, AND A CULT ROSE UP AROUND THEM, THE BETI-MA, THEY WERE CALLED."

"BUT AFTER HATSHEPSUT'S DEATH, HER NEPHEW THUTMOSE THE THIRD CLAIMED THE THRONE AND DESTROYED THE TEMPLES.

"WORSHIP OF MAAHES AND BETI WAS OUTLAWED.

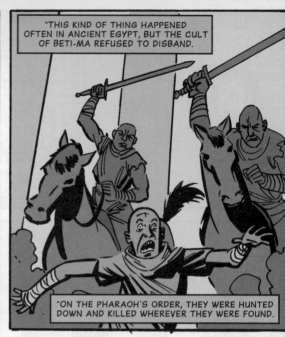

"THIS KIND OF THING HAPPENED OFTEN IN ANCIENT EGYPT, BUT THE CULT OF BETI-MA REFUSED TO DISBAND.

"ON THE PHARAOH'S ORDER, THEY WERE HUNTED DOWN AND KILLED WHEREVER THEY WERE FOUND.

"THEIR NUMBERS DWINDLED, AND THEY WENT INTO HIDING.

"THE OCCASIONAL WHISPER WOULD TELL OF SECRET UNDERGROUND TEMPLES WHERE THEIR WORSHIP CONTINUED.

"THEN, DURING THE REIGN OF RAMSES A STORY SPREAD OF A BREAK IN THE CULT BETWEEN THOSE WHO WORSHIPPED BETI AND THOSE WHO WORSHIPPED MAAHES.

"THE TWO SIDES HAD DECLARED WAR ON EACH OTHER..."

... EVENTUALLY, IT WAS ASSUMED THESE WARRING FACTIONS HAD WIPED EACH OTHER OUT, BECAUSE NEITHER HAS BEEN HEARD FROM IN OVER THREE THOUSAND YEARS.

THAT IS, UNTIL THE TWO OF YOU STUMBLED UPON A TEMPLE OF BETI SOMEWHERE IN THE MIDDLE OF MANHATTAN LAST MONTH.

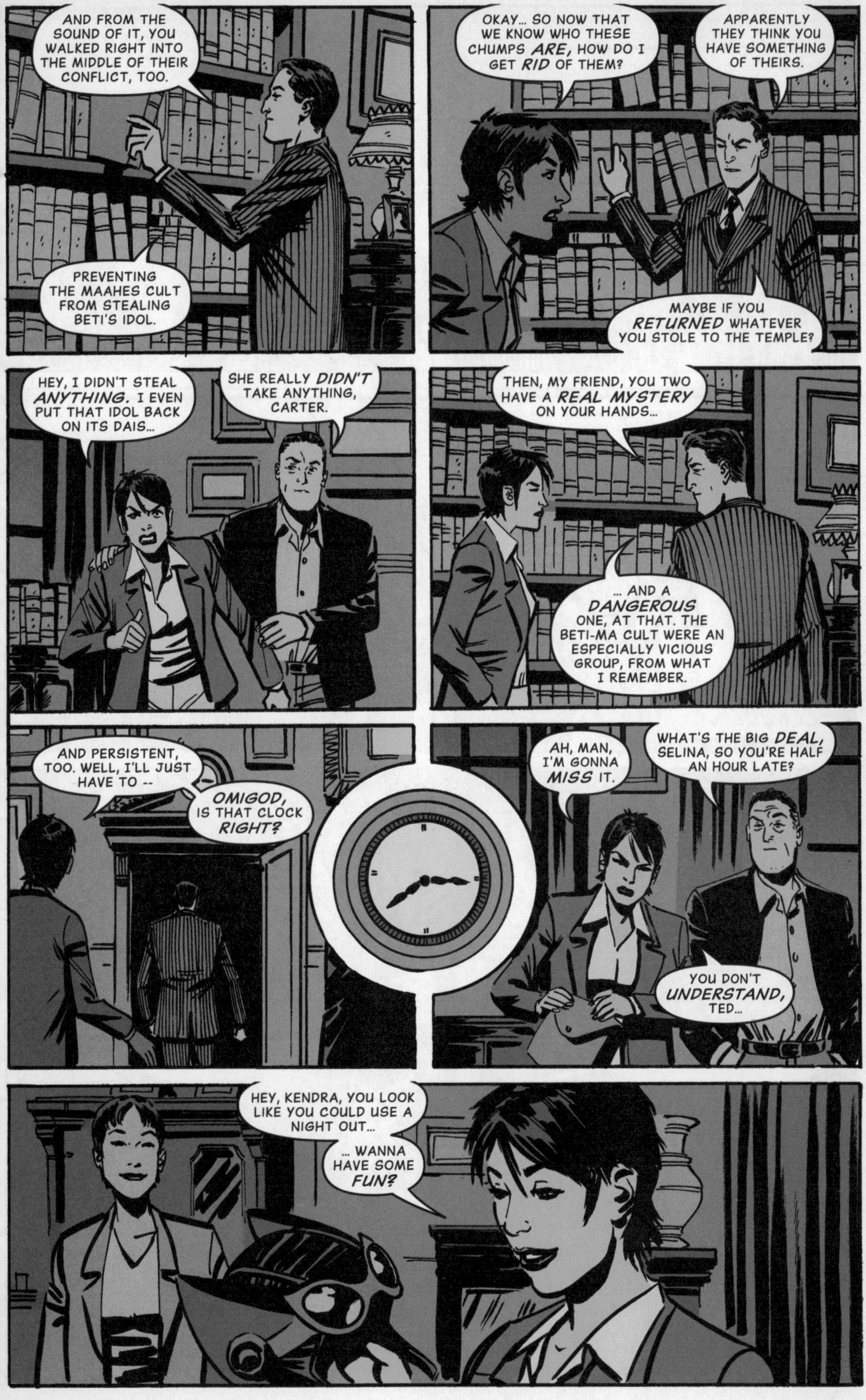
AND FROM THE SOUND OF IT, YOU WALKED RIGHT INTO THE MIDDLE OF THEIR CONFLICT, TOO.
PREVENTING THE MAAHES CULT FROM STEALING BETI'S IDOL.
OKAY... SO NOW THAT WE KNOW WHO THESE CHUMPS ARE, HOW DO I GET RID OF THEM?
APPARENTLY THEY THINK YOU HAVE SOMETHING OF THEIRS.
MAYBE IF YOU RETURNED WHATEVER YOU STOLE TO THE TEMPLE?
HEY, I DIDN'T STEAL ANYTHING. I EVEN PUT THAT IDOL BACK ON ITS DAIS...
SHE REALLY DIDN'T TAKE ANYTHING, CARTER.
THEN, MY FRIEND, YOU TWO HAVE A REAL MYSTERY ON YOUR HANDS...
... AND A DANGEROUS ONE, AT THAT. THE BETI-MA CULT WERE AN ESPECIALLY VICIOUS GROUP, FROM WHAT I REMEMBER.
AND PERSISTENT, TOO. WELL, I'LL JUST HAVE TO --
OMIGOD, IS THAT CLOCK RIGHT?
AH, MAN, I'M GONNA MISS IT.
WHAT'S THE BIG DEAL, SELINA, SO YOU'RE HALF AN HOUR LATE?
YOU DON'T UNDERSTAND, TED...
HEY, KENDRA, YOU LOOK LIKE YOU COULD USE A NIGHT OUT...
... WANNA HAVE SOME FUN?

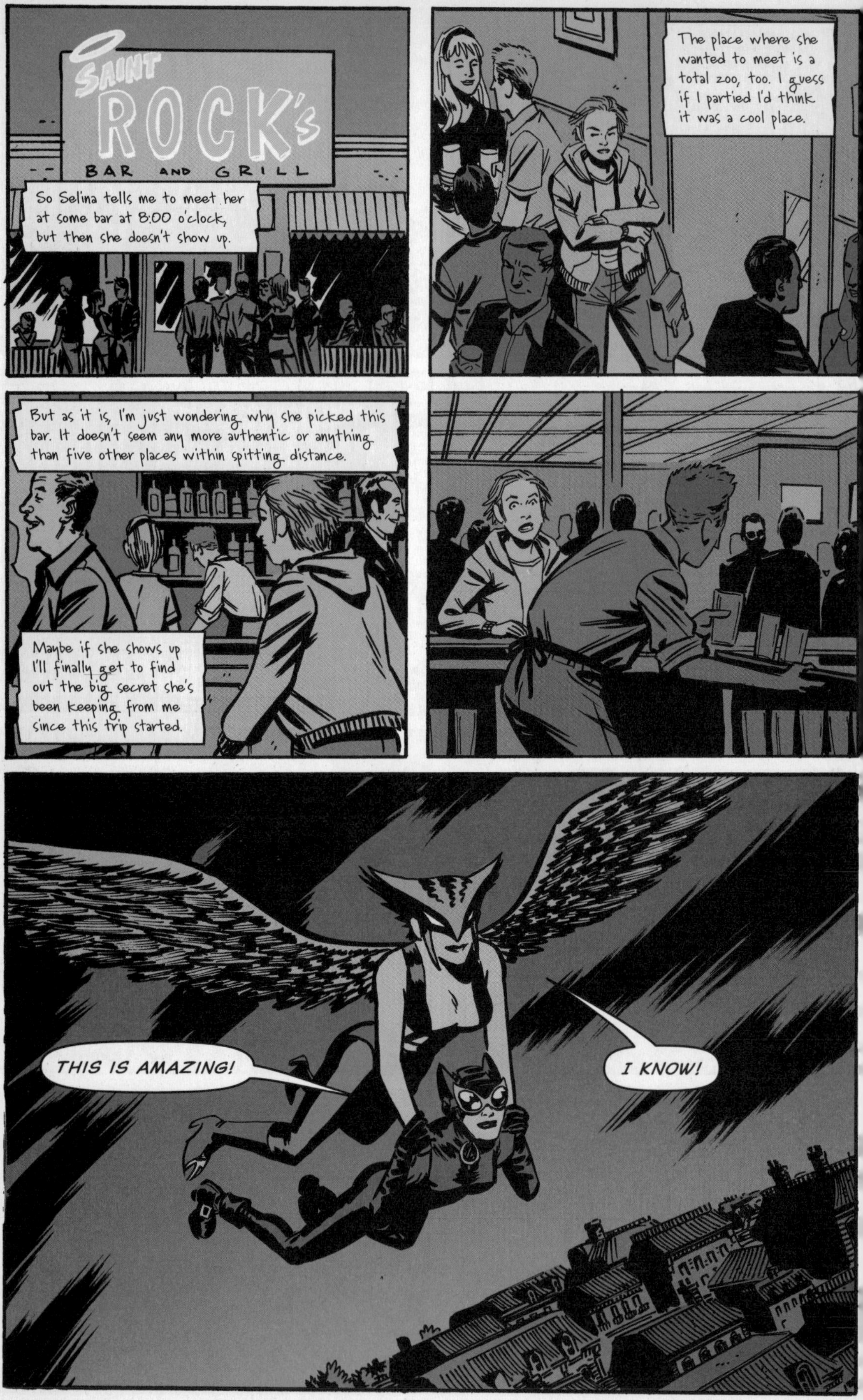
SAINT ROCK's
BAR AND GRILL
So Selina tells me to meet her at some bar at 8:00 o'clock, but then she doesn't show up.
The place where she wanted to meet is a total zoo, too. I guess if I partied I'd think it was a cool place.
But as it is, I'm just wondering why she picked this bar. It doesn't seem any more authentic or anything than five other places within spitting distance.
Maybe if she shows up I'll finally get to find out the big secret she's been keeping from me since this trip started.
THIS IS AMAZING!
I KNOW!

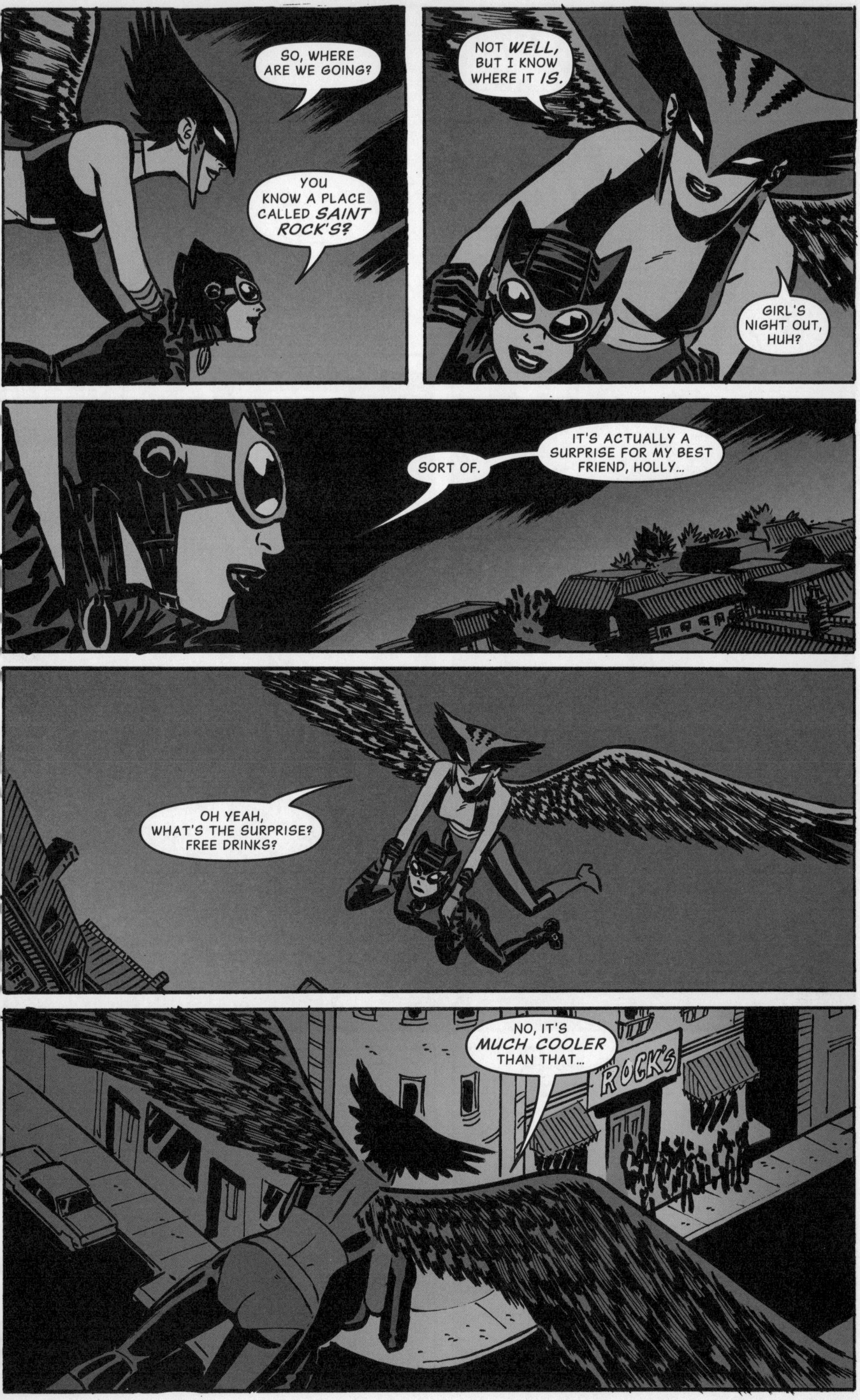
SO, WHERE ARE WE GOING?
YOU KNOW A PLACE CALLED SAINT ROCK'S?
NOT WELL, BUT I KNOW WHERE IT IS.
GIRL'S NIGHT OUT, HUH?
SORT OF.
IT'S ACTUALLY A SURPRISE FOR MY BEST FRIEND, HOLLY...
OH YEAH, WHAT'S THE SURPRISE? FREE DRINKS?
NO, IT'S MUCH COOLER THAN THAT...
ROCK'S

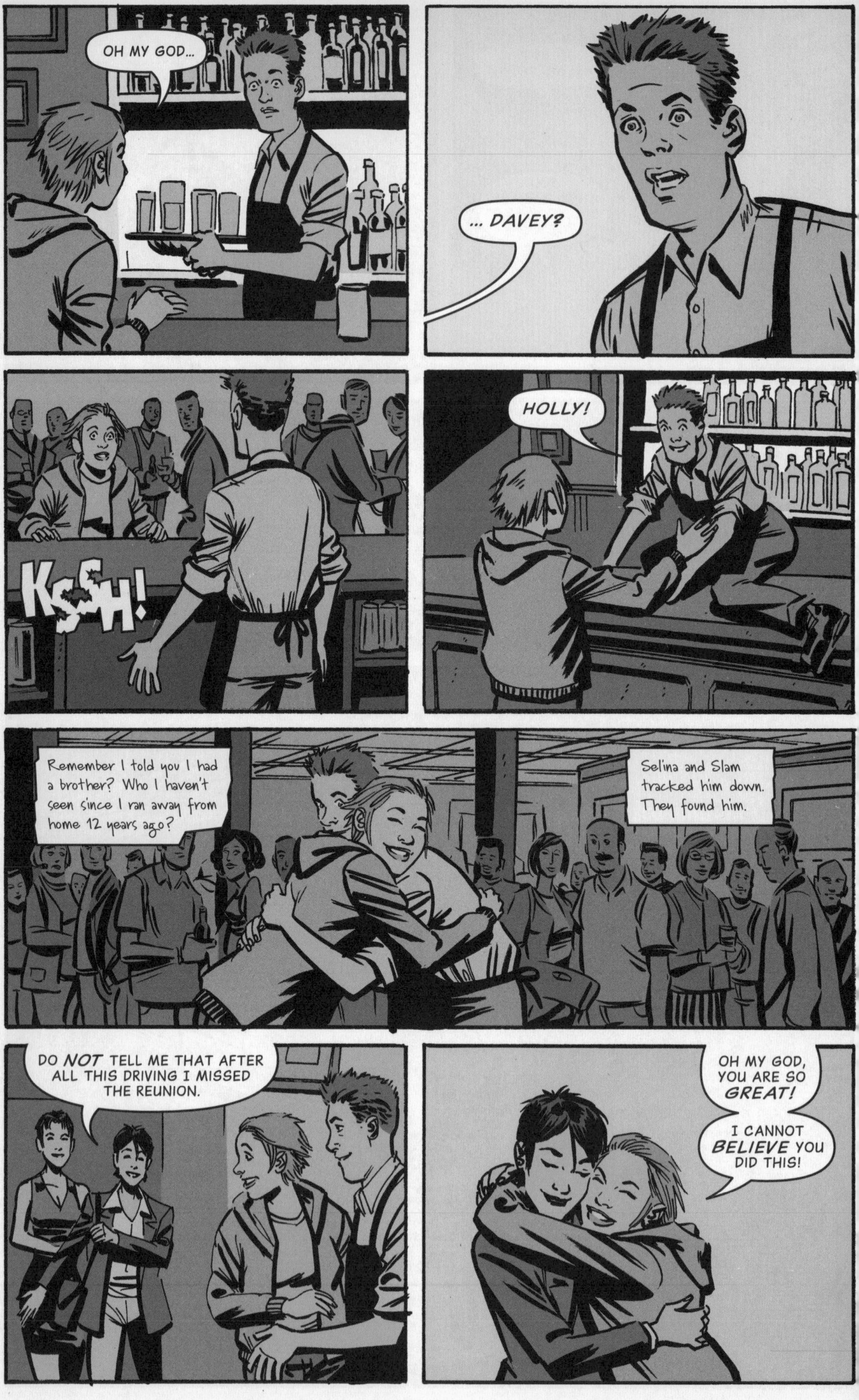
OH MY GOD...
... DAVEY?
KSSH!
HOLLY!
Remember I told you I had a brother? Who I haven't seen since I ran away from home 12 years ago?
Selina and Slam tracked him down. They found him.
DO NOT TELL ME THAT AFTER ALL THIS DRIVING I MISSED THE REUNION.
OH MY GOD, YOU ARE SO GREAT!
I CANNOT BELIEVE YOU DID THIS!

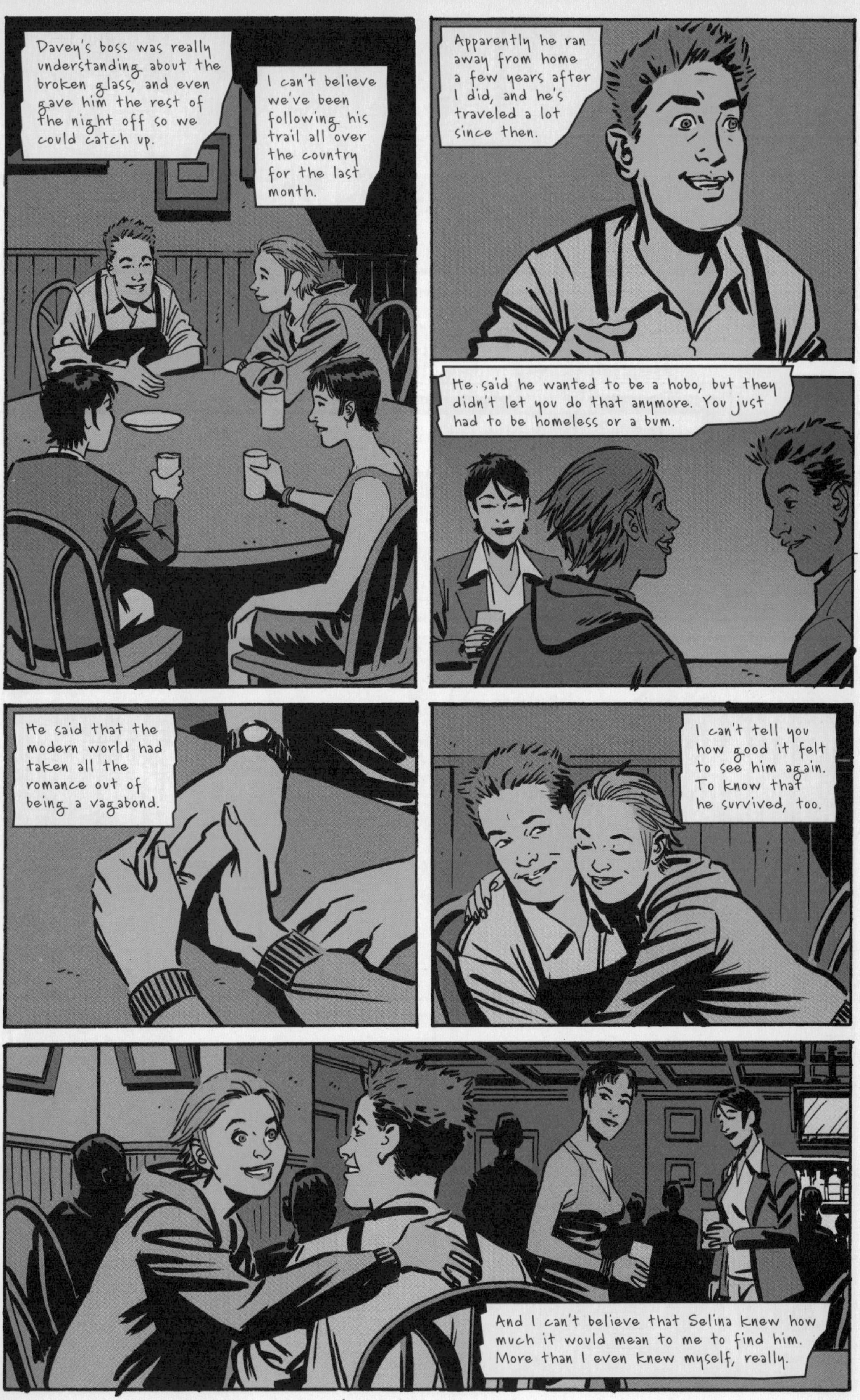
Davey's boss was really understanding about the broken glass, and even gave him the rest of the night off so we could catch up.
I can't believe we've been following his trail all over the country for the last month.
Apparently he ran away from home a few years after I did, and he's traveled a lot since then.
He said he wanted to be a hobo, but they didn't let you do that anymore. You just had to be homeless or a bum.
He said that the modern world had taken all the romance out of being a vagabond.
I can't tell you how good it felt to see him again. To know that he survived, too.
And I can't believe that Selina knew how much it would mean to me to find him. More than I even knew myself, really.

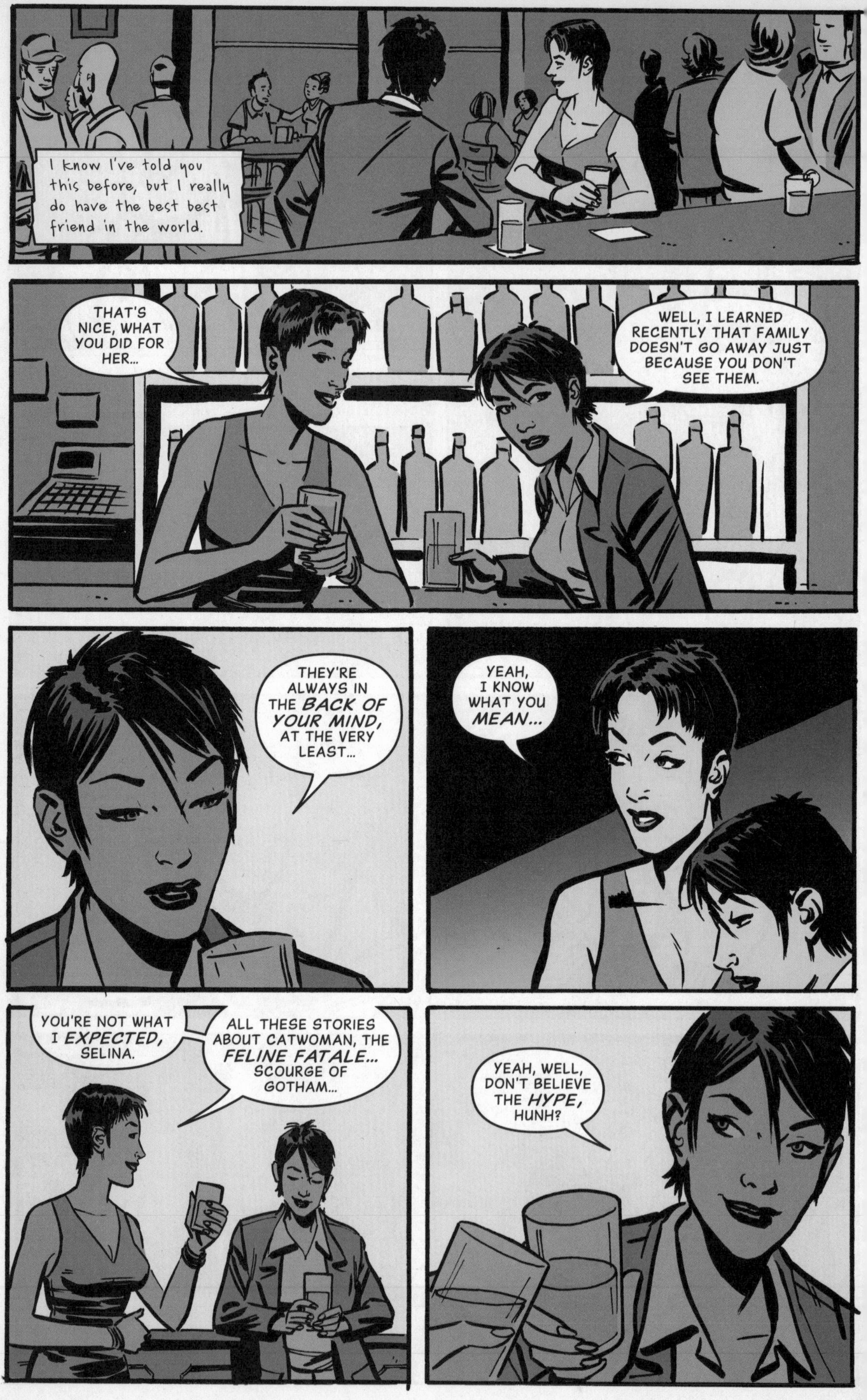
I know I've told you this before, but I really do have the best best friend in the world.
THAT'S NICE, WHAT YOU DID FOR HER...
WELL, I LEARNED RECENTLY THAT FAMILY DOESN'T GO AWAY JUST BECAUSE YOU DON'T SEE THEM.
THEY'RE ALWAYS IN THE BACK OF YOUR MIND, AT THE VERY LEAST...
YEAH, I KNOW WHAT YOU MEAN...
YOU'RE NOT WHAT I EXPECTED, SELINA.
ALL THESE STORIES ABOUT CATWOMAN, THE FELINE FATALE... SCOURGE OF GOTHAM...
YEAH, WELL, DON'T BELIEVE THE HYPE, HUNH?

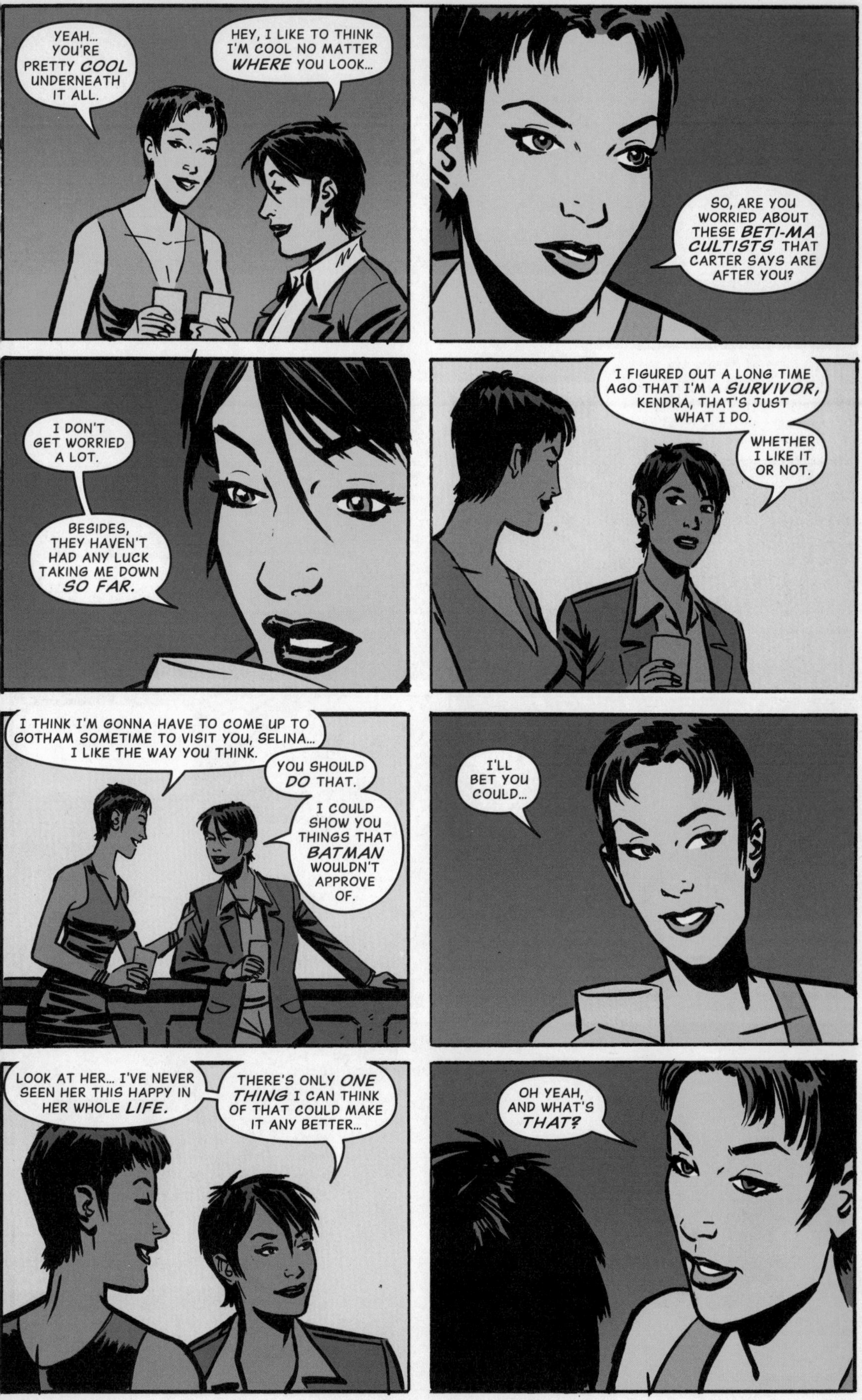
YEAH... YOU'RE PRETTY COOL UNDERNEATH IT ALL.
HEY, I LIKE TO THINK I'M COOL NO MATTER WHERE YOU LOOK...
SO, ARE YOU WORRIED ABOUT THESE BETI-MA CULTISTS THAT CARTER SAYS ARE AFTER YOU?
I DON'T GET WORRIED A LOT.
BESIDES, THEY HAVEN'T HAD ANY LUCK TAKING ME DOWN SO FAR.
I FIGURED OUT A LONG TIME AGO THAT I'M A SURVIVOR, KENDRA, THAT'S JUST WHAT I DO.
WHETHER I LIKE IT OR NOT.
I THINK I'M GONNA HAVE TO COME UP TO GOTHAM SOMETIME TO VISIT YOU, SELINA... I LIKE THE WAY YOU THINK.
YOU SHOULD DO THAT.
I COULD SHOW YOU THINGS THAT BATMAN WOULDN'T APPROVE OF.
I'LL BET YOU COULD...
LOOK AT HER... I'VE NEVER SEEN HER THIS HAPPY IN HER WHOLE LIFE.
THERE'S ONLY ONE THING I CAN THINK OF THAT COULD MAKE IT ANY BETTER...
OH YEAH, AND WHAT'S THAT?

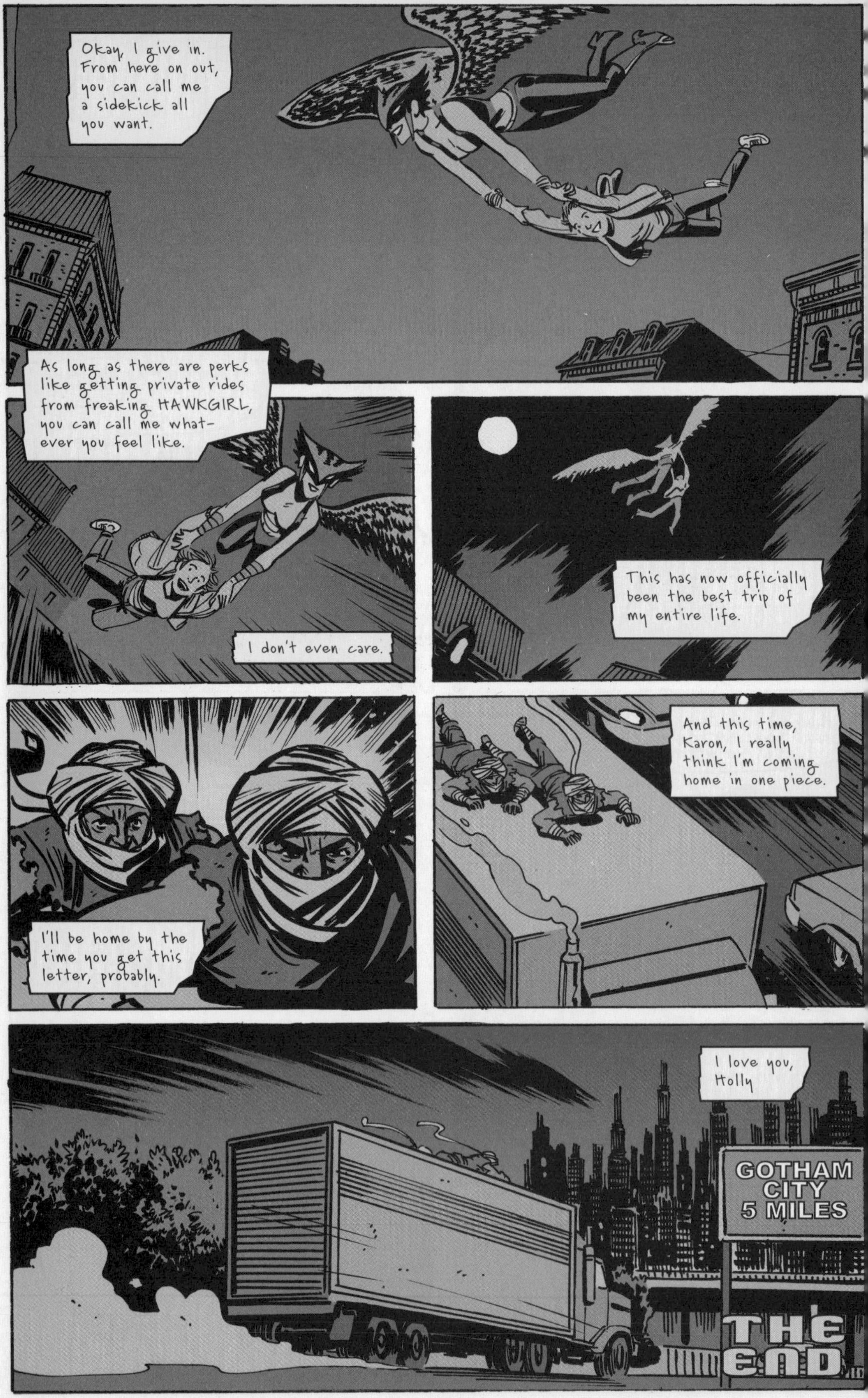
Okay, I give in. From here on out, you can call me a sidekick all you want.
As long as there are perks like getting private rides from freaking HAWKGIRL, you can call me whatever you feel like.
I don't even care.
This has now officially been the best trip of my entire life.
I'll be home by the time you get this letter, probably.
And this time, Karon, I really think I'm coming home in one piece.
I love you, Holly
GOTHAM CITY 5 MILES
THE END

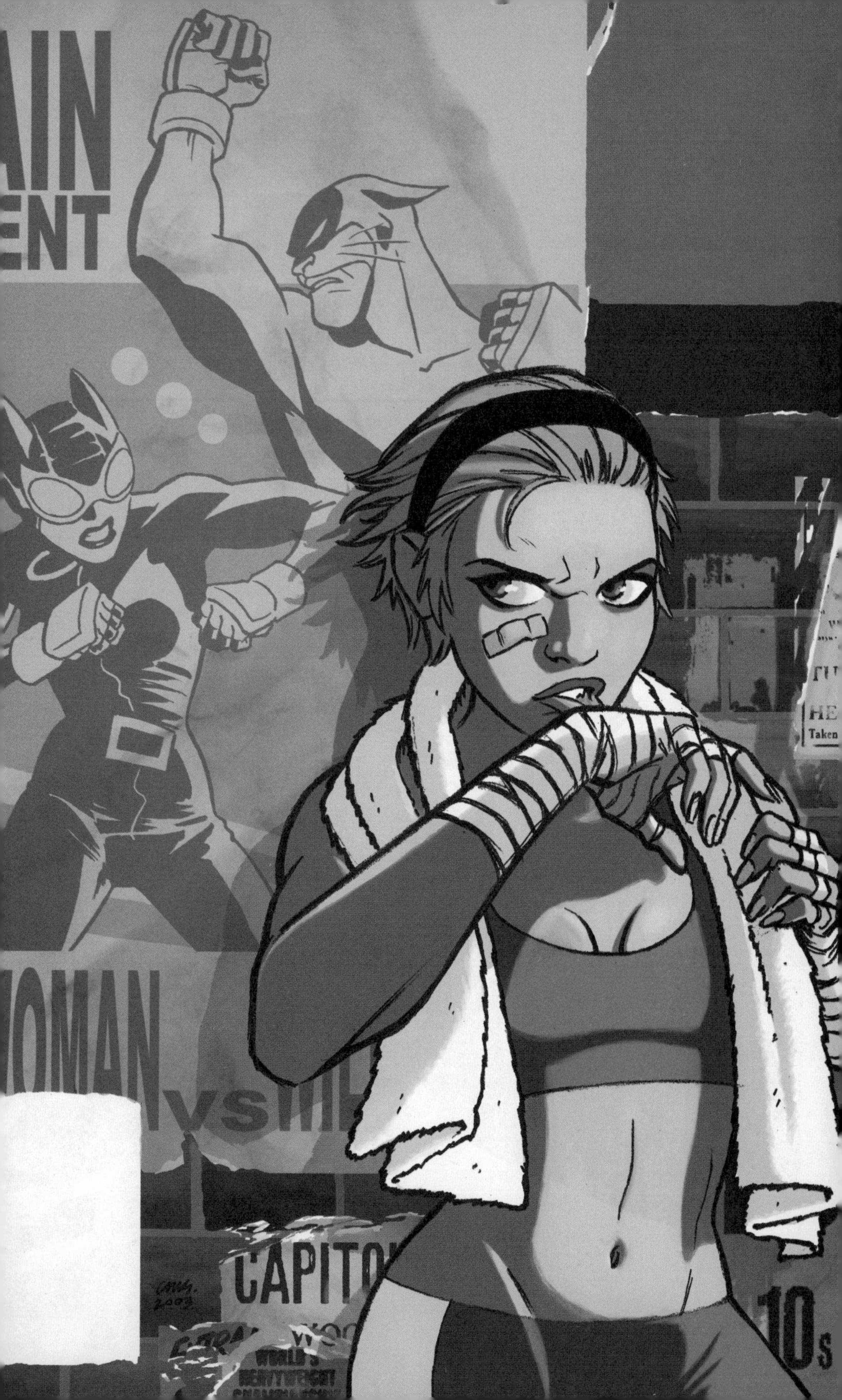

AIN
ENT
OMAN
VS
CAPITO
10s
Taken

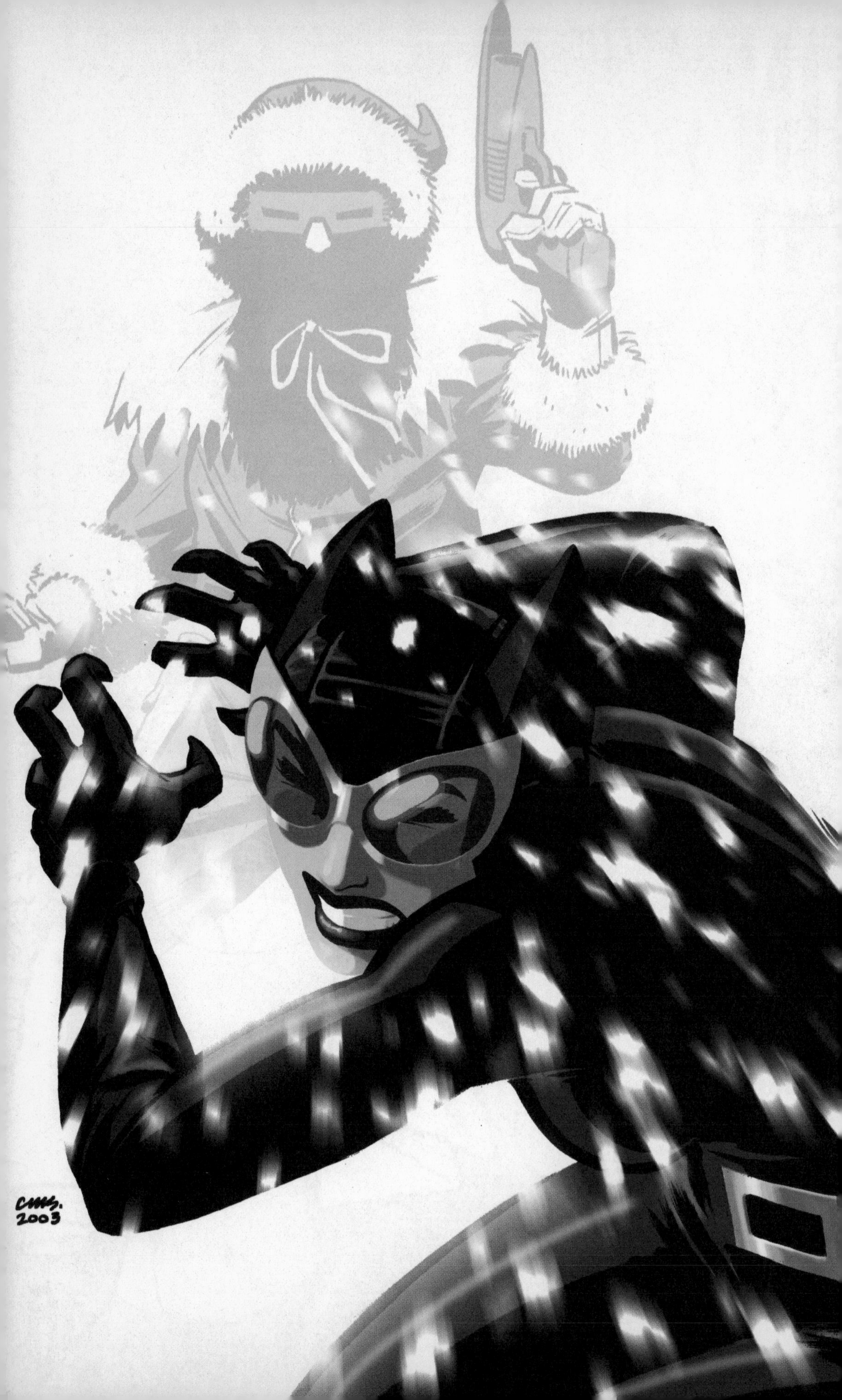
CMS.
2003

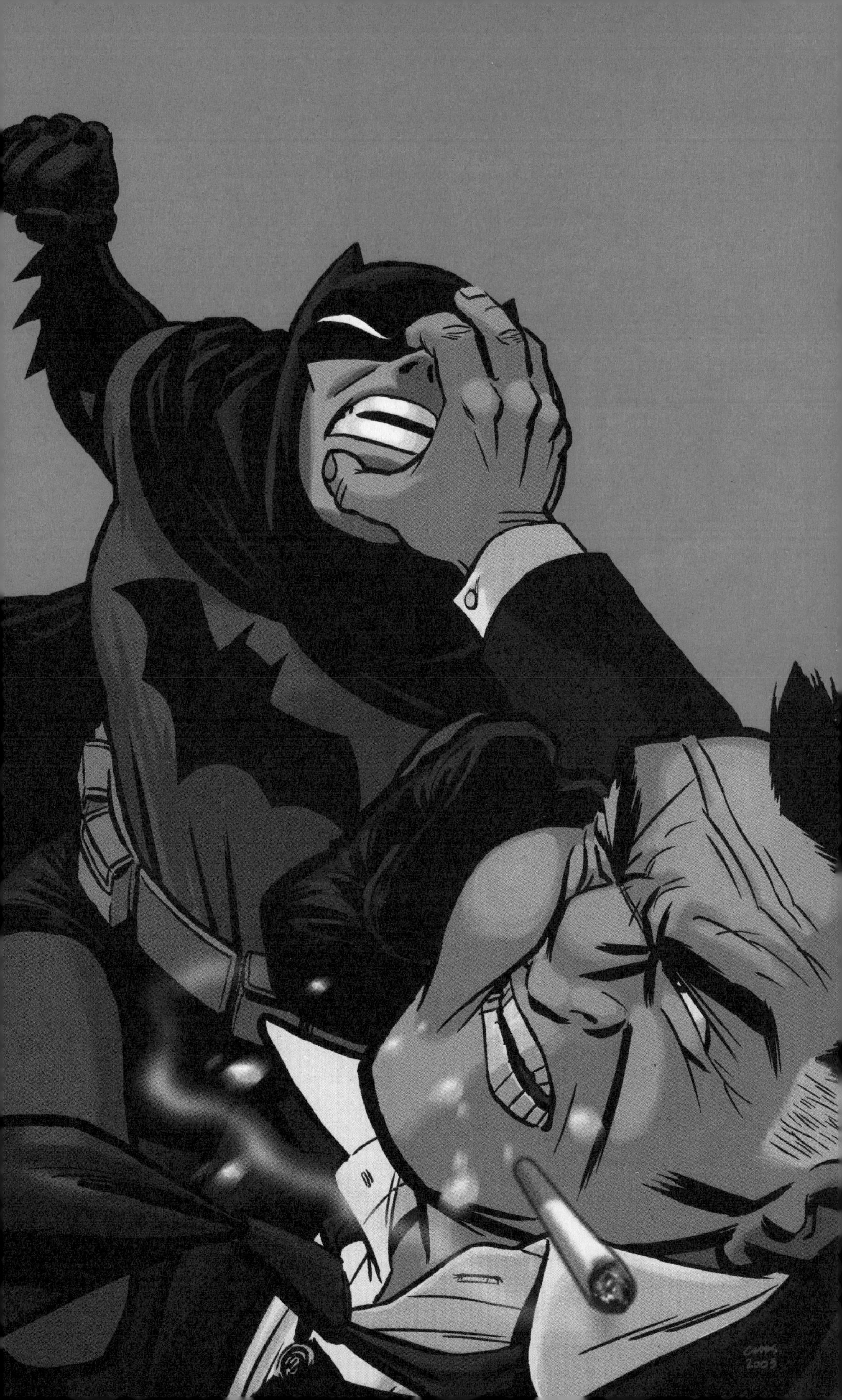

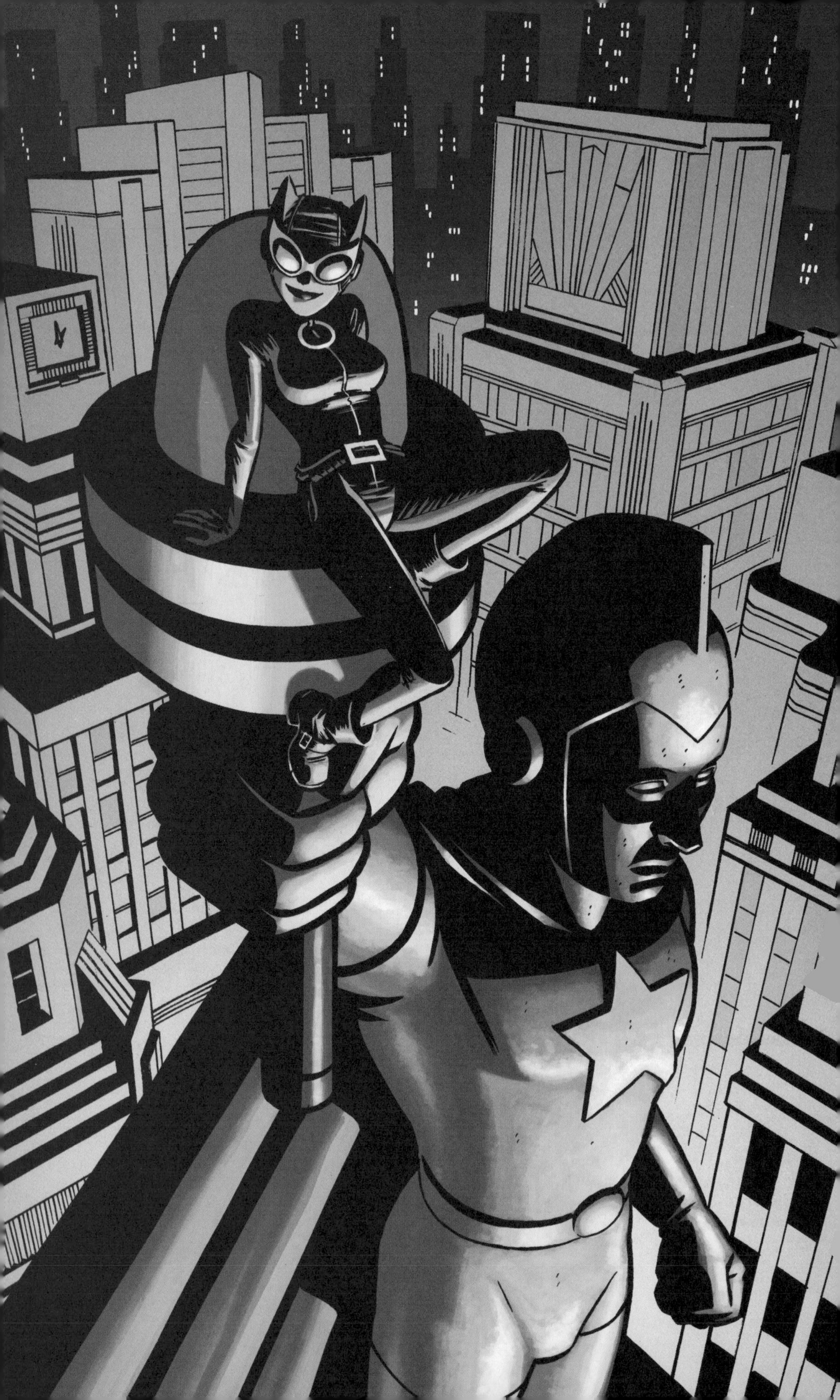

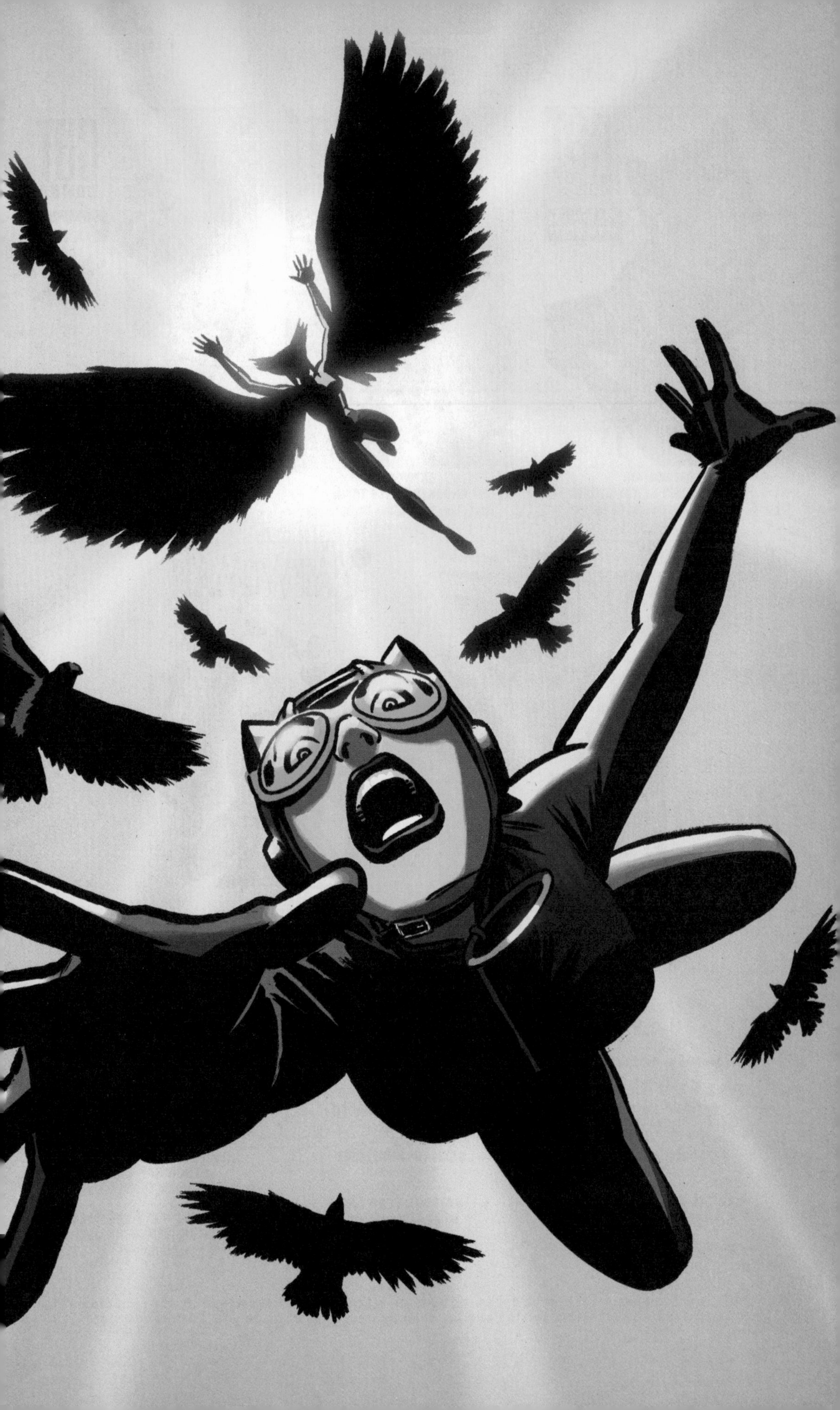

CATWOMAN LIBRARY

**CATWOMAN:
THE DARK END OF THE STREET**
Brubaker/Cooke/Allred

**CATWOMAN:
CROOKED LITTLE TOWN**
Brubaker/Rader/Stewart/Burchett

**CATWOMAN:
RELENTLESS**
Brubaker/Pulido/Stewart

CATWOMAN: SELINA'S BIG SCORE
Cooke/various

**CATWOMAN:
NINE LIVES OF A FELINE FATALE**
various

Sink your claws into these dynamic collections featuring CATWOMAN!

BATMAN: CATACLYSM
various

BATMAN: CONTAGION
various

BATMAN: DARK VICTORY
Loeb/Sale

BATMAN: HUSH VOLUME 1
Loeb/Lee/Williams

BATMAN: HUSH VOLUME 2
Loeb/Lee/Williams

BATMAN: THE LONG HALLOWEEN
Loeb/Sale

BATMAN: THE MOVIES
various

BATMAN: NINE LIVES
Motter/Lark

BATMAN: YEAR ONE
Miller/Mazzucchelli

BATMAN IN THE FORTIES
various

BIRDS OF PREY
Dixon/Haley/Frank/Raffaele/various

CATWOMAN: THE CATFILE
Dixon/Balent/B. Smith

**CATWOMAN: THE MOVIE AND
OTHER CAT TALES**
Austen/Derenick/DeKraker/various

**JUST IMAGINE STAN LEE CREATING
THE DC UNIVERSE VOLUME 3**
Lee/various

Search the Graphic Novels section of dccomics.com for art and info on every one of our hundreds of books!
Call 1-888-COMIC BOOK for the comics shop nearest you, or go to your local book store.